Wrestling with Alligators, Prophets and Theologians

Peter and Doris have pioneered much in calling the prayer movement forth in the nations through the 1990s. They laid a foundation for the necessity and value of prayer, on which many prayer ministries such as IHOP has been building ever since. We are very grateful for their labors.

Mike Bickle, President, International House of Prayer of Kansas City

Few who know Peter would question that his lifelong passion has been to obey and fear the Lord. This is a book about paradigm shifts in implementing God's mission that often moved Peter and others who followed his teaching from old to new wineskins. Whether you agree with him or not, you are likely to be challenged by what you read.

Luis Bush, International Facilitator, Transform World Connections

Peter Wagner is one of the most remarkable men I have ever known. One does not have to agree with all of his theological positions in order to love him deeply as a brother in Christ and recognize him as one of the most influential Christian leaders of our generation.

Paul Cedar, Chairman, Mission America Coalition

Wrestling with Alligators, Prophets and Theologians is an astute compilation of the life and times of one of the most esteemed and educated men of God in our time. Dr. Wagner is a masterful writer, theologian, researcher, professor and a wonderful friend. I highly recommend the reading of this book as an inspirational and rewarding learning experience.

David Yonggi Cho, Chairman, Church Growth International

I had an incredible vision of a multitude of thousands of souls standing around the heavenly throne room. In spirit, I heard these words: "These are here because of this man!" The Holy Spirit made it clear to me He was looking at C. Peter Wagner!

Apostle Jim Chosa, Founder, Day Chief Ministries

Since the time I came under the covering of Dr. Wagner in July 1999, my life and ministry have forever changed. I have been blessed to serve thousands of people through an international ministry—if it were not for the prophetic unction of Dr. C. Peter Wagner, I would still be ministering locally in my city! His spiritual posterity produces fruit that remains.

Kim Daniels, Founder, Spoken Word Ministries

Recently, I composed a list of the 10 people who have thus far impacted my life the most. As you might guess, Peter Wagner made my top 10 list. I have seen remarkable characteristics in this man that I wish to model in my own life. You have in your hands tales of the ways of God in modern Church history. This book is full of life, as it comes from one who has lived life to its fullest. May his shadow continue to be cast upon the multitudes for Jesus Christ's sake!

James W. Goll, Co-founder of Encounters Network and Director of Prayer Storm

Throughout C. Peter Wagner's long career, he has been both a researcher and activist and has maintained a passionate concern for the global Church's fulfillment of the Great Commission. *Wrestling with Alligators, Prophets and Theologians* reveals that he has remained at the frontiers in identifying the obstacles to the progress of the gospel and in seeking to overcome them and provides a fascinating account of his insights and struggles.

Eddie Gibbs, Senior Professor of Church Growth, Fuller Theological Seminary

Peter Wagner is one of the few great Church leaders who have obtained worldwide acclaim yet maintained holy living, a healthy marriage, and a progressive revelation with doctrinal purity. Peter has raised up more ministries and advanced the kingdom of God more than any other man in his generation. His memoirs will be a great blessing and inspiration for generations to come.

Bill Hamon, Founder and Bishop, Christian International Apostolic Network

Peter's remembrances cover a season of sweeping divine grace throughout the Church and rapid evangelism around the world—a season during which God made him an instrument of reporting revival and seeking to advance it.

Jack W. Hayford
Chancellor, The King's College & Seminary; Founding Pastor, The Church On The Way

Among Christian leaders both in this generation and before us, there are few like Peter Wagner. He is a legend in Christendom, yet he maintains a teachable spirit and humility that few can attain. *Wrestling with Alligators, Prophets and Theologians* will have you laughing, stretch you in your calling as a believer, and leave you longing to be a trailblazer.

Cindy Jacobs, Co-founder, Generals International

God has used Peter to encourage, teach, mobilize and stir up the Church to reach its highest calling and greatest impact in the world. He is a groundbreaker and galvanizer who has modeled leadership marked by integrity, authenticity and spiritual acumen. Follow the journey of Peter's life through this transparent memoir and be inspired and challenged to pursue excellence as you follow the destiny that God has in store for you.

Jane Hansen Hoyt, President and CEO, Aglow International

Reading *Wrestling with Alligators, Prophets and Theologians* is a refreshing experience. Rarely does one have such an opportunity to look into the life of one of the Church's most important leaders. Peter's transparent approach makes this book both an inspirational journey and great training for an overcoming life. I highly recommend this book.

Bill Johnson, Pastor, Bethel Church

We ordinarily don't expect much from a book of remembrances written by an old guy. But when the memoirs are about the crucial part played by a person during what may be the biggest movement of God in centuries, a book like this is worthy of attention.

Charles H. Kraft, Professor of Anthropology and Intercultural Communication, Fuller Theological Seminary

It is a joy for me to reminisce with Peter Wagner about my days at Skyline Wesleyan, Fuller Seminary and the National Church Growth conferences that we did together. Peter tells these stories, and so many others, in this enthralling and informative book. I'm anxiously looking forward to his fourth career!

John C. Maxwell, Leadership Expert

Peter is one of those rare individuals who touches lives in varied ways. His leadership in the church growth movement and insights on evangelism have aided thousands of church leaders to effectively fulfill Christ's command to make disciples. There are many lessons that we can learn from his lifetime in the Church, but perhaps the greatest lesson—after determining what God desires of us—is to have the courage to follow Christ wherever He leads.

Gary L. McIntosh, Professor of Christian Ministry and Leadership, Biola University

Peter Wagner is a delightful human being, and I would not be where I am today had God not brought this father of the faith into my life. I know of no man in the kingdom of God who has given as much liberty to as many to develop their gifts. *Wrestling with Alligators, Prophets and Theologians* is full of teaching, joy and history of the last 80 years of a developing saint's life and accomplishments. Read closely, as you might find that you are included in his account of modern Church history!

Chuck D. Pierce, President, Global Spheres, Inc.

Peter has been a forerunner for the Lord, establishing many organizations in the charismatic movement. *Wrestling with Alligators, Prophets and Theologians* is not a read-it-once-and-then-put-it-down book; it's a keep-it-handy resource for whenever there is a need to check something in recent charismatic history. It will be a treasured resource for all who value remembering the lessons of history.

John Sandford, Founder, The Elijah House

Peter Wagner's life, conduct, compassion, ability to forgive and courage to stand against ecclesiastical storms of opposition will hold you in its grip as you read through the pages of this modern-day Church history of our times. Much of the greatness of God in the author is in the way he honors his wife, Doris, and in their ability to complement each other. This is evident not only in this book but also in their life and ministry.

Gwen R. Shaw, Founder and President, End-Time Handmaidens, Inc.

Peter and Doris Wagner have left an imprint on the Church like few others. *Wrestling with Alligators, Prophets and Theologians* is a rare, candid and inspiring piece. Those of us whose lives have been blessed by Peter and Doris will be energized by their memories, but the greatest beneficiaries will be the generations to come who will benefit from the wisdom and practical advise poured into this book.

Ed and Ruth Silvoso, Founders, Harvest Evangelism

Some men are shaped by their generations; others shape their generations. Dr. C. Peter Wagner has shaped our generation. His life and literature have impacted Christian leaders worldwide. No doubt this informational, inspirational tome of Peter's life story will reveal to you what God is doing today and prove a valuable historical record for future generations.

Dr. Alice Smith, Co-founder, Eddie and Alice Smith Ministries

C. Peter Wagner will be remembered as one of the great apostolic leaders of our generation, and I'm thrilled he is finally writing his story so that those of us who look up to him can understand his perspective on God's dealings in his life. Few have had as interesting a life as C. Peter Wagner. Knowing him has enriched my life.

Steve Strang, Founder and Publisher, *Charisma* Magazine

Peter Wagner is one of the original thinkers in church growth and foreign missions. He learned from Donald McGavran, added his insights and has influenced the face of missions around the world. Leaders from most denominations came to Fuller to learn the latest in church growth and evangelism from him. If you want to trace what God has been doing in the world during the past 50 years, read *Wrestling with Alligators, Prophets and Theologians*.

Elmer Towns, Co-founder and Instructor in Church Growth, Liberty University

Wrestling with Alligators, Prophets and Theologians reveals the unique factor that in my opinion makes Peter a phenomenon: He combines the scholastic discipline of a professor with the rugged individualism of a farm-raised missionary and blends it with the restless intellectual curiosity of youth. Once Peter is convinced of the credibility of a new idea, he becomes the point man in its advocacy, even if it is politically incorrect and costly. His memoirs, like the man himself, are a burning light.

Lance Wallnau, President, Lance Learning Group

Wrestling with Alligators, Prophets and Theologians reveals the heart of a reformer who has helped shape the destiny of the Church. His humor, ability to overcome personal difficulties and zeal for life will captivate your heart. I highly recommend this book for anyone serious about understanding God's unfolding purpose for His Church.

Barbara Wentroble, President, International Breakthrough Ministries

Peter is an amazing man of vision and faith with both intellectual and practical brilliance. He is knowable, as well as the most positive and unoffendable leader I have ever known. I never cease to be amazed by his refusal to stay the same and to let any of us around him remain the same. To know Peter is to know one of the most godly and brilliant leaders in our lifetime—one who persistently and intentionally leads us into the future.

Barbara J. Yoder, Senior Pastor and Lead Apostle, Shekinah Christian Church

Wrestling with Alligators, Prophets and Theologians

Lessons from a Lifetime in the Church—A Memoir

C. PETER WAGNER

Regal

From Gospel Light
Ventura, California, U.S.A.

Published by Regal
From Gospel Light
Ventura, California, U.S.A.
www.regalbooks.com
Printed in the U.S.A.

Library of Congress Cataloging-in-Publication Data
Wagner, C. Peter.
Wrestling with alligators, prophets, and theologians : lessons from a lifetime in the church—
a memoir / C. Peter Wagner.
p. cm.
"Books published by C. Peter Wagner"—P.
ISBN 978-0-8307-5531-8 (hard cover)
1. Wagner, C. Peter. 2. Christian biography. 3. Missions. 4. Church growth. I. Title.
BR1725.W26A3 2010
277.3'082092—dc22
[B]
2010006191

1 2 3 4 5 6 7 8 9 10 / 15 14 13 12 11 10

Rights for publishing this book outside the U.S.A. or in non-English languages are administered by
Gospel Light Worldwide, an international not-for-profit ministry. For additional information,
please visit www.glww.org, email info@glww.org, or write to Gospel Light Worldwide, 1957 Eastman
Avenue, Ventura, CA 93003, U.S.A.

To order copies of this book and other Regal products in bulk quantities,
please contact us at 1-800-446-7735.

Contents

1

Born and Raised

(1930–1950)

Why not start at the beginning?

This was at the Columbia Presbyterian Hospital located at the foot of the George Washington Bridge on Manhattan Island. My father walked into the hospital, excited to see his newborn son for the first time. He got my mother's room number from the reception desk, located the elevator and pushed the button for the tenth floor. On the way up, the elevator stopped on the fourth floor, and a nurse wheeled in a crib containing a little baby.

Here's the way I heard my father tell the story: "I looked at the baby. It was so ugly! It had a pointed head and it was all covered with hair. I said to myself, *I'm sure glad it's not mine!*"

You guessed it! It was! It was me.

True, I don't remember the incident, but I heard my father tell that story so many times that I feel like I do. Whenever he told it everybody would laugh, including me. Fortunately, the way I turned out, I have a fairly round head and not much hair where it shouldn't be. It didn't take long for my father to be glad that the baby he saw was actually his after all. We ended up having a great relationship.

That was back in August 1930. My parents had married on what turned out to be the infamous Black Tuesday, when the stock market crashed on October 29, 1929. This was more than unfortunate for the new Wagner family because, at the time, my father, fresh out of college, had landed a job on Wall Street. They lived in nearby Greenwich Village. Ten months later, I came along. I was born in the Presbyterian Hospital because that's where my mother, originally from North Adams, Massachusetts, happened to be working at the time.

Why This Book?

Eighty years have gone by since then. For most of those years, writing a book of memoirs never even crossed my mind. In fact, I never had much of a taste for either biographies or autobiographies. As my personal library grew over the years, I ended up with a shelf of maybe 30 or 40 biographies, but I had read almost none of them. The moving story of missionary Jim Elliot, *Shadow of the Almighty*, was one of the few exceptions. I imagine that my anti-biography bias might have gone back to my early days as a Christian when I would read books like *Praying Hyde* or the story of David Brainerd, after which I would always feel miserable. Not only had I decided that I could never be like them, but deep down, I never really *wanted* to be like them. What did that feeling produce? A major guilt trip plus a gnawing sensation that I might be destined to end up a second-class Christian for the rest of my life because I could never live up to their standards.

So, a long time ago, I simply quit reading biographies. When I began thinking about it, I couldn't help but notice that the biographers, by and large, had apparently been conditioned to highlight the accomplishments and not the blunders of their subject. Yes, some failures were mentioned from time to time, but only those carefully selected in order to set the stage for a subsequent victory over adversity, which ended up actually making the subject a hero. To me there was an uncomfortable distance between what was on the pages and real life. So one day, I decided to give my whole shelf of biographies to my colleague at Fuller Seminary, Bobby Clinton. Bobby had determined to read all the biographies he could get because he was constantly distilling material for his courses on leadership. I'll get back to Bobby more than once in what is to come.

When I wrote my book *Humility,* I put my thoughts into print. I said, "My close friends and my publisher have known for a long time that I will not allow a biography to be written on my life. I personally cannot get interested in reading Christian biographies because of their propensity toward living in the achievements of the past."[1]

Not long after that, my publisher, Bill Greig III, began bringing up the subject of memoirs. My initial response was, "Absolutely not!" I referred him to what I had written in my book on humility that his own company, Regal Books, had published. However, that didn't seem to faze him. He was probably thinking that if I was humble enough, I could admit that I had made at least one mistake in my book on humility! For about five years he persisted. He argued that over the years many people had come to regard me as a leader in the Body of Christ, that I had accumulated a measure of wisdom, and that I had a responsibility for an intergenerational impartation. Because I was an experienced author, the best vehicle for that impartation would be a book. He also pointed out that autobiographies are different from biographies. He admitted that biographies are sometimes exaggerated, but he challenged me to do an autobiography that would reflect humility rather than exaggeration. When he had worn me down enough, Bill one day persuaded me to promise him I would pray about it. I promised, but I must confess that I didn't pray very much or too hard.

However, I must have prayed enough for God to enter the picture and begin to change my mind. I hadn't talked about it with others before, but then, at one point, I decided to begin asking a few close friends what they thought. Without exception they urged me to launch out with the project. Eventually, I opened up enough to concede to Bill Greig that I would agree to write a book of memoirs, but sometime in the distant future. *Mañana!* But then when I mentioned this to my friends, they gently reminded me of the biological facts of the aging process. They pointed out that some people around my age range were beginning to check into nursing homes and couldn't remember who visited them yesterday. They urged me to get going while I still had some of my wits about me. So when I was 76, I agreed to start moving on a book of memoirs; but I asked Bill to give me until my eightieth birthday to release the book.

Not long afterwards, my decision was reinforced by a word from Rick Joyner. I consider Joyner one of the most brilliant of our contemporary Christian leaders, so I pay careful attention to what he says. In one of his articles in *The Morning Star Journal*, Joyner promised his readers that eventually he would give them details of his early life, which is another way of saying that he would write memoirs. One of his reasons was based on Paul's admonition that believers should "recognize those who labor among you" (1 Thess. 5:12). Rick helped me to feel that I have good biblical justification for this book.[2]

Older and Wiser

The other thing about the aging process is that as we get older, we almost involuntarily get wiser. I realize that wisdom is relative, so I could not claim that I am particularly wiser than anyone else my age. But what I do know for sure is that I am wiser today than I was when I was 30 or 40. From that I can probably assume that if I do write some things that I have learned through the years, they might be useful to others who are still 30 or 40. I, hopefully, could help them avoid some mistakes and also encourage them to break some new ground and shift some paradigms that otherwise they might not be inclined to do.

It was only after I had gone through that lengthy process that God specifically gave me a verse of Scripture as the foundation for this book:

> Words from wise people are like spurs. Their collected sayings are like nails that have been driven in firmly. They come from one shepherd. Be warned, my children, against anything more than these.... After having heard it all, this is the conclusion: Fear God and keep his commands, because this applies to everyone (Eccles. 12:11-13, *GOD'S WORD*).

I can say up front that since the day I was born again, I have feared God and kept His commands. Perfectly? By no means! At times I have misunderstood Him, I have pushed ahead in my own ways before I heard His specific orders, I have shifted priorities upside down, I have made stupid decisions, and I could go on. But through it all, I did fear God, I kept the faith, I ran the race, and my foremost desire was to do His will 24/7. I can truthfully say with Paul, "I was not disobedient to the heavenly vision" (Acts 26:19).

Beginning Life

Back to the Great Depression. The decade of the 1930s was an unforgettable hinge point in American history. Never before had a modern industrialized nation suffered such an abrupt and prolonged economic free fall. Herbert Hoover was president when it began, and then he was defeated by Franklin D. Roosevelt in 1932, shortly after I turned two. I still clearly remember the words and music to the ditty: "President Mr. Hoover says now's the time to buy, so let's have another cup of coffee and let's have another piece of pie!" That is probably my earliest memory, along with dropping my cash-register-shaped coin bank out of the fourth-story window of our apartment in Jackson Heights, in the New York City Borough of Queens, and seeing it smashed on the sidewalk below. Those were the days when replacements for things like that were out of the question, but all of us in that generation learned how to "do without." Doing without became a very useful, ingrained characteristic; first, during the rationing of everything from sugar to shoes during World War II, and later, when Doris and I went to Bolivia as missionaries.

Although unemployment was hovering around 20 percent, my father somehow always managed to find enough work to make ends meet, even though our dinner at times consisted only of bread and gravy. Those were hard times, but I can't remember anyone in the family ever complaining.

My grandmother, a recent widow of a country doctor from Upstate New York, where my father was born and raised, spent a good bit of time with us in the city. She was a trained nurse, an immigrant from Great Britain. "Mum," as I called her, had a strong influence on my life. We never referred to the Bible, but she had me memorize some sound extra-biblical proverbs, such as, "Waste not, want not is a maxim I will teach. Let your conscience be your guide and practice what you preach. Do not let your chances like the sunbeams pass you by, for you never miss the water 'til the well runs dry." I still recite this mentally on a regular basis.

Part of my nature has always been to have a strong work ethic, and my grandmother played a key role in ingraining this in me. "One thing at a time, and that done well is a very good rule as many can tell" was another of those proverbs that I have taken seriously and practiced ever since. My friends know that I have a one-track mind, which is sometimes a blessing and sometimes a burden. Even minimal dual-tasking is for me all but out of the question. Another big favor my grandmother did for me was to teach me to read before I enrolled in kindergarten. I believe this, more than anything else, is what enabled me to stay at the head of my class most of the way through school. I recall that in second grade the teacher excused me from the daily reading class and allowed me to develop my own personal reading program.

Just before I enrolled in kindergarten, my family moved across the Hudson River to New Jersey. It was in New Jersey that my father eventually found his career niche, namely, in the retail business. Those were the days when dress codes were different. Men wore suits and ties and hats even when riding trains and attending baseball games. Women also wore hats, which were much more diverse and colorful and extravagant than the men's. Women's hats were called "millinery," and that became my father's business. He managed outsourced millinery departments in large department stores. Whenever he was promoted, it would be to a larger store in another city. Around this time, my sister, Margo, came along, and we ended up as the only siblings.

My father's frequent transfers established a family lifestyle that greatly benefited me for the rest of my life. I attended 13 different schools through my K-12 experience. Every time my parents would call a family meeting and inform us that we were going to move again, I would get excited. I loved the experience of making new friends, meeting new challenges, moving into a new home, studying under new teachers, trying out for new sports teams and exploring new cities on my bicycle. Even today I find that I have a hard time understanding parents who resist opportunities to move to a new location on the grounds that it might pull their children out of their comfort zone, although I realize that others have different sets of circumstances from mine.

I think that one of the reasons I have managed to find myself on the cutting edge of many new trends through the years is that as a youngster I never had the opportunity to settle very deeply into a comfort zone. Change for me was simply an acceptable and normal way of life, and I learned to enjoy it, even going so far as to desire it at times.

Choosing a Culture

One of the unusual privileges I had in life was the opportunity to choose my own culture. I grew up biculturally, namely, immersed in the cultures of both urban America and rural America. I found myself in an interesting situation. To some I was looked upon as a "hick," and to others I was regarded as a "city slicker." Those who don't recognize the cultural differences between the two would have difficulty passing a test in anthropology. They are very significant. From the beginning I leaned toward the rural culture. That is why when the time for college eventually came, I enrolled in the Rutgers University College of Agriculture, majoring in dairy production. I loved the sight and smell of cows!

How did all this come about?

My parents socialized, as was the custom of the day. In those simpler days, the stimulant of choice was alcohol. When they married, Prohibition was in effect, but where there was a will there was a way. Speakeasies were plentiful in New York City, and so was bathtub gin. Another of my earliest memories was watching my father use coiled copper pipes and funnels and burners to produce homemade liquor. It had to be the early 1930s, because Prohibition ended about the time I turned three.

Life in the city was very hectic, and my parents felt that I would be healthier physically, and probably mentally, if I spent some quality time in the country where my grandmother lived. When I was about five, I clearly remember my father taking me to Grand Central Station, accompanied by my teddy bear. He had pasted a sign with my name on my shirt and tipped the Pullman porter $20 (a very generous tip in those days), launching me on my first solo train ride to St. Johnsville, nestled in the Mohawk Valley and the foothills of the Adirondack Mountains eight hours to the north. I loved it! This became a greatly anticipated annual event for years.

My grandmother enjoyed a good social position in the town of St. Johnsville, population 1,500. She had always been like a second mother to me. But she saw a wider horizon for me than just being in town. She happened to be aquainted with the Claus family of the adjacent farming community of Oppenheim. One of the daughters, Kate, had worked for my grandmother for a time as a maid. Mum made arrangements with Charles Claus, a widower, and his two daughters, Mary Ann and Kate, to take me for the summer as if I were a member of their family.

Charles Claus, whose nickname of choice was "Shorty" (even for me!), farmed about 100 acres with horses and milked eight cows. I still stand amazed at how families like that could survive in the middle of the Depression with so little. But they had milk, cream, butter, cheese and eggs from their cows and chickens; and they had fresh fruit and vegetables from their garden in the summer and canned fruit and vegetables in the winter, fish from the creeks and lakes, a deer in the fall and canned meat from butchering hogs and calves. Trips to the grocery store were mostly for flour and sugar.

On this farm there was no electricity, no tractor, no running water, no indoor plumbing, no milking machines, no barn cleaner. The only internal combustion engine was in a 1932 Plymouth coupe with a rumble seat, which provided the bare essentials of transportation. Few things have had a greater influence on my life than my years on the Claus farm. Even though I had to go back to the city for school, by then my preferred culture was rural, somewhat to the consternation of my urban parents. Social scientists would label the culture of Oppenheim as Northern Appalachian; but in common language, it was pure hillbilly. I clearly recall one trouncing I received when I came back from the farm one year and started using some of the rather earthy rural vernacular in my parents' home!

What life-shaping influence did this have on me? I would say that first and foremost it taught me a solid work ethic. America was in a survival mode at the time, and on the farm, survival demanded work from dawn to dusk. There were no exceptions, not even for a five- or six-year-old boy. Play was reserved for occasions like Fourth of July picnics.

Left: I graduated from Suffield High School in Suffield, Connecticut, in 1948. This is my yearbook photo at age 18.

Below: My mother and father, Graham and Mary Wagner, are holding one-year-old Karen at Christmas, 1955.

At first, jobs were simple, like sitting on a stool and holding the cow's tail while Shorty milked. Then I graduated to carrying milk and dumping it through the strainer into the milk can. Then I could bunch hay in the windrow so it could be pitched onto the hay wagon. Then I could turn the wheel of the grindstone while Shorty sharpened the blades on the cutting bar of the mowing machine. Then I could go down the road to the day pasture by myself and bring the cows home for evening milking. Then the big day came when I could drive the team of horses and even harness them. Meanwhile, I could shovel manure and clean the barn with the best of them. I was happiest when I was working, and I still am.

When I first started on the Claus farm, my grandmother paid my room and board. Soon, however, I was useful enough to earn my own room and board. Later, I was elated when Shorty would give me $20 for my summer's work. In my mid-teens, I was offered a summer job by George Matis, who lived in St. Johnsville and farmed 250 acres, had electricity and a tractor and milked 35 cows. I took the job. George was paying me $20 per month, and I was feeling quite well off. I had been promoted!

While I did arrive there with a good work ethic, George taught me over several years how to work well. He taught me how to prioritize, how to persist until the job was done and how to pick up and put away my tools at the end of the day. Ever since then I have never been satisfied with a job half done or done poorly, and I have never been comfortable living in a mess. On Florence Littauer's "The 4 Temperaments" personality profile, I turn out to be a choleric–melancholy. This clearly indicates my bent to leadership and organization and reflects what I learned from George Matis. I'll tell more about the most important thing George and his wife, Frances, did for me in the next chapter.

Back to the City

While rural culture was my culture of choice, nevertheless, I was forced to live 75 percent of my life in the city. I have already mentioned that one thing that made this interesting to me was that our family kept moving to different cities and different states. Fortunately, my family was a functional family, which was still the American norm in those days. We loved each other, but we expressed our love by deeds rather than words. I never heard the words "I love you" from either of my parents, nor did I expect to. Neither my sister nor I found reason to display any serious teenage rebellion. Corporeal punishment was freely practiced in those days.

The work ethic I had developed was a bit more difficult to apply in the city than on the farm. In the city, children were supposed to play and grown-ups were supposed to work. I did manage to apply my work ethic to some extent in school where, combined with a desire for excellence, it pushed me to be first in the class for grade-point average, with only one exception that I can recall. In my freshman year in high school, in Buffalo, New York, I was beaten out by Richard Shushinsky. Richard happened to be Jewish, and ever since then, I have had a very high regard for Jewish people in general.

Later, a close call came as I was graduating from Rutgers University College of Agriculture, where the first in the class would receive the Borden Prize, given by the Borden Milk Company. Malcolm McVeigh and I were neck and neck, and I happened to squeeze him out by a point or two. That to me was justice, because Malcolm had never milked a cow, and I had been milking them since I was eight, so I felt I was the one who deserved the prize from the milk company.

Looking back, I must admit that my achievement at that point was a bit dimmed by the generosity of Mr. Keller, the professor of my senior course in agricultural economics. Somehow, I was not catching on to that course at all, and I was clearly headed for a C or worse. One day, Mr. Keller called me aside. He said, "Peter, why didn't you tell me that you had been elected to Phi Beta Kappa in your junior year?" I simply shrugged my shoulders. So he said, "I am not going to stand in your way of staying at the top. Your grade in this course will be an A!" By then, I was a Christian, as I will explain later, and that became one of my best real-life examples of grace!

Take Me Out to the Ball Game

One of my father's passions was baseball. In those days, baseball was regarded as the undisputed National Pastime. The National Football League had started in 1920, but it didn't gain public recognition until the 1940s. The National Basketball Association didn't even begin until 1946. The World Series then was equivalent to what the Super Bowl is today. Those were the days of Babe Ruth and Lou Gehrig and Christy Mathewson and Bob Feller. Sunday morning the family would go to the city park where Dad played softball. One of my milestones in life was when I was allowed to be the oficial scorekeeper of the games. I remember seeing the Yankees playing in Yankee Stadium, the Giants in the Polo Grounds and the Brooklyn Dodgers in Ebbets Field.

Naturally, I went out for baseball in high school. I earned a varsity letter in my sophomore year, then added basketball and soccer and had three letters my final two years. All were team sports. I couldn't get interested in individual sports such as track or tennis or golf or bowling or swimming. Looking back, I believe this helped to mold my character as a team player. I knew I could never win the game myself. Every win involved people on my team who could do some things better than I could. This made it relatively easy later on to understand what the Bible was teaching about spiritual gifts and also how apostolic ministry was to function. But more about those topics later on.

Sports teamwork also taught me about the true nature of leadership. Leadership is not all about the achievements of the leader; it is about helping every member of the team be all that he or she is supposed to be. The team is the winner, not any of the individuals, including the leader. This is the meaning of "servant leadership." Somehow, I was never a stranger to leadership. More often than not, when the class would vote for a president or a student council representative, I would be the one. I never campaigned for these offices; they just seemed to come to me.

The first time I learned about campus politics was in my freshman year in college. A vote for the class president was scheduled, and I hadn't been giving it much thought. One day a person I knew only slightly came up to me and told me he was running for class president. Would I be his campaign manager? I was a bit flattered, so I told him that I would, not really knowing what I was supposed to do. As it turned out, I didn't have to do anything. He was sharp enough to recognize that I might be his strongest competitor, so he skillfully took me out of the running, and he went on to win the election. It was one of my first lessons in manipulation. I decided then and there that campus politics was not for me!

Finding Work in the City

With all I had going on, I still maintained a lingering desire to work. I landed my first city job when I was 10 or 11. That was when every drugstore had a soda fountain where customers could get sparkling drinks or ice cream sundaes or milk shakes. A drugstore hired me to tend their soda fountain for 10 cents an hour plus all I could eat. I loved the job, but I soon began looking for something that would pay better. We lived in a suburb of Cleveland, Ohio, at the time, and I got word that a newspaper delivery route for the *Cleveland Plain Dealer* had an opening. I had a good bicycle and was ready to go except that the minimum age was 12, and I was only 11. However, my father was able to speak to a decision maker somewhere and convince him that I could handle the job. So every afternoon, I folded my papers, tossed them on the customers' porches and made the rounds once a week to collect the money. When I paid for my papers, what I had left over was mine, and it was not a bad income.

After we moved to Buffalo, New York, I expanded my business and landed two paper routes, one morning and one evening. That meant I had to get up at 5:00 every morning and deliver my papers before school. No problem for a boy who was accustomed to getting up to milk cows on a farm!

During my last two years in high school, we lived in the rural community of Suffield, in the Connecticut River valley just north of Hartford. The region was widely known for the highest quality of shade-grown tobacco used for cigar wrappers. I spent hours upon hours stripping leaves off the tobacco plants because it all had to be done by hand. Then I discovered an easier way to make spending money.

My dad had always been an avid poker player, and he taught me how to play. I became interested, so I bought some books and studied the science of the game, including the odds. Make no mistake about it, poker is much more a game of skill than it is gambling. It wasn't hard to get my circle of friends interested in playing poker on a regular basis. There was no such thing as Texas Hold 'Em back in those days. We played simple five-card draw. My friends all loved the game, but I was the only one who had studied the odds. I don't think anyone even noticed that over the period of maybe a year and a half, I never lost a sitting! They were having a good time, and I was enjoying their money! Everybody was happy.

Another job that lasted for more than a year came up at that time when, for some reason or another, radio station WTIC in Hartford asked me to appear on their Saturday morning teenage show, "Mind Your Manners." The host was Allen Ludden, who was just beginning his rather illustrious career in media. Mr. Ludden and I hit it off well, so I became one of the permanent members of the panel of six, while most of the other panelists changed from week to week. I attribute whatever skill I might have had in manners to my British grandmother who was very meticulous and proper about how all things should be done. In her home, for example, all men—no matter what they had been doing during the day—were required to dress in a suit and tie for cocktails and dinner! WTIC paid me

$10 per Saturday, and I think it was good training for the public speaking I would need to do later on in life.

Writing

English was always one of my favorite subjects, and I did most of my early writing for English classes. I was nine years old when I had my first writing published. Because so much of my subsequent career has been to write for publication, I think it would be interesting to some if I reproduced my first published article from the local newspaper:

The Day I Got Pneumonia
C. Peter Wagner, Fall 1939

One day I woke up with a little cough. We happened to have some cough drops. Mother thought I was just faking to get some so she sent me to school. At noon I had a high temperature and I went to bed. I woke up Saturday and I had a sharp pain in my left side. Mother called the doctor and he got here two and one-half hours later. He examined me and announced that I had pneumonia. He asked me if I wanted to ride in a car or an ambulance. I chose the car. I stayed in the hospital for ten days.

Well, you've got to start someplace!

Father and Son

If you have read this whole chapter, you will have concluded by now that the person who most shaped my character and my life during my first 20 years was my father. His full name was C. Graham Wagner. I have never been much of a counselor, and I think one of the reasons is that to this day I cannot understand the disproportionate number of people who are prone to complain about their fathers. Mine dished out plenty of discipline, and his tool of choice was the flat side of a huge wooden hairbrush applied to my bottom. "Sparing the rod" was something that never entered his mind. Looking back, however, I can't remember a spanking I didn't deserve!

One of our family crises came when I wrecked the family car. For most of the years during the Depression and World War II, we had no car. We simply walked, used bicycles or took public transportation. Finally, when we moved to Connecticut, the family could afford an automobile. It made a huge difference in our lifestyle, as one could well imagine. This was about the time I got my driver's license. I think I was a senior in high school when I was minding my own business (of that I am convinced!) and another car and mine crashed into each other at a good speed. Our family car was totaled! I had no idea what to expect from my father, but I thought I would be in real trouble. Instead, as we began to recover from the initial shock, there was no rebuke, no guilt trip, no scolding, no discipline. The whole event was "just one of those things that happens." At least for a couple of years, we once again had no family car. As much as anything else, this taught me how we could weather a family storm and keep relationships intact.

A similar memory goes back to a time, after the car wreck, when I was arrested for receiving stolen goods. This is why when I am asked if I have ever been arrested for a crime, I have to answer yes. We were playing a high school baseball game in another town, and while our team was up to bat and the players were on the bench, a man came up to me, showed me a nice wristwatch and said I could have it for $4. I had never owned a luxury item like a wristwatch, and I happened to have $4 of my poker money in my pocket. So I closed the deal, thinking I had just made the best business transaction of my life. A couple of days later, a police officer showed up at our house, demanded the watch and handed me a summons. I never needed my dad more than I did then. He took the day off work, called my uncle, who had a car, and accompanied me to court. The judge saw that I was remorseful, and he acquitted me. But through it all, my father never scolded me. He supported and encouraged me, knowing that I would not make the same mistake again.

Decision Making

Perhaps I am most grateful to my father for his ability to take a hands-off approach and allow me to make important decisions early in life. I now see that this enviable characteristic rested on two premises: (1) he himself harbored no personal insecurities, and (2) he trusted that I would learn valuable life lessons both from my good decisions and my bad ones. A memorable crossroads came when I graduated from eighth grade and was ready for my freshman year in high school. In Buffalo, New York, where we lived at the time, there happened to be an elite private preparatory academy called Nichols School. Probably because of my grade point average in elementary school, Nichols School got in touch with my family and offered me a full scholarship. Should I go to Nichols or should I go to the public high school?

This surfaced a fascinating difference of perspective between my father and me. At the time, we clearly were not affluent, but we were upwardly mobile. He was raised the son of a physician, so he was used to moving in the upper levels of society. The Depression was a severe setback, but he never lost his desire for social status. Because he had studied for a year in Union College, he qualified for membership in the University Club of the cities where he was working. That was where he always began building personal relationships. While never at the top of the social ladder, he at least was usually on one of its rungs. When his son was offered a scholarship to Nichols, this became a major status symbol in his circles. His friends who did have children in Nichols would all have been paying tuition.

My perspective? As I explained earlier, I had been given the choice of identifying primarily with either the rural culture or the urban culture, and I had chosen the rural culture. I never had any desire for social status. The simple life of the Claus farm in Oppenheim, milking cows and driving horses, was what I had in mind as good living. Upper-class people were not my kind of people, and Nichols School would be full of them. They probably thought that horses were for playing polo rather than for pulling manure spreaders. Even though I knew it would disappoint my father, I chose the more middle-class route of public high school. When I did, my father fully backed me, and I never heard a word of complaint about my decision.

The same creative tension persisted four years later when I chose agriculture as my college major instead of some more socially respectable profession. But it was my decision. It became a bit easier when Rutgers University in New Brunswick, New Jersey, offered me a full tuition scholarship, something my family could not have afforded. Things escalated considerably when, a few years later, I told my mother and father that I had decided to be a foreign missionary. That was obviously a huge disappointment for them, but they honored the principle they had established long ago, namely, that I was to be the one in charge of making important decisions for my life.

Now I was ready to move out of my home and make my own way down the pathway of life.

Notes
1. C. Peter Wagner, *Humility* (Ventura, CA: Regal, 2002), p. 96.
2. Rick Joyner, "A Prophetic History," *The Morning Star Journal*, vol. 18, no. 1, 2008, p. 86.

2

Born Again

(1950–1956)

During my freshman year at the Rutgers University College of Agriculture, I was pleasantly surprised when the American Guernsey Cattle Club invited me to join a special scholarship program that included a summer job for selected students. Although I had been expecting to continue working summers on the Matis farm in St. Johnsville, this seemed to be an offer I should not refuse. They would send me to McDonald Farms in Cortland, New York, arguably the number-one farm in the nation for Guernsey show cattle at the time. I would work under Henry Thomas, one of America's most respected herdsmen, to help prepare the show string for the New York State Fair in Syracuse and the National Dairy Cattle Congress in Waterloo, Iowa. This was an honor, and it would look very good on my résumé.

George Matis agreed, so off I went to Cortland. This set the scene for what became a life-changing and career-changing series of events.

It happened to be my nineteenth birthday, August 15, 1949. For me it was going to be another routine day on the farm. No one else would even know it was my birthday because I never have and still don't make birthdays special events. I would get up at 5:00 to feed and milk the string of Guernseys that had been assigned to me. Because they were show cattle, they were all milked three times a day and by hand. McDonald Farms had no milking machines. I would then clean the stable, shovel the manure, groom the cows, take them outside with halters for exercise and be available for odd jobs between milkings. This meant doing things like unloading hay bales, filling in for other milkers who called in sick, collecting semen from bulls for artificial insemination, mowing grass, assisting the veterinarian, and whatever else needed to be done. The last milking was around 7:00 P.M., so 14-hour days were common.

Honeybloom

This was the noon milking. The cow I was milking happened to be McDonald Farms Honeybloom, a beautiful Guernsey. How beautiful? Later that year she was judged to be the reserve grand champion aged cow at the National Dairy Cattle Congress in Waterloo, meaning that she was rated the second most beautiful cow of all breeds in the United States. I was minding my own business when, as a complete surprise, into the barn walked George Matis, with his wife, Frances, his two kids, and a young woman who immediately attracted my attention. They said that they had come to wish me a happy birthday. Their daughter, Jeanie, had also been born on August 15, and it was her birthday wish that they drive the 150 miles from St. Johnsville to visit me.

Not only was the cow beautiful, but the young woman they had brought along with them was beautiful as well. They introduced her as Doris Mueller from a neighboring farm, whom they employed from time to time as a baby-sitter. I knew the farm very well. In fact, I had baled hay with her two broth-ers, Buddy and Herbie. I had drunk a bit of hard cider with them in their basement. But I had never seen Doris before she walked into the barn. She did more than attract my attention—she instantly soared to the top of my list as a potential spouse. While we were having our first casual chat, I thought I should give her a little test. She had on a pair of sandals that ex-posed her bare toes, so I playfully squirted a stream of Honeybloom's warm milk on her big toe. When I saw that it didn't faze her a bit, I decided that she was the one for me! One of my characteristics has always been that I can make quick decisions when necessary, and this became a case in point.

However, the decision was one-sided. On the Kiersey temperament test, Doris comes out an "inspector." That means she has to look things over very carefully before she makes a decision about anything. A complicating factor for her was that only one week before she walked into the barn, Frances Matis had taken her to a nearby Bible camp where she had accepted Christ as her personal Savior and was born again. I tried to turn on the charm as I gave them a tour of the farm. But Doris was busy inspecting. Later, she told me that she saw a yellow flag when I took them into the room where I slept and where there happened to be a refrigerator. When I opened the door, she saw that the refrigerator was full of only two things: artificial insemination equipment and a large quantity of beer. Not good!

Beer Kegs and Canadian Club

At this point, I need to fill in some gaps. I have mentioned that my parents were accomplished socializers and that alcohol flowed freely in our family

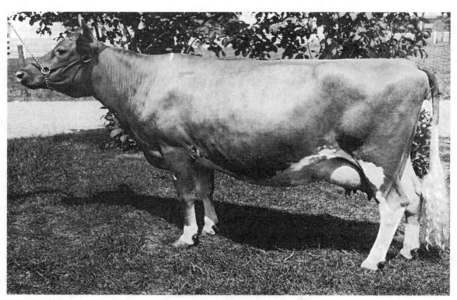

McDonald Farms Honeybloom is one of the most beautiful Guernsey cows on record. She was Reserve Grand Champion Aged Cow at the National Dairy Cattle Congress in Waterloo, Iowa in 1949, which means she was judged the second most beautiful cow in the nation. Besides, Honeybloom is the cow I happened to be milking when I first laid my eyes on Doris who walked into the barn with a friend. We feel like Honeybloom is part of the family!

The cow I am milking is one of Honeybloom's friends, but Doris loves this picture because this is what I looked like when she first saw me in 1949.

circles. However, unlike today, it was not the thing for teenagers to drink. I do not recall any of my high school friends who drank alcohol, including me. A little hard cider after baling hay would be an exception, not the rule. But when I left home for college, I thought it was time to broaden out and experiment a bit. With my father's encouragement I was rushed by the Phi Gamma Delta fraternity; I survived the humiliating initiation process as a pledge, and I moved into the fraternity house. My father had joined Phi Gamma Delta when he was a student at Union College in Schenectady, New York, and he was excited that I had become a "fraternity brother."

In those days, Rutgers University allowed only beer in fraternity houses, no wine or hard liquor. However, there were no limits on the amount of beer. It wasn't long before I decided that I liked both the beer and the exhilarating effect it had on my body and mind if I drank enough of it. I discovered that I greatly enjoyed getting drunk. My favorite drinking buddy, Vince Coyle, helped things along as well. His father was the manager of the Essex House hotel across the street from Central Park in New York City, and Vince had clandestine access to their vast liquor supply. He became proficient at breaking the school rules and keeping bottles of Canadian Club hidden in his dresser drawers. I paid him back by helping him pass his exams in the classes we had together, using means that I choose not to disclose. It became a toss-up as to whether Vince or I would be regarded by the rest as the heaviest drinker in the fraternity. I haven't counted how many mornings I could not remember who had put me into my bed the night before.

This was my lifestyle when Doris saw the beer in the refrigerator at McDonald Farms. Somehow she sensed danger when she saw it. I now realize that it was the Holy Spirit who had warned her, but I knew nothing of things like that at the time.

The County Fair

A few weeks later, when the summer's work was completed, I stopped off at my grandmother's house in St. Johnsville for a few days before continuing on to New Jersey. The obvious reason for this was to see Doris again and to get to know her. Our first date was to attend the Montgomery County Fair in Fonda, a very appropriate thing for farmers. I introduced her to my grandmother, who approved my choice. I got to know Doris's mother and father and other of her relatives, and I milked cows with her dad. We spent a good bit of time with the Matises, where we pitched corn together on their farm. The highlight for me was our first kiss under a tree near the cornfield. I was hooked!

Doris was still cautious. She began asking me questions about my faith, which was quite obviously nonexistent. Religion had been excluded from our family life. Why that was the case, I never did find out. Except for things like weddings or funerals or an occasional Christmas and Easter service, we never went to church. We did not pray. We avoided talking about Jesus or God. We were one of only 13 percent of homes in the United States that did not even have a copy of the Bible. I had never read the Bible or thought about religion my whole life. Looking back, I can't recall one Christian friend that I ever had growing up. But, strangely enough, when I left home for college, I went to a bookstore and bought two books that I thought I would need, a dictionary and a Bible. I may not have read it, but at least I owned a Bible, and I jumped at the opportunity to let Doris know that I had one.

Naturally, she asked me if I ever read my Bible, and I said that I hadn't. So she asked me if I would do something for her. At that point, after that kiss, I was ready to do *anything* for her. So she gave me a copy of a booklet called *The Upper Room,* which had daily Bible readings along with a devotional paragraph, and she made me promise I would read it every day. I know that I had plenty of faults, but at least I was a promise keeper, so I started reading my Bible. Even when I came into my room drunk I would still dutifully read the daily reading before I went to bed.

Not surprisingly, as our relationship developed, and I kept reading the Bible, I began to realize that if I were going to be successful in my pursuit of this woman, I would have to get saved some day. She had said, "I'm a born-again Christian, and I will only marry someone who also is born again." By then I began to understand what this would imply. Among other things, I suspected that when I was born again, I could no longer enjoy being a drunkard, so I postponed it as long as I could. I occasionally visited her farm where I slept in her brother's room with him. She came to Rutgers for what we called a "big weekend," when the members would move out of the fraternity house and our girlfriends would take it over. These meetings managed to produce a few more kisses, and by January of that school year, I was ready.

A Farm House Living Room

We were together in her living room one night when I told Doris that I was ready to become a Christian and asked her to help me. She said she would, but there was one more thing. She told me that she had promised God that she would be a missionary to Africa. My only question was, "Do they have cows over there in Africa?" When she assured me that they did, I told her that I would like to be a missionary too. So I accepted Christ and dedicated my life to be a missionary the same night there in that farmhouse. It was a powerful experience, and from that time, neither one of us has ever turned back.

When I returned to the Phi Gamma Delta house after that weekend, Vince Coyle invited me to his room where he said he had hidden a new bottle of Canadian Club. I said, "Vince, I'm on the wagon!" He looked at me in total disbelief and exclaimed rather vehemently, "Did you get religion?!" When I nodded, he yelled out and called all the fraternity brothers around us for a laughing party. Wagner, a teetotaler? Someone started a pool and they began betting money on how long it would last. I never did find out what happened to that money, but I should have gotten it. I totally abstained for the next 10 years.

I may have stopped drinking instantly, but other things took more time. It must have been six months before I cleaned up my foul language. I had a barnyard vocabulary that was not easy to change. When I did change my talk, I detested hearing it so much that even today when one of my friends naughtily drops a nasty word, I keep my peace, but inside I can't stand it.

About then I had one of my first experiences in seeing prayer answered. I had begun to develop a hunch that I should probably stop playing poker and gambling, but I wasn't sure, so I asked Doris. She advised me to ask God to show me if I should. I thought this was a novel idea, so I tried it. The next day I was dealt a hand, and every one of my cards was totally blank! I instantly realized that this God I was following was pretty insistent and pretty powerful. So I folded my cards, and that was the last time I played poker. From then on prayer was real to me.

When I was in St. Johnsville, I naturally attended the Lutheran Church with Doris and her family, but I knew nothing of churches in New Brunswick, where Rutgers was located. At college, I was actually the only believer whom I knew! That lasted until I took a class in public speaking, and for my class speech, I decided to tell the other students how I had been converted to Christianity. After the class, one of the students told me that he was also a believer and that he knew others like us. That is how I discovered InterVarsity Christian Fellowship. It was only a small group of 13, but they helped ground me in the things of the Lord. One member was Doug Smith who introduced me to his family in nearby Princeton, all of whom were believers.

The Smith family helped me to begin attending church and learn what the Christian life was all about. Doug and his wife, Audrey, have been friends ever since. I believe it is noteworthy that 12 of the 13 in our InterVarsity group ended up in what we then were calling "full-time Christian service," including me.

Man and Wife

The next summer, I was off once again to McDonald Farms. A vivid memory of that summer is how much time I constantly spent devouring the Bible. I couldn't get enough. The first couple of times through God's Word are an exhilarating experience!

A fellow worker and I each came up with $25 to jointly purchase a vintage Model A Ford, and we had transportation. I used the Model A to get me back and forth to the Mueller farm whenever I had a couple of days off.

By then I had decided that I would save the money I was making that summer to buy an engagement ring. I made around $200, and I found a used ring (the owner's engagement had not worked out) for that price. Doris came to the State Fair in Syracuse and bunked with all of us in the barns in front of the cows during the days we showed them. That's when I gave her the ring, on September 9, 1950. We had already agreed that we were meant for each other, but we needed to set a date. We didn't much care for long engagements, so we decided we should wait all of about six weeks. October 15 became our day.

Part of our affinity for each other grew out of our common historical roots as well as our shared rural culture. My ancestors had arrived in the British Colonies in 1710, from the Palitinate region of Germany. They made their way north up the Hudson River Valley, turned west up the Mohawk River Valley, and bought the Francis Harrington patent from the Mohawk Indians, for 900 beaver skins, in 1735. That later became St. Johnsville. Doris's father had emigrated from Germany, and the farm he acquired was on the very land that my ancestors had pioneered. Among other things, my ancestors built the Palatine Lutheran Church in 1770, and I was privileged to preach the two-hundredth anniversary celebration there in 1971.

But back to the wedding. There was very little time to prepare. I bought an 18-year-old Dodge sedan for $350. I played hooky from school for a week, and Jack Stover from the Phi Gamma Delta house came as my best man. Doris and I were married in the Mueller family's Lutheran Church in

Doris and I were married on October 15, 1950, in her family's church, Christ Lutheran Church, in Little Falls, New York.

Little Falls. My mother, dad and sister, Margo, were on hand, and the American Guernsey Cattle Club offered to pay for a honeymoon in Peterborough, New Hampshire, if we would agree to visit their national headquarters there. By then we were getting the idea that they might be leading up to offering me a job when I graduated, but they didn't know we were planning to be foreign missionaries.

Our home was a 28-foot box-like World War II surplus trailer with no indoor plumbing. We had to bring our water in to the sink in a bucket and throw out the drain water in another bucket. The common bathroom was a short walk down the road. Doris got jobs like clerking in a 5 & 10 cent store, checking customers out of a supermarket and peddling lunches to construction workers in an Italian lunch truck. By then I was milking a string of 35 cows in the College of Agriculture dairy herd, morning and night. This led to a memorable event that left no doubt that I had made a good choice for a wife.

I am not a sickly person. Good health has always been a blessing. One morning, however, when the alarm went off at 4:30 A.M., I woke up legitimately sick. I couldn't even get out of bed. What to do? Milking cows is extremely time sensitive. So I said, "Honey, how about milking my cows?" To complicate matters, she had never even been inside the dairy barn. She didn't know any of the other four or five students who were milking similar strings. Fortunately, however, we were using DeLaval milking machines, the kind she had been brought up with on her own farm. So, without missing a beat, she jumped in the '38 Dodge, introduced herself to the other milkers, found out which were my cows and how much to feed them and got the job done before breakfast! That's when I began saying, "What a woman!"

California, Here We Come

It's one thing to hear God's call to be foreign missionaries, but it's another thing to begin to take steps to make it happen. The spiritual climate of the whole Northeast was much more arid in those days than it is now. There were very few believers of the born-again kind; churches were small, pastors were struggling and we were such new Christians that we lacked good role models as well as specific instructions as to how to become missionaries. We had become aware, however, that we would need ministerial training in order to be prepared for the job. That meant that after Rutgers, we should plan to go to Bible school and seminary.

At that point, we had a close call, and my father came to the rescue. Right after I left home, my parents had moved from Connecticut to Springfield, Massachusetts. Surprisingly, they joined South Congregational Church, a prestigious colonial-era church, and became acquainted with Rev. James Gordon Gilkey, a community leader as well as their new pastor. In our enthusiasm for serving the Lord, Doris and I started entertaining the thought of quitting Rutgers and enrolling in a Bible school right away. My father was appalled when he heard of this, and he persuaded me to schedule an appointment with Gilkey before I made my final decision. Gilkey was a wise man. He told me how much agricultural missionaries were needed in today's world and that I should definitely finish my agricultural degree. That degree could also qualify me for entrance to a theological seminary, which would advance my career much more than a Bible school. I took his advice and, looking back, it is more than evident that I could not be where I am now without Dad's urging and Gilkey's good counsel.

By then we had discovered that we were evangelicals, and not liberals. New Brunswick Theological Seminary was located adjacent to the Rutgers campus, but it was geared for Reformed Church clergy. Princeton Theological Seminary was just down the road, but it was geared for Presbyterian clergy. Both were liberal. As we inquired, several evangelical schools in different parts of the country began to surface, but suddenly one seemed to rise up head and shoulders above the others, namely, Fuller Theological Seminary in Pasadena, California. For one thing, it was new, only 5 years old when I graduated from Rutgers in 1952. For another, it was founded by America's most famous radio evangelist, Charles E. Fuller of the "The Old Fashioned Revival Hour" radio program. And better yet, it was quite controversial. The faculty was composed of some of the most highly regarded evangelical scholars in the nation, but those who were not afraid to think outside of the box. This greatly disturbed many fundamentalist leaders across the country, but it seemed very attractive to me, even though I didn't know exactly what they were quarreling about. There was something inside me that made the possibility of new wineskins more appealing than the old wineskins.

A couple of bonuses were (1) the Bible Institute of Los Angeles (Biola), to which Doris could apply, was nearby, and (2) a trip across the country to California seemed almost irresistible to a pair of newlyweds. I was a bit apprehensive about being admitted to a respected theological seminary, having graduated from an "ag" school, but my grade point average probably helped. I was accepted as a Fuller student, and Doris was accepted in Biola as well. We would have three years to find out how to be missionaries and what mission field would finally be ours.

Learning to Cope

We would have no financial aid for this. Neither of our families could afford to help us. No scholarships were available. We knew we would have to launch out and live by faith, whatever that meant. The first thing was to get from New York to California in the days before interstate highways. Because both of us had been conditioned by the Depression, and then by wartime rationing, we had become savers, not spenders. Our saving vehicle of choice was $25 U.S. savings bonds, which we could buy for $18.75. By the time I graduated, we had saved enough of them to get us across the country.

I bought a trailer that had a plywood box and a back door, and with some hand tools I built in a bed and a table, turning out a homemade RV that we could pull behind the '38 Dodge. We packed in all of our belongings and set off on a month-long adventure across country, choosing a route through as many national parks as possible. Among other things, we saw our first palm trees in Southern California, and we were excited about living in a new part of the world for a time.

Our first lesson in what would become a couple of decades of living by faith came when we stopped in a campground in rural Iowa to spend Saturday night. Because the next day was Sunday, we would stay put. We scouted around and found a small Nazarene Church nearby, so we were in the service Sunday morning. When the parishioners found out that we were on the way to get training to become missionaries, they took up a love offering for us, which came out to a total of $18, the value of another savings bond! We've loved Nazarenes ever since!

Fuller had offered us a tiny three-room apartment located in a corner of a large remodeled home being used as a men's dormitory right on the Pasadena campus. We would have free rent as long as Doris agreed to be housemother to the 20 students who lived there, and to keep the toilets and other common places clean. We had spent all our savings bonds, so we needed income for tuition and necessities of life. I was a Fuller janitor, and I delivered baked goods and framed houses as a carpenter. Besides cleaning the dormitory, Doris was an assistant to the Fuller registrar and she operated the seminary switchboard.

Our Depression experiences helped us once again, because we were able to live on only $7 per week for groceries. That bought 1 pound of hamburger, 1 pound of hot dogs, 1 can of tuna fish and a box of Kraft Dinner, plus cereal, milk and bread for breakfast.

Bell Friends Church

Unlike Fuller, Biola required that their students undertake practical work assignments. Doris was assigned to Bell Friends Church in Bell, California, about 15 miles south of Pasadena. I checked it out with her and we liked it so much that Bell Friends became our home congregation for the three years we were there. They were excited about getting two students, one from Biola and one from Fuller, at the same time. Every Sunday a family from the church would invite us to Sunday dinner in their home. Our responsibility was to take over the junior church, which we did with a great deal of enthusiasm. This was the first official "ministry" assignment I ever had. Historical events like taking the kids to Disneyland the first week it opened were among the highlights. So also was leading many of the children to Christ. We still get phone calls from Eddie Main, who was one of those saved in junior church.

Before we arrived in Bell, we had never heard of a Friends Church. We soon discovered that it was another name for Quakers. Using virtually the only theological savvy we had at the time, we determined that it was a thoroughly evangelical church. So long as it wasn't liberal, we didn't care much that such things as water baptism or Communion were not part of their tradition. Before long, I was teaching an adult Bible class, which soon acquired the commendable habit of taking up a weekly offering for Doris and me. This gave us the wonderful opportunity to have a weekly night out and buy ourselves a hamburger with the trimmings on our way home after the Sunday evening service.

Theological Issues

Doris began driving down the Arroyo Seco Freeway (later the Pasadena Freeway) to Biola, located in the center of Los Angeles, every day for classes. She soon began to discover an interesting theological phenomenon. The Biola faculty recognized Fuller as a liberal seminary, and they would even occasionally criticize some of Fuller's theological positions in class. Living right on the Fuller campus, we had become a part of the Fuller community, and we were puzzled at what Biola thought could possibly be liberal about Fuller. My professors at Fuller explicitly identified themselves as evangelicals, and the presence of Charles E. Fuller and his "Old Fashioned Revival Hour" would seem to set that identity in concrete. If that weren't enough, Fuller's founding president, Harold John Ockenga, of Boston, also became the founder and first president of the National Association of Evangelicals.

I was hardly in a position to analyze what might be going on at the time. As a farmer and a fresh graduate of agricultural school, I was entering an ethereal theological world on the very bottom step of the ladder. I found myself rather overwhelmed when, during my first semester at Fuller, I was required to sign up for a course in epistemology taught by Carl F. H. Henry. For beginners, I didn't even know how to spell the word! Henry's first few lectures might as well have been in Japanese as far as I was concerned. Although it took me several weeks to comprehend it, I finally became aware that epistemology is a branch of philosophy that tries to figure out how we think. My initial response was, "Who cares?" However, I knew very well that the registrar would care and that if I were going to graduate, I would need to pass the course. By the grace of God, one of the students in our dormitory happened to be a fresh graduate in philosophy from Stanford, and he stayed up night after night tutoring a group of us who otherwise might have melted down.

Why do I tell this epistemology story? I am not by nature a critical person, but still, one of my purposes in this book is to examine and analyze certain past experiences in the light of where God has placed me now toward the end of my career. Epistemology as an entry-level required course for training to do Christian ministry is a case in point. I passed the course (with my only Fuller "C"!), but try as I might, I have never been able to make even a vague connection between the content of that course and anything I have done in the rest of my life so far. This was the beginning of a personal aversion to required courses, especially on the graduate level and up.

Disproportionate numbers of required courses ultimately serve the needs of the institution rather than the needs of the students. Courses like epistemology enhance the academic prestige of the school. They also help pay the salaries of professors who tend to teach irrelevant material. Many years later, when I started my own school, one of my first principles for curriculum design was to offer all elective courses, no required courses.

One consolation was that I was not alone. Theological education had become quite standardized, and the three years in an institution like Fuller were the most respectable pathway to ordination. I was determined to finish, and I did.

Doris, however, could not finish Biola. Toward the end of her second year, she unexpectedly became pregnant with our first daughter, Karen. Those were the days when motherhood trumped studenthood, so she was unable to go on to her third year.

The South America Indian Mission

Before I graduated, we had looked into many possibilities for missionary service, and we had settled on the South America Indian Mission, based in West Palm Beach, Florida. One of the deciding factors was that they had an opening for an agricultural missionary in eastern Bolivia, and we felt that such an opportunity would fulfill our calling. We went back to Doris's family farm in St. Johnsville to regroup, to connect Karen with her grandparents, to start packing for Bolivia and to arrange for my ordination.

While finishing Rutgers, we had joined New Brunswick (New Jersey) Bible Church, a small congregation of what we today would call fundamentalists. I say "today" because, in the 1950s, the terms "fundamentalist" and "evangelical" were generally synonymous. However, some of the evangelicals on the right also saw themselves as "separatists," which meant they taught that true Bible believers should not allow themselves to be associated at all with denominations or even local churches that were open enough to include liberals. They believed in guilt by association. Separatists also tended to follow more legalistic lines in issues of personal behavior, as well as keeping a distance between the church and the world. These strongly opinionated conservatives would eventually come to be labeled fundamentalists, while the more open ones would be known as the straight-line evangelicals.

These differences had been reflected in the opinions of some Biola faculty that Fuller Seminary was liberal. They saw themselves as the true evangelicals, while Fuller openly followed what came to be called the "new evangelicalism." My personal positioning at the time, even though I was a Fuller grad, was closer to the separatists like those in the New Brunswick Bible Church and the South America Indian Mission. I regret this now, as we will see in more detail later, but it is important to know that such were my convictions when we left for the mission field.

Christ's Two Natures

Because the New Brunswick Bible Church organized my ordination committee, these convictions of mine dovetailed nicely with those of the conservative pastors who were called upon to examine me in spite of the fact that most of them had concerns about the orthodoxy of Fuller. All seemed to be going well in my ordination questioning until we came to the matter of the relationship between the two natures of Christ. Suddenly, I found myself up against what turned out to be the first of many future disagreements with the religious establishment. Let me explain.

We all agreed that the Son, unlike the Father and the Holy Spirit, had two natures, a full divine nature and a full human nature. The standard view, held unanimously by those on my committee, was that Jesus switched back and forth, sometimes operating through His divine nature (e.g., stilling the storm or raising Lazarus) and sometimes through His human nature (e.g., getting hungry or weeping). My view, which I had learned from my theology professor, Edward John Carnell, was that during His incarnation, Jesus operated solely through His human nature and that His miracles were not done by His power but by the power of the Holy Spirit working through Him. This became a point of serious contention, and I cited Philippians 2, a major passage on Christ's incarnation. When I pointed out that Jesus "made Himself of no reputation, taking the form of a bond-servant, and coming in the likeness of men" (Phil. 2:7) and that He "became obedient to the point of death, even the death of the cross" (Phil. 2:8), I could detect that most of them had not given a great deal of thought to the matter, so they changed the subject.

During the discussion, I had tried to let all concerned know that I believed, as they did, that Jesus was forever and always fully divine. During His incarnation, He had not given up His divine nature; He had only suspended its use temporarily. Even so, the time the committee took in their private deliberations as to whether they would or would not approve my ordination was noticeably longer than usual. At the end of the day, they said I could be ordained, provided I would agree to spend a minimum of six hours in the Princeton Theological Seminary library, reading up on the subject of Christology. I agreed, and I was duly ordained.

After the six hours, I must say, I was more convinced than ever that my position was correct, and this helped me greatly in a later season of life when I began to experience more directly the power of the Holy Spirit. I explain my point of view in the chapter "Passing the Power" in *How to Have a Healing Ministry in Any Church*.

Once I was ordained, we were ready to set our sights on Bolivia.

3

Jungle Missionaries

(1956–1961)

We can easily divide our 16 years in Bolivia into two parts. We spent our first term in Eastern Bolivia, near the Brazilian border, which is a lowland jungle area. We spent our other two terms in Cochabamba, 8,500 feet above sea level, in the Andes Mountains. Back in those days, the accepted pattern for foreign missionary service was five years on the field for each assignment, separated by a one-year furlough in the home country. Typically, unlike today's missionaries, there was no expectation that a field worker would even think of visiting home between furloughs. International transportation before jet engines was difficult, time consuming and costly.

Short-Term Missions?

I find it interesting to note how the complexion of modern missions has changed in my lifetime. As I've already hinted, since the inception of the modern missionary movement with William Carey in 1792, missionary service was regarded by all as a career. When we set out for Bolivia, we fully expected to live our whole lives there. Our children would join the ranks of MKs, "missionary kids." Those who went to the mission field and ended up as "missionary dropouts" were considered nothing short of failures unless they were able to present a convincing case of physical breakdown.

Foreign missions as a lifelong vocation was the norm until the mid-1970s. At that time, some mission agencies began to appoint new workers for a limited period of a few months or a few years. Later, short-term missions began to come upon the scene and people would be sent to the field for missions trips lasting as little as a week or two.

Our first taste of this trend came in the mid 1960s when we agreed to host a group of short-termers taking a missions trip. It was a new idea, and we were among the pioneers. The rationale behind this was that committed young people wanted to find out firsthand what the mission field was like before making a career decision to become foreign missionaries. By and large they were in their late teens or early twenties. They would undertake certain odd jobs such as painting and building repairs, but as Doris and I looked back on it, we considered the experience a drag. Our personal role was mostly as tour guides and baby-sitters. In order to maintain good relationships with supporting churches back home, we, rather reluctantly, ended up doing this several times even though we felt that our time could be better used for concentrating on the work we had been called to do.

The results? Undoubtedly the mission trip was a life-changing experience for many who went to a foreign country for the first time. However, to our knowledge, few, if any, of the short-termers ultimately became career missionaries. Researcher Michael Jaffarian confirms that our suspicions were correct when he refers to "the hollow hope, expectation, and rhetoric about the impact of short-term missions activity on long-term missions commitment. The myth says that growth in short-term missions and mission trips leads to growth in long-term missions. The facts, however, say that growth in the one has not led to growth in the other."[1]

Nevertheless, the trend continues. To be precise, at this writing, North America is sending approximately 41,000 career missionaries as compared to 147,000 short-termers.[2] And those who take mission trips? Today "for every long-term missionary serving overseas there are more than sixty mission-trip participants, nearly all of them untrained."[3]

Missionary Training

Although we had prayed about it a good deal, our choice of the South America Indian Mission was not a result of extensive knowledge of the mission fields of the day or options for service. Missionary training in seminaries and Bible schools at that time was minimal. Yes, missionaries were generally regarded as spiritual hero figures, but they were largely on their own. For example, none of my professors at Fuller Seminary had been missionaries. In fact, few had ever traveled outside of the United States. Textbooks and other literature on missions were scarce. The word "missiology" was unknown in our academic circles. I was offered one course in missions, taught by Harold Lindsell, a church historian. He was considered qualified because he had taught courses in missions and had written one of the popular missions textbooks, *Missionary Principles and Practice* (Fleming H. Revell, 1955). That, along with an elective course in reading missionary biographies, was the extent of the professional training available for what was to be my lifetime career.

Our bathtub was the river. Here our daughter Karen gets the functional equivalent of a shower.

In San Jose, Doris developed a very popular form of outreach—a cooking class for neighborhood women. She is the one with a wooden spoon in her hand.

In the midst of this paucity of systematic instruction in missiology, one bright and shining source of missions information was the Urbana Missions Convention sponsored by InterVarsity Christian Fellowship (IVCF), held at the University of Illinois campus in Urbana-Champaign between Christmas and New Year's every three years. During my senior year at Rutgers, some of us from our tiny IVCF group packed into two automobiles, one of which was our 1938 Dodge, and managed the drive through extremely snowy weather from New Jersey to Illinois before the days of Interstate highways. This 1951 Convention was the third (it's a triennial conference begun in Toronto in 1946), and an amazing 1,500 students showed up. We listened to some of the best missions speakers of the day and perused scores of displays set up by almost every missions agency known. We had no idea then that the Urbana Convention would endure to this writing and draw 20,000 to the 2009 event. We returned highly motivated to pursue our missionary call.

"Faith" Missionaries

After we signed up with the South America Indian Mission, we needed to face the stark reality that it was a "faith mission," and that we would be personally responsible to raise all the funds needed for transportation to Bolivia, shipment of our goods to the field and our personal financial support during our career. As the years went by, raising support became by far the most personally draining aspect of missionary life. This was particularly difficult for such things as medical emergencies, vehicles and even transportation to the field. When we returned to Bolivia for our second term, for example, we actually had to borrow money for our travel expenses, and we were forced to stretch our meager resources to repay the debt over the next two or three years. Existing on a subsistence income or worse had become a painful but necessary way of life for us.

One of our drawbacks was that neither Doris nor I had roots in a Bible-believing, missionary-minded church with a missionary budget that might see fit to underwrite our family's missionary support. However, by God's grace, our affiliation with Bell Friends Church, while we were going to school, provided us with such a group. While their denomination wouldn't allow us to be supported as an official project of the church, numbers of individuals and families to whom we had ministered agreed to send monthly contributions to the mission. Many of our family members and friends supported us as well, but the bulk came from Bell Friends.

Because we had agreed to be "faith missionaries," the experience of always being short of funds naturally raised the question in our minds as to whether we actually had the necessary level of *faith* for this missionary task. What was going on? While we were on the field, we had no comfortable answer to that question. We certainly believed God and believed that we were where God wanted us to be; but from today's perspective, I would now be inclined to confess that we probably did fall short of the godly faith for finances that we otherwise might have had.

Christian leaders such as Kenneth Hagin and Oral Roberts had just begun to surface when Doris and I went to Bolivia. Because I had identified with the cessationist evangelical camp at the time, everything I heard about them was negative. My professors had relegated them and their colleagues to the lunatic fringe of pseudo-theologians. Later in the book I will explain some of the positive influences that I believe the Word of Faith movement has contributed, but at this point I simply want to say that our "faith missions" circles might have benefited greatly if they had been listening more closely to the message of biblical prosperity that Hagin, Roberts and others were preaching. Instead we unwittingly allowed ourselves to be dominated by an evil spirit of poverty; and as a result, I am convinced that we actually forfeited a good bit of the potential that we had for spreading the gospel in those days.

Culture Shock

When Doris, one-year-old Karen and I boarded the four-engine, propeller-driven Douglas DC-6 in Miami, bound for South America, we knew that we were headed for a place called Santiago de Chiquitos in Eastern Bolivia, the only South America Indian Mission (SAIM) station with a substantial agricultural project. We were excited finally to be launched into our full-time service for God. However, we had little inkling of the huge cultural adjustment we would face once we arrived in Santiago. We were so naïve that I don't think the term "culture shock" was even a part of our vocabulary at the time. However, it would very soon become a conspicuous part of our experience.

We changed planes in Lima to a two-engine Douglas DC-3 and stepped off in the Bolivian town of Roboré to what I still remember as the hottest blast of air I had ever experienced. The temperature must have been well over 100 degrees, and the humidity near 100 precent. George W. Haight was waiting for us with his stake-bed truck, which would take us 12 miles through the jungle, crossing three small rivers without bridges, to Santiago. Haight was a World War I veteran of the Canadian Cavalry. He was a tough, hardened, no-nonsense missionary from a generation that has not since been replicated.

To give you an example, about a decade before we arrived, a group of five young New Tribes Mission workers had set off from the Santiago mission station in search of the fierce unreached Ayoré Indians. Haight strongly admonished them to take firearms, but they refused. All five were massacred! When Haight went to search for them, he did take his rifle, and, sure enough, he found it necessary to put an end to one of the Ayoré warriors. Some would want to debate as to whether he did the right thing, but there was no room for debate in George Haight's mind. He once said to me, "My life was clearly more important to God than the savage's!" Such was our senior missionary, and he ran his mission station with an iron hand.

Assignment Number One was to learn Spanish. We had never previously been in a foreign country without knowing the language, except for a few benign visits to the tourist sections of Tijuana, just across the Mexican border from Southern California. Yes, we could speak English from time to time with the five other missionaries at the station, but not often. They were all over their heads with their own responsibilities. Our language teacher was Flora Balcázar, whom the childless Haights had all but adopted as a daughter and sent her to study at Moody Bible Institute in Chicago. We soon began to realize that we had an advantage over other new missionaries who were first assigned to Spanish language school in places like Costa Rica. After class, we were out there with the people on our own, not socializing with other English-speaking language students. This sped up the learning process and helped us to avoid much of a foreign accent. Eventually we were even dreaming in Spanish. Poor Karen started life not knowing much English at all.

Isolation

By far, our most difficult challenge was isolation. Initially, without the language, there were few people to talk to. Smiles and sign language go only so far, especially since neither one of us is a sanguine temperament. We had no radio, no newspapers, no Internet, no telephones of any kind. Mail to and from home took from three to six weeks. Doris had to learn to cook with a wood stove and bake in a beehive oven. Without electricity, refrigeration was unknown. They would butcher one cow a week on the mission station to feed the students in the mission school as well as the rest of us. On the first day, we had wonderful filet mignon. By the end of the week, however, the

Walking barefoot through a jungle swamp full of alligators with only a .22 rifle is a memorable experience. When Doris cooked the tail that you see, the gourmet result could hardly be matched in Paris!

Off on an evangelistic tour in the jungles. My mule, Betty, was 18 years old, and I could depend on her to get me where I wanted to go.

meat became rather ripe hanging in the tropics amidst swarms of flies. At the end of the first week in Santiago, we were served a hot bowl of soup with the bottom of the bowl lined with cooked maggots. That is when we were thankful that bananas, around 15 different varieties of them, were abundant, so we heartily ate bananas until we finally got used to our new cuisine.

That reminds me of a joke. How do you tell the difference between a first-term missionary, a second-term missionary and a third term missionary? The first-term missionary sees an ant in his soup and throws the soup away. The second-term missionary sees an ant in his soup, takes it out and eats the soup. The third-term missionary sees an ant walking across the table, grabs it and puts it in his soup!

But seriously, the food at first presented a severe problem to our lower intestines. Our chronic diarrhea progressed into severe dysentery, which lasted for one-and-a-half years "running," as I like to say! The uncomfortable situation was further complicated by the lack of indoor plumbing, and toilet paper in the form of old issues of *Reader's Digest*. The bad news was that this dragged us down a bit physically. The good news was that when we recovered there was hardly any food that we couldn't eat or water we couldn't drink from then on. We had stomachs of iron!

Alligator Tail

Besides all the beef we could eat, and an occasional chicken, one of the rare culinary delicacies of the Bolivian lowlands was alligator tail. My coworker, Luís Bravo, told me he knew where there were some alligators, so we each took a .22 long rifle, some cartridges, our machetes and set off through the woods on horseback. About two hours later we found the swamp. I wondered what we would do next. Luís told me that we would take off our pants and our shoes and socks and walk barefoot into the swamp to find the alligators. Looking back on this as an old man, I find it unbelievable that without a moment of hesitation, I undressed and was walking in the water. Soon we saw them, namely, three spots—their nose and two eyes—on the surface of the water. Alligator skin is so thick that a .22 bullet would bounce off, so we had to hit the alligator exactly in an eye. Fortunately, like many farm boys, I was a good shot. I fired one round, the alligator flipped, floated on his back on the surface, and I pulled him out.

On about the third or fourth attempt, my shot was a bit off, and the alligator flipped once but submerged instead of floating. Now, I'm walking in a swamp barefoot with a wounded alligator that I can't see. I'm not by nature a fearful person, but I openly confess that this was one of life's moments when I was thoroughly enveloped by fear. I was so confused that I grabbed my small 22-caliber revolver, my machete, as well as my rifle, with only two hands, not stopping to realize that I could not have used any of the weapons if the need ever appeared. I was walking slowly, and to top it off, I stepped right on the back of the wounded alligator! When he moved under my foot, I think I set the Olympic high jump record! Somehow I got out of the swamp. Luís also had two or three alligator tails by then, so we headed home with a good supply of meat after some frightening but successful alligator hunting. I'll admit that I never hunted alligators again!

Delayed Baggage

One of the most upsetting aspects related to our culture shock had to do with our personal belongings. On the DC-6 from Miami, Doris and I were each allowed 22 lbs. of checked baggage, and Karen none, because as an infant she had no seat of her own. To compensate a bit we layered. I recall that I wore three sets of underwear plus two shirts, two sweaters, and so on. However, we were allowed to also take a moderate number of foot lockers or trunks in which we could pack some personal belongings and ship them by sea. Naturally, we shipped many of our sentimental items like pictures, wedding gifts and favorite clothing as well as household goods, because we considered it a lifetime move. We began looking forward to receiving our baggage almost as soon as we arrived and had begun to feel the severe isolation. We badly needed a touch from home!

What a disappointment when weeks and then months went by without word of our goods! Finally, news came somehow that the shipment had been waylaid on the docks of Montevideo, Uruguay. After some more time, it became evident that the only way we could ever claim our belongings was for me to travel to Montevideo. The expense of flying was out of the question, so I boarded a coal-burning train from 13,000 feet in La Paz for the three-day journey to sea level in Buenos Aires, crossed the Río de la Plata to Montevideo, found the luggage and brought it up the Paraguay River on a boat to nearby Corumbá, Brazil. It was a year and a half late, but by the grace of God it was all there! Fortunately, before we received our baggage we had successfully emerged from our culture shock even without our precious memorabilia. We had learned how to live off the land!

"Your Mother Has Died!"

Speaking of isolation, undoubtedly the most severe communications breakdown came when we had been on the field for a couple of years. A New Tribes missionary, whom we did not know, stationed in a different part of the jungle, was among the few who had a ham radio and could communicate with North America. One day a stranger knocked on our door and said he had a message from that missionary. Word of mouth was the major communications medium in that part of the world, and one never knew through how many mouths the message had been passed before it reached us. The message was that our mother had died! Our immediate question was, "Which one of our mothers?" The stranger had no idea!

It took us the better part of two weeks to discover that it happened to be my mother who had died. Next question: "What did she die of?" No one this far from the ham radio knew a thing about it. As expected, my sister, Margo, had immediately written me a letter telling me all about Mother's sudden premature death of pneumonia and the subsequent family funeral. However, just at that time the postal service of Bolivia had happened to go on strike! When mail arrived in the capital city of La Paz, it was simply thrown onto a huge pile. By the time the strike had ended, the pile was so massive and discouraging that someone decided to pour gasoline on it and set it on fire! It took six months for us finally to know what had happened. I realize this sounds strange to today's missionaries who have cell phones and who will often make a quick trip home for something like a mother's appendectomy, but we calmly took the whole scenario in stride as simply a part of the life to which God had called us.

Working to Live

Without a doubt, one of the most valuable lessons we soon learned was that the American culture in which we had been raised had some inherent weaknesses. Although it was not always easy, both Doris and I had an inward desire to learn and appreciate and participate in the Bolivian culture without making the foolish mistake of "going native." I wouldn't have been able to verbalize it at the time, but I now realize that God, by His grace, had given us the "missionary gift," which I describe in detail in some of my other books, such as *Your Spiritual Gifts Can Help Your Church Grow.*

As we became more open with our Bolivian friends, we heard this observation of American culture more than once: "Americans live to work; we work to live!" I will not forget how this was demonstrated by a friend of mine named Bernardo. Bernardo had a business of cutting firewood in the jungle and selling it to the railroad as fuel for their wood-burning locomotives. At one point, a friend of mine in the United States sent me a chain saw, the first such tool ever to appear in the region. Bernardo was one of the first ones for whom I was anxious to demonstrate the chain saw. He was amazed! Do you know what he said? "Peter, if I had that saw, I could get all my week's work done in one day!" It never entered his mind that he might be able to produce five times as much firewood!

Which reminds me of another joke that is in my book *Let's Laugh!*

A boat docked in a tiny Mexican village. An American tourist complimented the Mexican fisherman on the quality of his fish and asked how long it took him to catch them.

"Not very long," answered the Mexican.

"But then, why didn't you stay out longer and catch more?" asked the American.

The Mexican explained that his small catch was sufficient to meet his needs and those of his family.

The American asked, "But what do you do with the rest of your time?"

"I sleep late, fish a little, play with my children and take a siesta with my wife. In the evenings, I go into the village to see my friends, have a few drinks, play the guitar and sing a few songs. I have a full life."

The American interrupted, "Look," he said, "I have an MBA from Harvard and I can help you! You should start by fishing longer every day. You can then sell the extra fish you catch. With the extra revenue, you can buy a bigger boat."

"And after that?" asked the Mexican.

"With the extra money the larger boat will bring, you can buy a second one and a third one and so on until you have an entire fleet of trawlers. Instead of selling your fish to a middleman, you can then negotiate directly with the processing plants and maybe even open your own plant. You can then leave this little village and move to Mexico City, Los Angeles or even New York City! From there you can direct your huge new enterprise."

I am sharing my *yerba mate*, an Argentine tea, with daughter Karen, 2, in Santiago de Chiquitos, Bolivia. Ever since then I have enjoyed *yerba mate* every afternoon for 55 years!

Luis Bravo (back row left) and me with our students in the Eastern Bible Institute in San Jose de Chiquitos, Bolivia. The picture was taken in the inside courtyard of our home.

"How long would that take?" asked the Mexican.

"Twenty, perhaps 25 years," replied the American, "but you'd be making millions!"

"Millions? Wow! And after that?"

"After that you'll be able to retire, live in a tiny village near the coast, sleep late, play with your children, catch a few fish, take a siesta with your wife and spend your evenings drinking and enjoying your friends!"

Let's Get to Work

While we were learning Spanish, we could still be useful in some ways. Doris had some medical background, so she took care of the sick, including extracting teeth at times with no anesthetic. Once she gave an injection to a child whose father showed his gratitude by bringing us a freshly skinned boa constrictor. Doris cut it up, boiled it, then fried it, and we enjoyed a tasty dinner! Because I had gone as an agricultural missionary, I plowed with the small tractor, planted, made a trench silo and prepared to assemble the first dairy herd in the region. One of the more humorous incidents came when we happened to secure a bit of commercial fertilizer and I experimented with it on a few rows in a field of corn. The crop in those rows more than doubled anything that had ever been grown in the area, but we ended up with very little of it. Why? Local farmers were so amazed that they could not help but steal our large fertilized corn for seed, expecting that if they planted it they could duplicate our production!

I may have started with agriculture, but that venture was short-lived. Only about six months after we arrived, and with very rudimentary Spanish, I was asked to direct the Eastern Bolivia Bible Institute (*Instituto Bíblico del Oriente*) that was located in Santiago. That set the course for the rest of my life. Although I have ministered in many other areas, ever since then, teaching has been my passion.

Regretfully, however, the Bible school never did well. I attribute that to my utter ignorance of what we would later call "contextualization." I was a cross-cultural missionary, but I had never been trained in cross-cultural missions. Consequently, I made the serious mistake of designing the school, from the scheduling to the student body to the curriculum, on the pattern of Fuller Theological Seminary, albeit at a lower academic level. Needless to say, such a school never made a powerful impact on Eastern

Bolivia. As I will explain later, my view of equipping the saints for the work of the ministry has radically changed, and I would have certainly done it differently if I had to do it over again.

Church Planting

Mixed with teaching were the traditional missionary roles of evangelism and church planting. Planting a new church, however, came rather suddenly when, for reasons that I never discovered, George Haight experienced a severe falling out with SAIM. We found ourselves in the midst of a classic mission split, and we felt the Lord would have us stay with the mission instead of siding with the Haights. We were assigned to move the Bible institute to the town of San José where a church had been started but gone dormant several years previously. We did find some struggling believers, and we planted a new church that became our base for the remainder of our first term.

The church grew, but it was a struggle. Jesuit missionaries had founded all the towns and villages of the area in the seventeenth and eighteenth centuries. Called "Jesuit reductions," the entire social fabric of each community was tightly woven around the Catholic Church, based in an imposing cathedral on the central plaza. Religious boundaries were virtually impenetrable. By the time the evangelical, or Protestant, missions arrived, the Franciscans had taken over from the Jesuits, but what I now see as the spirit of religion had continued to maintain its powerful demonic oppression over the people. Evangelical congregations of 20 or 30, but never more than 50, were the norm. We were there before Vatican II, when Protestant persecution by Catholics was still unrestrained.

On more than one occasion our street evangelism meetings were stoned and broken up by mobs organized by the local nuns. Once, we were holding a meeting with a converted priest in the backyard of our home when a nun persuaded a young man to hurl a large construction block over the roof of the house into our backyard. Karen, 3, who was sitting on a small wooden bench suddenly decided, undoubtedly with the help of an angel, to get up and walk over to where Doris was playing the organ. The first thing we heard was a thunderous "bang!" and the bench where Karen had been seated moments before had been smashed into three pieces! Thank God for His angels!

Three Arrived, but Four Left

While we were in San José, Doris discovered that she was pregnant. With no doctors or nurses or medical facilities available in the jungle, the normal pattern was for missionary wives to go to the city of Cochabamba about six weeks before the due date and consult a gynecologist. Since the baby was due in March, our plans were to send Doris in January. Karen and I would join her when the date was closer to the baby's arrival.

Our plans did not work. It was Christmas Eve. We held a barbeque party for our congregation in our backyard and everyone had a wonderful time. At about 2:00 A.M. on Christmas morning, we were sleeping on our four-poster bed, with plastic stretched over us to keep out the dirt from the numerous rats that traveled back and forth every night on the beams of our adobe house. I suddenly felt Doris's elbow poking me in the ribs. I said, "What's the matter?" She said, "The baby's going to be born!" Groggy, I muttered, "How do you know?" She replied, "I've done it before!"

So there we were with our new baby coming. No doctors or nurses. We hadn't contracted a local midwife because Doris was supposed to give birth in Cochabamba. Fortunately, we were both dairy farmers and the birth process was no mystery to us. I don't know how many calves I had pulled from their mother cows, but I had never tried it with a human baby! There were enough similarities, however, and Ruth was born, 10 weeks premature, weighing 2 lbs. 14 oz. Doris had no luxury of staying in bed, so she was up fabricating an incubator out of a footlocker, a hot water bottle and a mosquito net. She, of course, had no milk, but a member of our congregation and a dear friend who worked with us was nursing an infant and she dedicated one breast to her child and one to Ruth. She milked herself daily, so we had a supply of mother's milk. Little Ruth couldn't drink even from an eyedropper, so Doris fed her with soaked cotton for a week, every hour and a half, with milk one time and water the next. She thrived! By her original birth date, Ruth weighed over 7 pounds!

Our furlough was coming up soon. We had arrived in Bolivia as a family of three, but we left as a family of four.

Notes

   1. Michael Jaffarian, "The Statistical State of the North American Protestant Missions Movement," from the *Mission Handbook*, 20th Edition," *International Bulletin of Missionary Research*, January 2008, p. 36.

   2. Ibid., p. 35.

   3. Ibid., p. 36.

4

The McCullough Era

(1961–1971)

To keep things as simple as possible, when people occasionally ask me what I have done in my life, I often say that I have had three careers. I was a field missionary in Bolivia for 16 years, I was a professor at Fuller Seminary for 30 years, and I am now President of Global Harvest Ministries as my third career.

When I begin to slice my life more thinly, the names of certain individuals invariably come up. I could not possibly be where I am today without God's allowing my path to cross with many, many key persons, six of whom were so important that I have chosen to use their names in chapter titles for this book. I will mention the others in the proper places in due time. The biblical analogy of the church being a "body," namely, the "Body of Christ," has been a directive concept for me. As I mentioned previously, I have always gravitated toward team sports in which no individual, by himself or herself, could win the game. In light of this, understanding the biblical dynamics of spiritual gifts was a natural.

The key person for helping to mold my career during the season of ministering as a field missionary was Joseph McCullough. Joe was a businessman in central New Jersey, who had committed his life to Christ and was subsequently called into the pastorate. He had notable gifts of leadership, and his Baptist church in Plainfield grew well. His ministry developed a strong appeal, especially to men, and many men from his region were attracted to the church. But his overriding passion as a local church pastor was foreign missions. His church became widely known as a missionary-sending and a missionary-supporting church.

Missions eventually became so much a part of McCullough's life that he resigned from his pastorate to take the position of General Director of the Bolivian Indian Mission (BIM) with their field offices in the city of Cochabamba. As I will soon explain in detail, Joe had little influence on the first phase of our missionary career, which was in the jungles, but he is the one whom God used to help us transition to the second phase when we lived in the mountains, and I believe that he was the one who actually saved us from ending our missionary career after only one term.

Changing Mission Boards

By the time we left Bolivia after our first term, we had decided that SAIM was not a good fit for us. While we were strong evangelicals, Fuller Seminary had molded us more into what were being called at the time "neo-evangelicals" rather than the more traditional fundamentalist evangelicals. We have never been inclined toward the fundamentalist legalism that was then prevalent and that largely characterized SAIM. My inclination, as evidenced, for example, by my problems with the ordination committee in 1955, was to color outside the lines at times. I usually gravitated toward new wine, and therefore sought new wineskins. Some even considered me a maverick.

Writing for Publication

I had begun writing for publication before going to Bolivia. After I arrived, however, I discovered that the home office of the mission in Florida insisted on approving every article before it was submitted for publication. This became a point of irritation because I kept pushing boundaries that sometimes would provoke animated discussion of relevant issues. The mission office was more phlegmatic than I am. Above all, they wanted to stay in the good graces of its financial supporters, most of whom were fundamentalist evangelicals. This was a reason why, at one point in time, I had written and sent to Florida no fewer than 14 articles that our mission director would not allow me to submit for publication. This was not the way I wanted to live the rest of my life.

Enter Joseph McCullough, for whom I have named this chapter. As mentioned earlier, Joe had pastored a church in Plainfield, New Jersey, a city near New Brunswick, where Rutgers was located. He had spoken to our tiny IVCF group on occasion. He later was also a member of my ordination committee. Then he had become General Director of the Bolivian Indian Mission whose headquarters were in Cochabamba. Whenever we had traveled from the jungle to Cochabamba, we stayed in the BIM Guest Home and came to know Joe and Elizabeth quite well. As our relationship developed and I told him about some of the difficult things we were going through with SAIM, I found a sympathetic ear. I also noticed that Joe leaned toward our neo-evangelical point of view.

When we arrived in the United States and went back to the farm (incidentally, Karen, our first daughter, then 6, needed a crash course in English before she could communicate with her grandparents!), one of the first things we did was to resign from SAIM. Our resignation was cordially accepted, with no hesitation, by return mail. I think the SAIM leadership was greatly relieved. At least I could then publish my articles, which I proceeded to do. But what would our future be? If it weren't for Joe McCullough, there is a high probability that we would have joined the ranks of missionary dropouts. McCullough, however, promised to help us and be our friend. He gave us application papers, and before long we were accepted as missionaries under the Bolivian Indian Mission. We were ready to switch from jungle missionaries to mountain missionaries.

Princeton Seminary

Besides visiting our friends at Fuller and renewing relationships with our supporters at Bell Friends Church in California, we needed direction on how best to use the year of furlough we had been granted. By then I had begun building a reputation as a teacher. Joe McCullough wanted to assign me to teach in his Emmaus Bible Institute, one of the most prestigious evangelical schools in Bolivia. I agreed that this was what God wanted me to do. So after consulting with Joe and with some other friends, such as Clyde Taylor of the National Association of Evangelicals, I decided to enroll in the ThM program of Princeton Theological Seminary. Clyde suggested that if I were going to move forward as an educator, it would look good on my dossier. That turned out to be excellent advice, because it certainly helped open doors to my later second career at Fuller Theological Seminary.

My two major tasks during the 1961-1962 school year were to earn my degree at Princeton and to raise the funds necessary for this "faith missionary" to return to Bolivia. I did receive the degree. My thesis was *The Marian Theology of Thomas Aquinas.* I wanted to develop some professional expertise in Roman Catholicism, and this gave me the opportunity. I was excited when I found that they decided to permanently catalog my thesis in the Princeton Seminary library.

On the other hand, the fundraising wasn't so successful. With the help of members of Bell Friends Church, we were able to raise the minimum support necessary for returning to the field; but as I've mentioned before, we had to borrow money for our travel expenses back to Bolivia.

Speaking of money, Princeton Seminary was affiliated with the Presbyterian Church USA, which had as its doctrinal foundation the Westminster Shorter Catechism. The seminary had a standing endowment fund that enabled them to offer a stipend of $120 to students who agreed to memorize the catechism. That was a huge sum of money to furloughed missionaries at the time, so I signed up. The first thing I discovered is that the Westminster Shorter Catechism isn't very short! It is quite long! But I succeeded in memorizing it, and I passed the test. The only catechism question I still remember is the first one, which I consider excellent. "Q: What is the chief end of man? A: The chief end of man is to glorify God and enjoy Him forever." I've never been able to improve on that. Anyhow, I used the $120 to buy Doris her first-ever sewing machine, and it was well used for years and years.

Training Workers

When we arrived in Cochabamba, 8,500 feet above sea level, and settled down in our missionary apartment, I began teaching in Emmaus Bible Institute. This was the fall of 1962. Emmaus Bible Institute was simply an upscale version of the Eastern Bible Institute that I directed in San José, modeled after most Bible schools and seminaries in the United States. As I have mentioned, the Eastern Bible Institute was so culturally irrelevant that the student body had dwindled down to zero before I left for furlough. The larger evangelical constituency in the highlands provided enough students to keep Emmaus going, but the philosophy of the school was still pre-service education. It was a place where bright young men and women who seemed to have some promise for future ministry could spend two or three years studying religious subjects at a high school level. Students who came from churches of the *Unión Cristiana Evangélica* (UCE), the denomination affiliated with BIM, received a scholarship toward their training.

I was very happy with this, since, at least in my mind, there was no alternative. All the missionaries that I knew around the world were doing the same thing. For us it was the only way. In 1965, I was appointed the

Joe McCullough (left) was one of the chief molders of my ministry career. Verne Roberts (center) served as the mission director from the 1930s to the 1950s. He decided to remain in Bolivia after he was replaced by McCullough, and remained there until his death several years after this picture was taken.

Organizing the 1965 World Vision Pastors' Conference in Cochabamba, Bolivia, was a highlight of my missionary career. One thousand pastors (practically every single pastor in the nation at the time) attended. Nothing like it had ever been seen, and it contributed greatly to the year-long Evangelism in Depth effort that followed it.

director of Emmaus, and "theological education" became the core of my ongoing professional career. I spent a large amount of my time preparing lessons and syllabi for my courses and mentoring students personally. I appointed myself librarian and succeeded in securing, cataloging and shelving thousands of volumes for the school. And, of course, I supervised the school's administration.

Meanwhile, Doris moved into another area of training by taking over the BIM correspondence school. She could set this up in our home, which was necessary because Ruth, our second daughter who was born in the jungle, had been diagnosed with cerebral palsy (from which she has now recovered!), and she needed close attention. Doris was able to obtain correspondence courses in Spanish from another mission and offer them throughout the country. There were only a couple of dozen students when she took it, but she was able to build it up to the place where she was sending 700 courses per month and seeing 100 students graduate every month as well. She had 1,700 students when she turned it over to someone else and became my personal assistant a few years later.

Postgraduate Bible Institute

Several graduates from Emmaus Bible Institute, who were pastoring churches in different parts of Bolivia, began asking me about the possibilities of further training. These were mature, experienced Christian workers who felt that there was much more they could learn to help them advance in their ministry. I agreed. I was very much an advocate of helping to bring Latin American leaders to a theological level that would make them peers of the foreign missionaries rather than inferiors. So I started a short-term Emmaus Postgraduate Bible Institute geared for in-service students rather than the pre-service students we were teaching in the undergraduate school. Pastors had to agree to leave their churches for three months, September through November. Courses and assignments were intense. We were able to draw faculty from other schools in Bolivia as well as professors from Costa Rica, Peru and other places. This was the first educational program in Bolivia on a true seminary level, and it was by far my most personally rewarding teaching assignment.

In order to build relationships with other ministry training schools in Bolivia, I started convening what came to be called the Bolivian Theological Education Association (*Asociación Evangélica Boliviana de Educación*

Teológica—AEBET). I was pleased that eight schools, arguably the top eight in the nation, joined and connected with each other at the annual meetings. All this was designed to raise the levels of integrity, mutual appreciation, accountability and camaraderie among the members. AEBET also helped the Postgraduate Bible Institute with faculty and students.

It is important to keep in mind that we missionaries at that time were not missiologists. Even though a few might have taken a course or two in anthropology in college, there was little or no overt attempt to bring professional-level understanding of cultural dynamics to the practical arena of cross-cultural missionary ministry. That has now been corrected, as I will explain in due time. Meanwhile we were doing the best we could in attempting to superimpose the theological education models under which we had been trained on the unsuspecting evangelical leaders in Bolivia. One consolation is that, while we didn't see great growth of the churches throughout that season, not a few of those we trained found their places in the years to come among the most highly respected and influential evangelical leaders of the nation.

Written and Unwritten Rules

Down in the jungle we needed no licenses to ride our bicycles or our horses or to drive trucks or any other vehicle. However, driver's licenses were required in the more urban environment of Cochabamba. While we may not have been missiologists, we nevertheless did develop some practical skills in playing by Bolivian cultural rules. In every society there are written rules and unwritten rules, often of equal importance. In America, for example, this applies to traffic laws, among other things. I have driven in all 50 states, and I find differing sets of unwritten rules under the same written rules. In all 50 states, the written rule is that pedestrians have the right of way. They actually do in California, but if California pedestrians do not understand the unwritten rules when they go to Chicago, they put their lives at risk. All states, as well, require that drivers slow down for yellow lights and stop for red lights. Again, they do in California, but not in Colorado. In Colorado, you double-check the cross street in front of you before you start up when the light turns green. Hedging on red lights is common.

But back to Bolivia. Remember the trouble we had getting our baggage through Montevideo to Santiago years ago? We had no problem this time. Why? We had learned that money helps make certain things happen.

So we hired a lawyer who specializes in customs. We paid the lawyer what he required, but asked for no receipts. What he did with the money and who ended up with what we never knew and never cared. We got our baggage in no time. We also found that all real-estate transactions were closed with two prices. One price was what you paid and one was what was reported to the government. Everybody, including government officials, knew and respected that unwritten rule.

The driver's license was similar. We learned that the best (and virtually the only way) to get a driver's license was to have a friend in the Motor Vehicles Department. You could make a friend for about 30 pesos, so we did. This allowed us to receive an otherwise unavailable instruction manual. We read it, took our tests and got our driver's licenses. On the other hand, I remember one young Methodist missionary who had come to Bolivia primarily to clean the country up and remove corruption. He decided to look up the laws and get his driver's license the legal way according to the written rules. After six frustrating months, with no results, he also decided to go by the unwritten rules and make a friend in the Motor Vehicles Department!

How do things like this work out? One day, after getting my license, I was driving up to one of the city's plazas. It was rather amusing. I had been there numerous times over the years, and the traffic went around the plaza counter clockwise. But as soon as I had turned right, like I always did, I heard a police whistle and stopped. The policeman walked up to my car and said I was going the wrong way. I thought he was kidding until he pointed to the sign. Sure enough, he had switched the arrow to point the other way! So he got into my car and told me to take him to the police station. We had gone about two blocks when he said, "Señor, I know you're a busy man and you have a lot to do. I'll tell you what. If you don't have time to go to the police station and fill out all the papers, I'd be willing to go and do it for you. The fine for going the wrong way is 20 pesos, and I can take it over there and fill out your forms." I told him how much I appreciated him going out of his way, so I gave him the 20 pesos, let him out of the car and he went over and paid my fine! What? Sure, but he's got a wife and kids to support as well. The unwritten rule works for all concerned!

It may be that some could draw wrong conclusions from stories of unwritten rules like these, especially when we move from traffic laws where we Americans have a considerable amount of flexibility, to government representatives who may pocket some money on the side. I want to go on record as opposing systemic corruption, which unfortunately character-izes many nations of the world today, and I want to join any forces I can to eradicate it. There is no corruption in the kingdom of God. Mean-while, however, we are forced to live in an imperfect world, and our choices are often limited not to good and bad, but rather to bad and worse. Learning to function in a society plagued by systemic corruption isn't always the way we would prefer. The other choice, however, is not to function at all.

Spreading the Gospel

A large part of what most missionaries do is to spread the gospel. Al-though it was not our primary calling, no matter what else we did, we also constantly evangelized. The UCE Calle Bolivar Church in Coch-abamba, pastored by Jaime Rios, was the largest in the city. It became our home church. Every Sunday night the church sent out one or more open-air evangelistic teams, and our whole family would go out with one of them. Doris played the accordion, and I played a drum. Someone had given me a Bolivian drum made out of cowhide with the hair still on it and the sticks holding hard balls of rawhide. I learned to play it, keeping time with the Bolivian music we were singing. Others had guitars and trumpets, and other instruments. We would go out to where the action was, namely, the open market. Sometimes I would preach, sometimes others would. Every week between 2 and 15 unsaved people would make a decision to follow Christ.

Evangelism in Depth

On a broader evangelistic scale, the Latin America Mission (LAM) based in Costa Rica, one of the highest profile missions in all of Latin America, had started a movement called Evangelism in Depth (EID) in the early 1960s. This quickly gained the reputation of being on the cutting edge of innovative cooperative evangelism initiatives. It promised much more than the traditional citywide evangelistic campaign, because it had the vision of mobilizing the whole Body of Christ in a nation for an intensive year-long program of evangelism, which hopefully would be sustained indefinitely. Because Joe McCullough had been a long-time friend of Ken-

neth Strachan who led LAM, Bolivia was chosen to be one of the early nations outside of Costa Rica to attempt a year-long EID effort in 1965.

The massive project started less than a year after we had arrived in
Cochabamba. Actually, Cochabamba would then have been recognized
as the evangelical headquarters of the nation, far ahead of such cities as
La Paz, the capital, and Santa Cruz in the lowlands. An obvious person for
McCullough and Strachan to suggest as one of the EID leaders would be
the pastor of the large Calle Bolivar church, Jaime Ríos. Jaime's first assignment was to travel the nation and attempt to bring the full spectrum
of evangelical leaders from all missions and denominations together for
an initial Evangelism in Depth Institute. This was a huge challenge because nothing of the sort had ever been attempted before. A long history
of, sometimes aggressive, disunity had been a blight on the wider Body of
Christ in Bolivia. But Ríos, with God's help, was up to the task.

My contribution to the effort would be to agree to take Ríos's place
as interim pastor for the Calle Bolivar Church for three months, which I
did. This was my second pastoral assignment after pastoring the small
church I had planted in San José de Chiquitos. That was all the experience
I needed to come to the definitive conclusion that God had not given me
the gift of pastor! Nevertheless, the church did not fall apart, the Evangelism in Depth Institute turned out to be a resounding success, and EID
for 1965 was a go in Bolivia. I was glad to get back to teaching.

World Vision Pastors' Conference

Providentially, World Vision International, based in the Los Angeles area,
at that time had launched a worldwide ministry of sponsoring national
pastors' conferences. Under Paul Rees, then recognized as one of America's most outstanding Christian leaders, they would bring together as
many practicing national pastors as they could for a week of prayer, inspirational messages, relaxation, connecting with one another, good food and
hearing from God. The World Vision Pastors' Conferences had been gaining an international reputation of being one of the most unifying initiatives of the day for the Body of Christ in a given nation. Undoubtedly,
because of Joe McCullough's visibility and integrity, and with his encouragement, I was approached to head up a World Vision Pastors' Conference
for Bolivia. I jumped at the opportunity because by then I was beginning
to discover that, rather than pastoring churches, this was the sort of thing

I loved to do, and I could do it well. I didn't suspect it then, but looking back, I realize that this was my spiritual gift of apostle coming into action. I will explain more about that later.

My first move was to persuade World Vision to allow their conference to become an official part of Evangelism in Depth as well. They hadn't done such a thing previously, but they agreed. That is why I used the word "providentially" in the previous paragraph. Only the hand of God could have brought these two high-profile international ministries together in the same place at the same time. I consider leading this event as my major contribution to the EID effort. The nuts and bolts of the EID program were in the capable hands of national Bolivian leadership such as Jaime Ríos.

One of the joys of coordinating this meeting was that, for the first time in my life, I could work with an unlimited budget. World Vision would pay for the transportation, housing, food and all other expenses for the conference. Cochabamba was the obvious place to hold the event, but an immediate problem arose. At the time, there were slightly more than 1,000 churches with pastors in Bolivia, but there was no auditorium in the entire city with such a seating capacity. So what I did was confiscate the soccer field on the property of our BIM Missionary Children's School on the outskirts of Cochabamba and hire a contractor to build a pole-type auditorium that would accommodate a conference of up to 1,000 people. When it was over, we simply demolished the building and resold the building materials. It was soon a soccer field again!

More than one seasoned missionary wept as they watched the trucks, buses, trains and automobiles unload crowds of pastors from every corner of the nation. It was for them like a dream come true. They were seeing the fruit of their labor with their very eyes! For the 800 pastors who gathered, the experience was unforgettable, and the impact was beyond encouraging and energizing. They were ready to shout "Bolivia for Christ!" as they moved together toward the Evangelism in Depth program.

What Really Happened?

Now let's analyze this. There is no question in anyone's mind that 1965 was the high point of the evangelical work in Bolivia that had started in 1895, 70 years previously. Never had there been more excitement; never had there been more unity; never had there been more public pronouncement of the gospel. For the first time, Bolivian evangelicals took to the

Doris, along with her assistant, Martha, oper-ated the largest Christian correspondence pro-gram in Bolivia for many years. Thousands of students received training.

In my Cochabamba office around 1965. I am at work on the manuscript of one of my early books. My first book was published in 1966, and I have been writing them ever since.

An action picture of faculty and students of our George Allan Theological Seminary in Cochabamba, Bo-livia. Cochabamba is in the Andes Mountains, but I am talking to a student from the Beni in the lowlands, a jungle area similar to the one where we spent our first term.

streets en masse with peaceful demonstrations in all the major cities in contrast to the frequently violent political manifestations. Some Christian Bible schools even closed for the year so the students and faculty could be active in EID. The hope? Reach Bolivia for Christ!

Unfortunately, however, the hope was not realized. When I later returned to Fuller, in 1967, to study missiology and church growth under Donald McGavran, I acquired research tools that enabled me to dig under the enthusiasm and excitement of evangelistic initiatives and discover what was really happening. Much to my surprise and dismay, I found that the Evangelism in Depth program had actually made little difference in the pattern of church growth in Bolivia. In 1964, the year before EID, the annual growth rate was 15 percent. During the EID year of 1965, it dropped to 12 percent. The following year it rose to 14 percent, and in 1967 it was down to 11 percent. Simply put, churches grew more rapidly before EID than during and after! I attempted to analyze the reasons for this unexpected development in my book *The Protestant Movement in Bolivia*.

While we are on the subject, I later made a study of the Evangelism in Depth program worldwide and I came to similar disheartening conclusions, which I reported in *Frontiers in Missionary Strategy* and later in *Strategies for Church Growth*. For a number of understandable reasons, the strategic design of EID, known also as "saturation evangelism," could not be shown statistically to have helped the effectiveness of evangelism and church growth on a broad scale.

Separation!

The year 1964 turned out to be a complicated year for our family. One day we noticed that Ruthie, who was then three, was not only struggling to walk, but her knees started bending backward! We knew that she needed serious medical help, so Doris took her to Bolivia's best in Cochabamba and La Paz, but to little avail. They told Doris that the only place she could find adequate specialists for Ruth was in America. Sadly, we faced the reality that we would have to separate for a while. The estimated time for Ruth's treatment was six to eight months. Karen, who was entering fourth grade, would need to go with them; and to further complicate matters, Doris was pregnant with our third daughter, Becky. But Doris rose to the occasion and left for the United States, not having a clue what she would do once she got off the plane and arrived at my sister, Margo's, home in Buffalo, New York.

This precipitated one of the most dramatic, shocking and pleasant surprises of my life. It was now mid-September. Doris had left in late June, two-and-one-half months previously. The last I had heard was that she would be gone at least until December, which meant that Becky would be born in the meantime. One afternoon, I happened to be at the Cocha- bamba airport to greet a visitor who was coming to see the mission. I am going to tell the rest by quoting three paragraphs from the letter I sent home to our friends:

> Well, it would be impossible for you to imagine the shock that came over me to see Doris, Karen and Ruth step off the same plane! The age of miracles certainly has not passed. I had no idea that they were coming—Doris's letter telling me all about it arrived the next day! Praise to God for answered prayer, and thanks to each one of you who has been praying for us during the time of separation.
>
> All during the months of July and August, Doris took Ruthie on the average of twice a week to the New York State Children's Re- habilitation Center in Buffalo, where a battery of specialists in al- most every phase of modern medicine examined her. The first answer to prayer was getting her into the center at all—waiting time is ordinarily one year.
>
> The final diagnosis, a thorough piece of work, pinpointed the source of Ruthie's trouble. A combination of being born 10 weeks premature and a severe case of jaundice at two weeks of age left some bile on her brain and permanently damaged the section that controls equilibrium. There is no therapy at all that could help her, and she will just have to grow up with the disadvantage of having a sub-normal sense of balance. Her legs are okay, and her intelligence is "high normal." The recommendation is that we should raise her just like any other child and that she can go to our Missionary Children's School here in Cochabamba. The doc- tor in charge, who is not a Christian, admitted to Doris that only a miracle of God kept her both alive and then from becoming a hopeless case of cerebral palsy! Thank you, Lord!

Before Ruth became an adult, she had outgrown most of her handicap. Speaking of balance, she unbelievably had the fortitude to teach herself to ride a unicycle at age seven! She soon arrived at the place where it would be impossible for anyone to know that she had childhood problems unless they were told. She is now the mother of three and serving the Lord as an expert in information technology and foreign exchange.

Mission Administration

Probably the major tool I have used through the years to understand what I do in life, why I do some things well and some things poorly, the degree of personal satisfaction I derive from attempting certain things, and the inner witness of the Holy Spirit, who moves me in specific directions, is a personal application of the biblical teaching on spiritual gifts. I mentioned awhile ago that I think my gravitation toward team sports rather than individual sports in my athletic days helped condition me to grasp the practical implications of the metaphor of the Church functioning as a human body better than I might have picked up otherwise. The tasks of quarterbacks and wide receivers in the game of football, for example, require totally different skill sets, but both are needed to win the game.

The practical outworking of spiritual gifts will come up frequently in these memoirs. If anyone were to ask me which book, of all the books I have written, has been the most helpful to the Body of Christ in general, I would not hesitate to say *Your Spiritual Gifts Can Help Your Church Grow*. It first was published in 1979, is now in its forty-sixth printing and has sold more than one-quarter million copies in English, plus countless copies in 16 other languages. I actually started writing on spiritual gifts back in 1967, with a series of articles in *Eternity* magazine. Now I have a smaller book out—*Discover Your Spiritual Gifts*, a study guide for teachers; and the popular *Finding Your Spiritual Gifts*, a 135-question survey to help people discover their gifts, which so far has circulated more than 1 million copies throughout the church. Denominations from Episcopalians to Baptists to Presbyterians to Pentecostals are using it. All of these resources provide concise, dictionary-type definitions of 28 spiritual gifts.

Why am I mentioning all of this? It is because I have long recognized that I have the spiritual gift of leadership. Here is my definition: The gift of leadership is the special ability that God gives to certain members of the Body of Christ to set goals in accordance with God's purpose for the future and to communicate these goals to others in such a way that they voluntarily and harmoniously work together to accomplish those goals for the glory of God. As soon as I say this, some jump to the conclusion that I must be bragging or I'm egotistical. If I had suggested that I had spiritual gifts of service or hospitality or helps or mercy or tongues or even teaching or pastor, few eyebrows would be raised. But leadership? Some might accuse me of thinking of myself more highly than I ought to think, as Romans 12:3 warns against. But this is absurd. In baseball, nine players play the game, but only one, the pitcher, goes on record as either the winner of the game or the loser. The same is true in the Body of Christ. Many saints play, but one has to take the responsibility of leadership. More often than not, I have found myself in that role.

Directing the Mission

Toward the beginning of this book, I mentioned that in school I would often be elected president of the class or student council representative. There was little opportunity for this to surface again in the jungle, but with the BIM it was a different story. I arrived in Cochabamba in 1962, and by 1964, two years later, Joe McCullough asked me to serve as Assistant Director of the mission. Perhaps I should explain a bit about the BIM government. Formally, it was a democratic government, and I needed to be elected Assistant Director at the annual field conference by votes of the 100 or so missionaries in BIM. We were the largest mission in Bolivia. McCullough also had the gift of leadership, and he was usually able to influence the votes at field conference in the direction he thought they should go. I say "usually" because the missionaries came from America, Canada, the U.K., Australia, New Zealand, Jamaica and Germany. On occasion, as might be expected, voting on certain issues followed national lines; but fortunately for McCullough and me, the majority of the missionaries were Americans.

The reason given for creating the office of Assistant Director was that Joe and Elizabeth felt that they should spend some time promoting the interests of the mission in the United States and Canada. Someone needed to fill in and lead the Field Council, which was the decision-making group between field conferences; so that became my temporary assignment along with my teaching responsibilities. However, things escalated! For different reasons, the McCulloughs decided to move permanently from Bolivia to the United States. As expected, Joe turned the leadership of the mission over to me and had me elected to the new office of Associate General Director in 1968. The central international office of BIM was in Cochabamba, so

Joe McCullough and I are standing in a boat on the waters of Lake Victoria, the mission leprosarium in the lowlands region of the Beni. Hundreds of victims of leprosy owed their quality of life as well as their eternal salvation in Christ to the faithful workers who sacrificed to be in this difficult place.

Did you know that I was a drummer? I was drumming while Doris was playing the accordion in an open air meeting in Cochabamba. We were on the streets spreading the gospel every Satuday night.

I became de facto leader of the mission, except for the finances, which Mc-Cullough as General Director kept under his control in Plainfield, New Jersey, the U.S. office of BIM. At that time, I had to give up my regular Bible institute teaching post.

My tenure as mission director, beginning in 1964 and ending when I left the field seven years later in 1971, was not a tale of outstanding success. While I might have been the best choice for the job among the personnel we had available at the time, I'm sure that McCullough would have done better than I had he remained on the field. Why would I arrive at such a conclusion, since we both had the spiritual gift of leadership? I couldn't have explained it then, but I think I can attempt it now.

My first thought is that not all of those who have the same spiritual gift have been assigned the same ministry by God. I get this from 1 Corinthians 12:4-6: "There are diversities of gifts, but the same Spirit. There are differences of ministries, but the same Lord. And there are diversities of activities, but it is the same God who works all in all." An obvious application of this is the gift of evangelist. Some with the gift have the ministry of public evangelism, like Billy Graham, but others with the same gift have the ministry of personal evangelism, like Bill Bright. The principle will also apply to the gift of leadership.

I will explain much more about this later on, but my second thought has to do not only with the gift of leadership but also with the gift of apostle. Not all with the gift of leadership have the gift of apostle, but all those with the gift of apostle have the gift of leadership. I now think I could argue that both McCullough and I had the gift of apostle as well as leadership, although there was no talk about such a thing in those days. What I have only recently learned is the difference between vertical apostles and horizontal apostles. Vertical apostles, in this particular context, would have the oversight of a number of missionaries and the ministries they represent. McCullough could do this better than I. Why? I have since discovered that I am not a vertical apostle. Horizontal apostles could be excellent in convening events like the World Vision Pastors' Conference. I could probably have done that better than McCullough. I now know that I am a horizontal apostle, and I function primarily with that ministry today as I write this book.

So here I was, a horizontal apostle, attempting to minister as a vertical apostle, and the results were not as I would have wished. Oh, I held the mission together, but mostly it was maintaining the status quo rather than breaking into new, exciting horizons of fulfilling the Great Commission. Having said that, the good news is that I was still able to initiate a few important changes.

The Financial Pool

Financially, the mission was using the "pool system." This meant that all the contributions toward the support of individual missionaries went, not directly to the workers, but into a pool. At the end of each quarter, the pool was divided equally among all the missionaries, up to a set amount. If the pool was over the needed amount for "distribution," the balance that quarter went into the general fund. This sounded good to us when we first joined the BIM, but once we arrived on the field, we discovered that there were certain inequities. We Americans were required to raise the full amount of pledged support before we were allowed to come to Bolivia. But the same rule did not apply to the Canadians or the Brits or the Australians or the New Zealanders who could come to Bolivia with whatever they might or might not be able to raise.

This did not become an issue when the pool was sufficient to provide full distribution. However, on my watch one quarter, I had to reduce distribution by 10 percent, and then I had to do the same the next quarter. This was particularly troublesome to us Americans whose full support continued coming in each quarter. It dawned on us that we were subsidizing our coworkers from other nations. We were sure that if this news got to our supporters it would not be well received. I decided that it was a battle I should fight, and the fight was not easy. I believed that justice demanded that all workers should follow the same rule and raise their full support before coming to the field. You can imagine the fireworks in the annual field conference when it came up for a vote! Many at that time decided that someone other than I should be Associate General Director, and I almost was not reelected. Still, the change went through!

Another change, which was as radical as the first but not as difficult, was changing the name of the mission. When missionary George Allan left his homeland of New Zealand in 1907, his calling was to reach the Indians of Bolivia. "Bolivian Indian Mission" fit the situation well. In fact, there were relatively few Bolivians who were not Indian. Many more were monolingual in the Quechua or Aymara language than were monolingual in Spanish. But as time went on the processes of urbanization and modernization began reshaping the nation until the name "Indian" was no longer politically correct. It was time for a change. The new name "Andes Evangelical Mission" not only eliminated the word "Indian," but it also opened the geographical door for expansion into neighboring nations. We had already assigned a couple to Peru. BIM was now AEM.

Time for Writing

No matter what other responsibilities I might be carrying, I have always seemed to find some time for writing. I think this is an outgrowth of my gift of teaching. I teach through the spoken word and I teach through the written word. In fact, sometimes I think that I might need to be psycho-analyzed. It seems that I can't stand to live with an unpublished thought! I began my writing career with articles for magazines such as *Eternity* and *Christianity Today* and *Sunday School Times*. While in the SAIM I wrote arti-cles on a regular basis for the mission magazine *The Amazon Valley Indian*. Once I had joined the BIM, I was asked to become the editor of *The Bolivian Indian*. When we changed the mission name, I soon changed the name of the magazine to *The Andean Outlook*. I also came alongside Héctor Torres, who owned a printing press, to help him edit Bolivia's first monthly Span-ish language Christian magazine, *Visión Evangélica,* in which I wrote a monthly editorial, *"En Esto Pensad"* ("Think about This"), under the pen name of Eutychus, the man who went to sleep and fell out of the window while Paul was teaching (see Acts 20:9).

I had never written a book, but I had the desire to do so. When I was doing my ThM in Princeton during furlough, I believe the Lord told me to cut my first book-writing teeth on missionary biographies. I remember discussing this with one of my professors who encouraged me. The per-son who first came to mind was one of my missionary heroes, Bill Pencille, who had been called to reach the savage Ayoré Indians. The Ayorés are the ones who had murdered the five New Tribes missionaries in 1943, about 13 years before Doris and I arrived in the jungle on our first term. Soon after we got settled in Cochabamba, I started doing the research, meeting with Pencille as he came out from the lowlands to stay in the BIM Mission Home from time to time, and I produced my first manu-script, *Defeat of the Bird God*.

I just mentioned that the BIM was founded by a New Zealander, George Allan. Predictably, many of the first BIM missionaries came from

New Zealand and Australia. One of the Australians, Wally Herron, turned out to be a history-making individual. A bush pilot, Herron acquired a one-engine Cessna and based it in the jungle town of Magdalena. Arguably, he became the literal pioneer of missionary aviation. While agencies such as Missionary Aviation Fellowship have since made air service for remote missionaries commonplace, such a thing was unheard of when Wally Herron first started flying in Bolivia. His rather amazing exploits drew the attention of the Bolivian government, which awarded him the highest honor for a foreigner, The Condor of the Andes.

Not long after Doris and I arrived in Cochabamba, Wally Herron perished in a tragic airplane crash, not in the jungle where he was based, but high in the Andes. While we were still grieving, Joe McCullough suggested that I undertake the task of writing his biography. I agreed provided he would be a coauthor, since his name was widely known and mine was not. The title of our book was *The Condor of the Jungle*.

Let me deviate for a moment. We now live in a day when the notion of field missionaries being supported not only by donations but also through for-profit businesses on the field is gaining acceptance. This was far from the case when we were in Bolivia. Later I'll say more about it, but the spirit of poverty had maintained a tight grip on the worldwide missionary community until very recently. Subsistence income or below was the norm for missionary families, and anything that exceeded it was to be contributed directly to the "work." Interestingly enough, two of the older missionaries with whom I served in the 1950s and the 1960s were among the few who at that time were coloring outside the traditional missionary poverty lines, George Haight of Santiago de Chiquitos and Wally Herron.

In order to do them justice, I will reproduce a paragraph from my history book *The Protestant Movement in Bolivia*. In that book, I had just described the relative ineffectiveness of evangelical missionaries in the Jesuit Reductions of the lowlands of Bolivia (myself included), and then I said:

> There are two exceptions to this general rule. The first was George Haight of SAIM, who settled in Santiago and was able to disciple at least 10 percent of the population. The second was the renowned missionary, Walter Herron of AEM, known now as the "Condor of the Jungle." His Magdalena church is without doubt the outstanding Protestant church in the Jesuit reductions of

A family portrait taken in Bolivia just before we came home from the year I studied under Donald Mc-Gavran in the Fuller School of World Mission. Karen (left) was 11, Becky (center) was 2, and Ruth (right) was 6. Spanish was the primary language for all three girls, but Karen was the only one who ended up bilingual.

My colleague Doug Smith, whom I had known since Rutgers Inter-Varsity days, had a strong work going on among Bolivian university students. A number of them are gathered here in a training retreat.

Bolivia. Haight and Herron had much in common. Both of them became functional alternatives to the Jesuit or Franciscan padre. Haight established a school, a large agricultural project, a transportation service with the town's first truck, a tile factory, a cattle ranch, and a firewood industry, which supplied the railroad. Herron pioneered the first air taxi service for the region, founded a leprosarium, started a school, served as a medical doctor, operated a cattle ranch, and opened a canal. Both mixed freely with the local politicians, and both were deeply involved with the social and economic life of their villages. Both had strong personalities and were strong disciplinarians, maintained a formality in most social relationships, and were accepted as community leaders. Both handled large sums of local money, which in turn was used to support their projects.[1]

First Corinthians

As I taught in Emmaus Bible Institute, one of my favorite subjects was "First Corinthians." I had begun to specialize in this book of Scripture even before coming to Bolivia, when I taught that Bible book in an adult Sunday School class in Bell Friends Church in California. I then tested my writing abilities by expounding on what I thought were the main ideas revealed in Paul's epistle in a series of six articles. To my surprise and satisfaction, they were well received. The series appeared in English in *Eternity* magazine and in Spanish in *Visión Evangélica* and in *Pensamiento Cristiano*, circulated throughout Latin America from Argentina. The next step would be to draft a book manuscript, which I did. What happened to that manuscript turned out to be one of the most worrisome events I can recall.

Linking with Doris

First, however, I want to explain a hugely significant life transition for Doris and me. You will recall that Doris and I both have a background in a rural, farming culture. On the farm, husbands and wives invariably work together on the same job. They are partners in labor 365 days per year. When we were in school, and during our first years in Bolivia, Doris and I worked different assignments for the most part. In Cochabamba, I taught in the Bible school, and Doris ran the correspondence course, although each of us had many other different ministry activities as well.

When I took over as director of the mission, I was given a full-time bilingual secretary, and things went well until she married and quit her job. There was literally no other person in or outside of the mission who had the qualifications to replace her. A secretary was as necessary to me as a hammer would be to a carpenter. When we joined the mission, we had signed a document saying that ordinarily our personal desires and leading from the Lord would determine our field assignment except under unusual circumstances. In that case, we would willingly accept, at least for the time, whatever assignment the mission leadership would give us. Doris had signed that paper as well. I desperately needed a secretary. I happened to be the "mission leadership" at the time. So, you guessed it, I assigned her to become my secretary. Her first protest was that she had no training or experience in office work. My response was that she would have to learn on the job. So she turned the correspondence course over to another missionary, resigned from teaching her classes at the Bible school and installed herself in my office, reminding me that it was "only for the necessary time."

That was a major turning point in our lives. The "necessary time" has endured until today. We picked up on the lifestyle of the farm and became partners in whatever job we undertook from then on. At least Doris was a quite competent typist as well as being fluently bilingual, which gave her a clear head start. She learned basic office procedures on the job, and then she was boosted to a new level by a young short-term missionary, Pam Toomey (now Pam Marhad), who had professional training in secretarial work. Years later, when Fuller Seminary invited me to join the faculty, one condition was that they hire Doris as well. This caused ripples, because they had an anti-nepotism policy, but they ended up bending it, and we worked together at Fuller. As I write this, Doris serves as the COO, CFO, and office manager of Global Harvest Ministries, which she and I co-founded.

Back to the First Corinthians manuscript. After I finished my draft, I left for a two-month teaching assignment at Fuller Seminary. Doris stayed behind to type my manuscript for the publisher, and then she was to join me in California. Keep in mind that in those days there were no copy machines, to say nothing of computer memory discs. Unfortunately, Doris fell ill and underwent major surgery, so she hadn't quite finished the manuscript before the rush to get packed and leave. She put the manuscript in one of the suitcases that she checked through. When she landed, you guessed it—the suitcase did not arrive! The only existing result of months of work on the part of both of us did not show up. This was utterly disheartening. Our prayers for recovering the lost manuscript were intense. All of the Fuller faculty, the student body, and Bell Friends Church joined us. After three weeks of calling airlines, we had given up hope. But God came through. Where it had gone no one knows, but after 23 days, the suitcase with the manuscript showed up! The book, *A Turned-On Church in an Uptight World,* was published by Zondervan. We profusely thanked God for His goodness!

Our next big transition was moving from Bolivia back to the United States and Fuller Seminary. That will come in the following chapter.

Note

1. C. Peter Wagner, *The Protestant Movement in Bolivia* (South Pasadena, CA: William Carey Library, 1970), pp. 194-195.

5

The McGavran Era
(1971–1982)

It took four years to transition from Cochabamba, Bolivia, where Andes Evangelical Mission was located, to Pasadena, California, where Fuller Seminary was located. Changing careers in midlife is not easy. The beginning point was the Master's in Missiology that I earned during my 1967-1968 furlough from Bolivia. At that time, not only did I become a disciple of Donald McGavran, but I also met and established a personal relationship with Ralph D. Winter. Winter had served as a Presbyterian missionary to Guatemala, and then had been recruited as McGavran's third faculty member in the fledgling School of World Mission. For the record, Winter was honored toward the end of his career when he was selected by *Time* magazine, in 2005, as one of America's 25 most influential evangelical leaders.

The School of World Mission

Let me explain what was happening at Fuller. For years, David Allan Hubbard, president of Fuller Seminary, had harbored a strong desire to upgrade the missionary training that the seminary offered. Hubbard was, by nature, an innovator and a strong change agent. He sensed that God was raising up a new wineskin for missions, and he soon discovered that the most visible and innovative figure on the foreign missions scene at the time was Donald A. McGavran. McGavran, with roots in the Christian Church (Disciples of Christ), had served for 40 years as a third-generation missionary to India. When Hubbard met him, McGavran had left India after 30 years and was then doing research and teaching for the Disciples of Christ. As an academic base, he had established the Institute of Church Growth, attached to Northwest Christian College in Eugene, Oregon, in 1961. After many conversations, Hubbard invited McGavran to become the founding dean of the Fuller Seminary School of World Mission (SWM).

McGavran was interested, but by then his focus was more on the dynamic growth of churches around the world than on traditional, often ineffective, foreign missions in general. As a condition for moving to Pasadena, he insisted that Hubbard incorporate his budding Institute of Church Growth into Fuller's new school. Hubbard rather reluctantly agreed, because he was convinced that McGavran had become the leading missiologist of the day. Both were strong individuals, so the name of the new school had to please them both. Consequently it was officially founded as the "Fuller Theological Seminary School of World Mission and Institute of Church Growth." With that, McGavran, then 68 years of age, moved to Pasadena in 1965. I arrived from Bolivia to study under him two years later in 1967.

McGavran was commissioned to raise up an initial faculty of six outstanding missiologists. As a starter, he insisted that every one of them be a seasoned field missionary who had become fluent in the language of a second culture and who had a passion for the growth of churches worldwide equal to McGavran's.

His first choice was Alan Tippett, an Australian missionary to Fiji, who had been McGavran's student and potential colleague in the Institute of Church Growth in Oregon. Tippett's professional field was anthropology. The second was Ralph Winter, the Guatemalan missionary whom I have mentioned. Winter, who had been born and raised in Pasadena, and who had attended Fuller Seminary when it was first launched in the late 1940s, was well known by Charles E. Fuller, its founder, as well as by David Hubbard and others. Winter was to cover the area of the history of the Christian movement. I mention all of this because I believe that at the end of the day Winter, possibly even more than McGavran, was the most instrumental person in bringing me onto the SWM faculty.

Theological Education by Extension (TEE)

While in Guatemala, Ralph Winter had observed an extremely significant phenomenon. The pastors of countless Latin American evangelical churches were being selected from the ranks of their congregations without the benefit of formal ministerial training, and their numbers were rapidly growing. Furthermore, because these were typically mature individuals with family, jobs, houses and community responsibilities, there was no possibility that they could take time off for the usual months or years required by traditional residential Bible schools. The number of these individuals was estimated by some to be 100,000 or more at the time throughout Latin America. So Winter designed and implemented a new way of delivering training to these pastors, which he called "theological education by extension" or TEE.

I studied TEE under Winter while I was at Fuller in 1967 and 1968, including participating with him in a high-level consultation in Colombia where missionary educators from many Latin American countries gathered together. I soon found myself going through a radical paradigm shift. Taking training out to those who needed it rather than expecting them to come to you and your school made complete sense to me. While there, I connected with Peter Savage, a missionary to Peru from England, who had experienced the same paradigm shift, and I recruited him to come to Bolivia under AEM. When I returned to Bolivia, I assigned Savage to revamp the program of the George Allan Theological Seminary. He introduced TEE, and the enrollment doubled in each of the following two years.

TEE Around the World

Through all of this I had been gaining some international visibility as a strong advocate of TEE. Our two evangelical umbrella organizations for missions in the United States, Interdenominational Foreign Missions Association (IFMA) and Evangelical Foreign Missions Association (EFMA) had jointly formed a service agency called Committee to Assist Missionary Education Overseas (CAMEO). CAMEO had become so excited about TEE that, as one of their first projects, they asked Ralph Covell of Denver Seminary and me to do a tour of Taiwan, Vietnam, Indonesia, Singapore and India in order to introduce the concept to the mission leaders in those nations. One of the outcomes of this was a book that Covell and I co-authored, *An Extension Seminary Primer.*

As an outcome of the intense meeting of educators from many Latin American nations in Armenia, Colombia, in 1967, which I mentioned above, I helped organize and became the founding president of *Comité Latinoamericano de Textos Teológicos* (CLATT—Latin American Committee for Theological Textbooks). TEE required textbooks that were specially programmed to be interactive and that would help the adult students in the self-study part of their training. We designed these books so they could be used in all Spanish-speaking nations and on all academic levels. While I was still in Bolivia, we saw 20 of these innovative textbooks written, published and widely circulated.

Ralph Winter, of course, was well aware of all my pro-TEE activities and he helped persuade McGavran that I should come to Pasadena as the fourth professor in the School of World Mission (SWM). McGavran had approached me about this possibility when I graduated in 1968, but at the time, I felt responsible to continue as director of the AEM. McGavran soon afterward reactivated the process by inviting me to teach for one quarter at SWM in early 1970, which I accepted. Because I was teaching only one course on Current Strategies of Latin American Missions, I had time to write. My resulting book was *Frontiers in Missionary Strategy*.

With our children in missionary boarding school, Doris was able to join me in California, bringing with her the "lost" First Corinthians manuscript that I have told you about. That was when we had a number of serious conversations with McGavran and Winter about the possibility of leaving Bolivia. As we prayed hard about it, we sensed that this might actually be the direction the Lord was taking us for our future.

Would SWM Go in the Right Direction?

But we were not entirely sure. The one nagging doubt had to do with the theological direction that the Fuller School of Theology had been taking. When we were there as students in the 1950s it was uncompromisingly evangelical, especially with the presence of the founder, legendary radio evangelist Charles E. Fuller. However, by 1970, it had become more liberal than we were comfortable with, especially when it decided to remove the clause affirming biblical inerrancy from the seminary statement of faith. The School of World Mission itself was thoroughly evangelical, but McGavran, Winter, Alan Tippett and the newest addition, Charles Kraft, all belonged to denominations affiliated with the World Council of Churches. I would be the only one from the IFMA/EFMA stream. Added to this was the fact that McGavran, past the age of 70, had begun looking for his successor as dean. I felt that whoever replaced McGavran would undoubtedly set the theological direction for SWM's future.

Much to my relief, McGavran decided to invite Arthur Glasser as the next dean. Not only did I know Glasser's name very well through the many periodical articles that he had written and multiple news items about his activities, but I had also attended a meeting in which he was a speaker, and from that time on, he had become one of my missionary heroes. I wanted to be like Glasser when I grew up! Glasser had served as a missionary to China under China Inland Mission (CIM), later Overseas Missionary Fellowship (OMF). Then after being expelled by the Communists, he became the OMF home director in the United States. OMF, like AEM, was a member of IFMA, and Glasser's nomination became the tipping point for me. Doris and I agreed that we would begin arranging things in Bolivia so that we could make our move to California in the summer of 1971. I would visit Pasadena and teach one intensive course in February 1971, and then start teaching full-time in SWM that fall quarter.

Fuller Evangelistic Association

However, the plot began to thicken. When we started serious contract negotiations with Fuller, we informed David Hubbard that Doris and I were accustomed to working together and that one of the nonnegotiables would be that Fuller would agree to hire us both as a team. Surprisingly, this did not seem to faze him much in spite of Fuller's anti-nepotism hiring policy. Providentially, an amazing change had been taking place just at that time.

Charles E. Fuller's "Old Fashioned Revival Hour," under the Gospel Broadcasting Association (GBA), had become the most widely broadcast religious radio program of the day. It was bringing in the revenue to support his radio ministry with enough surplus to allow him to do such things as launch Fuller Seminary in 1947. Fuller had previously established the Fuller Evangelistic Association (FEA) in order to help evangelists in smaller communities and to distribute funds to strategic evangelistic programs worldwide. Just two years before Doris and I moved from Bolivia to California, Fuller had passed away. His heir was his only son, Daniel P. Fuller.

Dan Fuller had been one of the first students in his father's new seminary in the late 1940s. By the time I arrived as a student in the early 1950s, Dan was in the graduate program and was also serving as an adjunct professor. The school was small at that time, and we got to know each other. David Hubbard, also a graduate student and an adjunct professor, had become one of Dan's close friends, and we all had good relationships. In fact, Hubbard later told me that from the time I graduated in 1955, he had kept my photograph on his bedroom dresser and prayed for me every day as one of his favorite missionaries. These personal friendships, now almost 20 years old, became very important in my transition into Fuller Seminary.

Daniel Fuller

Dan had become the heir to both the Gospel Broadcasting Association and the Fuller Evangelistic Association. He ran them under a board of trustees composed of his father's friends, mostly from Lake Avenue Church where Charles and Grace Fuller had been members. By that time, David Hubbard had become president of the seminary and Dan had become dean of the School of Theology. Dan was a prototypical theological scholar. He had received his PhD under Karl Barth in Switzerland. He loved to teach classes and do research, but he was shy, and he never became an eloquent public speaker like his father. His friend David was all of that, however, and David had even filled in for Charles Fuller on "The Old Fashioned Revival Hour" from time to time. So Dan invited David to come on the board of GBA and take his father's place on the radio. Hubbard did so and soon changed the name of the broadcast to "The Joyful Sound."

That left Dan with the Fuller Evangelistic Association. With the help of his father's administrative assistant, Mae Douglas, he was able to keep things running, but he never had a particular calling to it. Dan had a normal interest in foreign missions, but never the passion that he had for theological research, writing and classroom teaching. When he heard that I might be coming to the faculty of the School of World Mission, he began to wonder if I might be interested in taking FEA off his hands.

All this helps to explain why Hubbard would tend to be more open than expected to my suggestion that Doris and I be hired as a team. He and Dan were ready to offer me a seat on the board as well as the position of executive director of FEA. It was an offer I couldn't refuse. Not only would I be in charge of building a staff that naturally would include Doris, but I would also have a travel budget to move around the world, as I felt necessary. This would be a dream come true for any budding missiologist!

Donald McGavran's chief desire was that his newest faculty member teach a full load in SWM as Associate Professor of Latin American Studies and supervise graduate students as professors normally did. This was my desire as well, as long as I could also give the necessary attention to running FEA and distribute funding to deserving missions projects worldwide. We all agreed that it could be done and that I would officially go on the SWM payroll, but two-thirds of my salary would be contributed to the seminary by FEA. I would have an office in both places, and Doris would be my full-time assistant based in FEA. Needless to say, I profusely thanked the Lord for opening a new season of ministry that exceeded my fondest expectations.

Evangelical Theology in Latin America

While we were still preparing to leave Bolivia, I had become very concerned about the direction that evangelical theology had been taking in Latin Amer-

Donald A. McGavran, the founding Dean of the Fuller Theological Seminary School of World Mission in Pasadena, California. He had served for many years as a field missionary in India.

Donald McGavran, one of the greatest missiologists of the twentieth century. I studied under him from 1967-1968. He invited me to join his core faculty, and I was able to make the shift from Bolivia in 1971.

ica. During my years there, I had expanded my areas of expertise quite far beyond Bolivia itself. I read voraciously through the missiological literature that was being produced on Latin America in general, and I was able to travel quite extensively throughout the whole continent. Because Doris and I were running a mission with more than 100 missionaries, we provided a substantial amount of business to our local travel agent. As an expression of gratitude, he once offered us a trip to wherever we wanted to go around South America, for whatever period of time. Needless to say, it turned out to be one of our most notable vacations!

As a result of the extensive international contacts I had been making, I was asked by IFMA/EFMA to edit their regional newsletter, *Latin America Pulse,* which I did every two months from 1967 through 1971, when I left Latin America and moved to Fuller. This forced me to stay informed as to what was going on. I had the privilege of serving as the International Press Coordinator for the high-profile Latin American Congress on Evangelization sponsored by Billy Graham in Bogotá, Colombia, in 1969. Before, during and after this historic event, I found myself producing a volume of press releases covering the whole continent.

Through this process, I could not help but notice some differences between the more liberal and ecumenical missions affiliated with the World Council of Churches and the more evangelical missions of the IFMA/EFMA stream, which I represented. Missionaries under the liberal denominations, for example, were almost invariably seminary trained and theologically astute as contrasted to most of the evangelical missionaries who had been trained in undergraduate or non-accredited Bible institutes. For example, I found myself to be the only missionary under AEM who had a seminary degree until I recruited Peter Savage while I was at Fuller. Since like tends to beget like, it was not surprising that the denominational missionaries had founded a disproportionate number of universities and graduate schools in many parts of Latin America.

In the initial stages of missionary work, the foreign missionaries by default serve as the theological spokespersons for the churches. While the evangelical missionaries in Latin America were concentrating on evangelizing and multiplying churches, the denominational missionaries were focused on training national leaders to replace them as soon as possible as the new theological spokespersons for their churches. Scholarships for graduate theological education in the United States and Europe were readily available for the more liberal Latin American leaders. Evangelicals, with the notable exception of the Latin America Mission in San José, Costa Rica, had little interest in either theology or higher education.

The predictable result of this was that, by my generation, some theologians had risen up in Latin America who were now being recognized as peers by those in the international theological community of the day. However, the most influential ones among them were from the more liberal Latin American churches. In fact, the theology du jour had become Latin American liberation theology, which was focused on social justice, leaving little or no room for the evangelical passion of saving souls and multiplying churches. This deplorable situation became a high agenda item for me.

The Theological Fraternity

Fortunately, our evangelical theological voice was not quite zero. Three Latin American theologians, in particular, had surfaced in our circles, René Padilla of Ecuador/Colombia, Samuel Escobar of Peru/Argentina, and Orlando Costas of Puerto Rico/Costa Rica, although they had not yet gained the international recognition that certain theologians of liberation enjoyed. With the help of Peter Savage, I convened these three along with some theologically oriented evangelical missionaries and other Latin American thinkers in Cochabamba in 1970. From this consultation emerged the *Fraternidad Teológica Latinoamericana* (Latin American Theological Fraternity), which Peter Savage agreed to lead. The organization has continued, under a succession of leaders, until the present time.

Directly related to this was one of my biggest disappointments. While I was studying at Fuller, 1967-1968, and becoming a diehard advocate of Donald McGavran's theories of church growth, I spent considerable time researching and working on the theological issues I have been describing. I expanded a research paper I did there into a book manuscript, *Latin American Theology: Radical or Evangelical?* that was published in Spanish in 1969, before it was released in English in 1970. The Spanish version came out just at the time I helped organize the Latin American Theological Fraternity. I honestly thought that my friends, Padilla, Escobar and Costas, would welcome the book with open arms and that they would congratulate me for it.

Wrong! None of the three liked it, and, in fact, all of them became vocal critics of the book and also of me! What was going on? Ironically, they had no quarrel with the main theme of the book, which advocated training Latin American evangelical theologians who would have as strong or stronger an international voice than the liberals had gained. However, their attention had been diverted by my interspersed church growth theories. What they accurately read between the lines was my argument that our primary mission under God was evangelism and church planting, while our social involvement should be relegated to a secondary, or inferior, undertaking. They felt that social action should never be secondary, but that it should at least be placed on the same level as evangelism.

This precipitated a 40-year theological controversy between us, heightened especially in the International Congress on World Evangelization, which was to come in the mid-1970s. We always respected each other personally, but we sharply disagreed. The debate, at least in my mind, formally ended in 2008, when I published my book *Dominion!* and in which I found myself apologizing to them in print.[1] My position is now much closer to theirs, but more on that later.

Making the Move

When the time came, making the move to America from Bolivia, where we had formerly presumed we would spend the rest of our lives, carried its share of challenges. Karen was 17 and had a steady Bolivian boyfriend. Ruth and Becky were not that attached, but they had their circles of friends as well. All three were bilingual, although only Karen subsequently went on to maintain Spanish throughout her life. We left virtually all of our personal possessions in Bolivia except for our rustic one-of-a-kind dining room table that had been homemade out of mahogany slabs from a sawmill and the trunks of a hardwood tree from the lowlands where we spent our first term. In fact we still have it, although it now serves as an outdoor picnic table.

Donald and Mary McGavran were some of the most gracious people we have ever known. Fully aware of the reverse culture shock that would be involved in our reentry process, they opened their home in Pasadena to the five of us. Not only did they give Doris and me their master bedroom, but also we later discovered that Mrs. McGavran ended up sleeping on a couch, and Dr. McGavran was sleeping on the floor in another small room! They had come from that bygone generation of post-World War I missionaries who, like George Haight and Wally Herron, were tough as nails. They had never learned the meaning of the word "hardship."

We wanted to find a tile-roofed Spanish colonial house, which was common in Southern California, so we stopped on the way back to the United

States in Cuernavaca, Mexico, where we purchased a quantity of unfinished bedroom, dining room and living room furniture handcrafted from beautifully grained Mexican cedar. I sanded it down and finished it with hard varnish in the McGavrans' backyard. Much of it adorns our home today, almost 40 years later, and the finish still looks new!

We were to live with the McGavrans until we found a home of our own. By the time we had purchased the furniture and made a down payment on a Datsun station wagon, we were down to nothing. We were more than 40 years old, with no savings account or investments or real estate or other assets. We had to start from scratch. We did find a house that we liked, but all we could do was pray that God somehow provide the down payment. The numbers sound strange today, but the house cost $32,500, and the down payment was $1,500. Our prayers were answered! A wonderful couple from Bell Friends Church, Maynard and Alison Chapin, offered to loan us the $1,500 on a handshake and a promise that we would repay it as soon as we could. With profound thanks to them and the McGavrans, we moved into 2440 Santa Rosa, which was our home in Altadena for the next 25 years. Before we left, we had totally paid off the Chapin's loan and the mortgage, and we were out of debt!

Contextualizing Church Growth in America

My year of studying at the School of World Mission, beginning in 1967, helped me initiate my change from a simple field missionary to a professional missiologist. Not only had I absorbed Church Growth from McGavran and TEE from Winter, but I had also begun to understand how anthropology intersects with the missionary vocation from Alan Tippett. For the first time, I had begun hearing the word "contextualization," and I came to understand how the gospel and all of its ramifications needed to be adapted, or contextualized, according to the culture into which it was being introduced. Some of my first field experiments in doing this were in Bolivia, where I had attempted to help contextualize worship music through organizing the Bolivian Hymnology Committee; to contextualize theology through the Theological Fraternity; and to contextualize ministerial training through TEE.

When I arrived on the faculty of the School of World Mission, I soon became aware of a new challenge for applying the missiological principle of contextualization. McGavran's focus had been exclusively and unswervingly on evangelizing and multiplying churches on the mission field, namely, in Africa, Asia and Latin America. His interest in church growth in North America and

Europe was very near to zero, if not past zero to the negative side. In fact, he had protected the School of World Mission from any possible infringement on the part of pastors or church leaders from America by requiring applicants for admission to have spent at least three years ministering in a second culture verified by fluency in the vernacular of that culture. He wanted leaders for whom missions was not a hobby, but a career.

When I returned to America after 16 years in Bolivia, I suddenly felt somewhat like a cross-cultural missionary to America. I had taught church growth in Bolivia, and I asked McGavran if he believed that church growth principles would also work in America. His response carried undisguised irritation. "Of course!" he replied. "They will work anywhere. But as far as applying them to a missionary sending nation like America, someone else will have to do it! I have no interest!" I did not say anything at the moment, but I believe the Lord spoke to me inwardly and said, "You will be that 'someone else.'"

I did, in fact, become the "someone else" to eventually light the fire for contextualizing church growth into the American religious culture, but it was not easy, because McGavran's irritation persisted under the surface. I never made any major moves without McGavran's consent, but while he was always cordial and outwardly proper, there was no doubt that my "diversion" into American church growth, as he would have seen it, became an ongoing disappointment to him. This is not to say that I neglected the Third World. My missiological publications, my rather extensive international ministry, my 15-year involvement with the Lausanne Committee for World Evangelization, my work on unreached peoples, my travel to up to 15 nations per year, and my teaching load at SWM should have been enough to allay his fears, but they weren't. Nothing less than 100 percent focus on the foreign mission field would have pleased him fully.

The Elburn Consultation

The process that led to introducing church growth into America began, as I am going to describe it, with a consultation called for Elburn, Illinois, in 1970. This specially convened emergency meeting of 50 top executives from the IFMA/EFMA missions was precipitated by the publication, in 1969, of the epochal study, *Latin American Church Growth,* written by William R. Read, Victor M. Monterroso, and Harmon A. Johnson, while they were studying under McGavran at SWM. Some, including myself, still consider it the best field study of church growth ever written.

Among the many revealing findings of the research was one particularly disturbing to those of us who were part of IFMA and EFMA, regarded a bit arrogantly, by us who were members, as the most biblical and God-aligned mission agencies of the day. The study compared the number of missionaries deployed in Latin America to the number of resulting church members. Much to our dismay, the IFMA/EFMA missionaries had the lowest rate of church members to missionaries when compared to mainline conciliar missions, Seventh-Day Adventists and Pentecostals. While a full 42 percent of missionaries in Latin America were IFMA/EFMA-related, only 5 percent of the church members could be traced to their efforts.[2] What a shock!

Fortunately for all concerned, the reaction of the leadership of IFMA and EFMA to this rather startling church growth research was constructive. They called the 50 executives to Elburn, Illinois, and appointed Vergil Gerber and me as co-chairpersons of the meeting. They chose me because I was the only IFMA mission executive in Latin America who had earned a degree under McGavran, who was seen as the ultimate source of these disturbing findings. They chose Gerber because he was the executive director of the Evangelical Missions Information Service (EMIS), an agency based in Wheaton, Illinois, sponsored by IFMA/EFMA. Gerber had served as a Conservative Baptist missionary in Ecuador, Argentina, Costa Rica and Mexico, so he knew Latin America well. Vergil and I had previously connected and become good friends through several international meetings we had attended together; and in 1967, he was the one who had invited me to edit the bimonthly EMIS newsletter, *Latin America Pulse*, which, as I have mentioned, I did until I moved to the United States in 1971.

As I recall, I do not have pleasant memories of those three or four days of meetings in Elburn. The executives were in somewhat of a surly mood. The morning Bible studies and prayer time led by Melvin Hodges of the Assemblies of God were a high point, but the rest of the sessions were little more than organized confusion. The Church Growth Movement itself came under serious scrutiny, and I found myself being cross-examined with numerous questions that I as yet could not answer well. Mostly out of frustration, the closing mandate of the Elburn Consultation was that Vergil Gerber and Peter Wagner would somehow undertake the implementation of church growth principles in IFMA/EFMA circles in Latin America and report back the results. Period!

When the meeting was over, Vergil and I looked at each other with blank stares. What did we do to deserve this? The only thing we knew to do was to pray for God's guidance. I returned to Bolivia, and Gerber to his office in Wheaton, not having any idea of all that God had in store for us in the 1970s. But God knew, and He showed it to us in His time.

Bible Fellowship Church

Arthur Glasser had taken McGavran's place as the dean of SWM by the time I had arrived to begin teaching in the fall of 1971. Because technically he was my boss, I had little choice when he came to me one day with an unusual request. He had been scheduled to speak on church growth to the annual conference of the pastors of the Bible Fellowship Church, a denomination of some 40 or 50 churches centered in Eastern Pennsylvania and New Jersey, early in 1972. For some reason, he decided he couldn't make it, so he asked me to take his place. I have a sneaking hunch that Glasser actually got cold feet and decided to toss the ball to the rookie on his staff! My required answer was, "Sure I will," but my mind was totally blank.

Keep in mind what I have said about McGavran and American church growth. Nothing had been done at SWM related to the American church. I had no books I could read, no research reports, and no role models. I found myself on my own. I had no prepared talks for American pastors other than urging them to send out and to support foreign missionaries, which was not the requested subject of the day. To put it mildly, I was more than apprehensive about this assignment.

As I prayed about it, however, God impressed me to write to the denomination and request the membership statistics for each of their churches over the past 10 years. While on the airplane, I put together a 10-year statistical chart with these figures. When I landed, I asked the person who was driving me to the conference to stop in a drugstore where I bought a supply of simple graph paper. A format for the meeting was beginning to take shape in my mind.

In the seminar itself, I spent a day or so teaching basic church growth principles, as best I could at that time, to the pastors of 46 local American churches. Some thought my teaching was helpful; others weren't so sure. Then I passed out graph paper and told them that I wanted each of them to draw a 10-year graph of growth of their own church. They said, "We don't have the statistics!" So I gleefully replied, "I do!" and proceeded to

David Barrett is arguably the number one Christian researcher of our generation, producing the two editions of the legendary *World Christian Encyclopedia*. I am with him in his Nairobi, Kenya, office, looking at some of the material for the first edition. As a result of this visit, I helped him acquire his first computer.

Those of us in the second row are School of World Mission students in 1968, all experienced field missionaries. Three of the men in the front, from left to right, are Ralph Winter, Alan Tippett, and Donald McGavran, the initial core faculty. I was to join that core faculty three years later.

write them on the blackboard. As they were drawing the graphs, I began to detect a new sense of excitement in the room. It was as if God was finally showing up in the seminar. The lines drawn across the paper were providing new information and insights about the churches they had been pastoring. I now had their attention.

When they finished, we added up the total membership of the 46 churches in 1961, 1966 and 1971. It came out to be 4,500 for each date! The Bible Fellowship church was on a distinct plateau! I then challenged each of them in prayer and faith to extend their graph of growth for five years into the future on the basis of how many new members they believed they could trust God for. When these were added up, the flat graph of growth took a sharp swing upward. So far as I know, this was the first "faith projection," as I labeled it there, ever made in a church growth seminar. It certainly would not be the last!

What were the results of this first experiment in American church growth?

Daniel G. Ziegler, director of the Church Extension Department of the Bible Fellowship Church, wrote a report in 1981, "How Did the BFC Do in the Seventies?" On the first page he references our 1972 faith projections. Then he reports that in the 1970s "the membership of the Bible Fellowship Church rose by 1,205, the largest numerical increase in any decade of our history." He goes on to say, "But percentage growth is a more accurate measure of comparison than raw numerical increase. In the decade of the '70s, the church grew 26.5 percent. One would have to go back to the '30s to find a higher percentage of growth. . . . The one decade, the '70s, outgrew the previous *three* decades by 777 members, a phenomenal 282 percent!"

Although it didn't happen immediately, this remarkable experience confirmed in my mind that I was probably the "someone else" to whom McGavran had unintentionally relegated the task of lighting the fire of church growth in North America. But first I needed to do more work on developing the basic concept.

The Venezuela Experiment

Back to the Elburn Consultation. Although I had not yet received Dan Zeigler's report, God had still given me a notable degree of faith and hope that the Bible Fellowship Churches would now get off their plateau. So I called Vergil Gerber and suggested that we might actually have a church growth seminar design that we could test in Latin America. I asked him to activate his EMIS network and see if he could locate a group of church leaders somewhere in Latin America who would be willing to set up three church growth workshops, one year apart. The two of us would teach church growth principles to the pastors, challenge them to make faith projections and then return for two successive years to measure what had happened. By then I was Executive Director of Fuller Evangelistic Association, so I could finance the project.

Vergil soon called back and said he had found a group of five IFMA/ EFMA missions in Venezuela that would invite us to do it. This "Venezuela Experiment" paid off. Fifty-two churches cooperated. Their combined growth rate for the previous 10 years was 60 percent DGR (decadal growth rate). Their rate for the two years following the first church growth workshop had soared to 250 percent! We knew that God had given us a workable model, and we reported the results to those who had attended the Elburn Consultation.

This revolutionized Vergil Gerber's ministry. He became so excited about church growth that he used a large portion of his time through the decade of the 1970s conducting church growth workshops in more than 50 nations of the world! I helped him in the second one, Haiti, but after that he was on his own. For years he was logging at least one church growth workshop every six weeks in different parts of the world. Few evangelical leaders, if any, have been more widely used of God than Vergil Gerber in stimulating grass-roots, church-based outreach that has produced measurable fruit, and fruit that remains.

After Venezuela, it had become obvious that a standard guidebook of some sort needed to be produced and used in each church growth workshop. Vergil was a novice at writing books, but I had been producing them for years. Ordinarily it would have been my task to write the book, but by then I knew that with the other responsibilities I had in SWM and FEA, I would not be doing many of the workshops. I strongly urged Vergil to put the book together and he tried but did not succeed. So, for the first and only time in my life, I decided to ghostwrite a book under Vergil Gerber's name. I helped him sign a contract with Regal Books, and the result was *God's Way to Keep a Church Going and Growing*, otherwise known as "The Gerber Manual." The book was translated into more than 50 languages, and arguably it became the number-one instrument for making church growth principles known throughout the world, even surpassing McGavran's magnum opus, *Understanding Church Growth*.

Without the Elburn Consultation, the Bible Fellowship Church and the beginning of the Venezuela Experiment under my belt, I could not have moved as strongly as I felt I should in promoting American church growth.

Our Course at Lake Avenue Church

For the first year after we moved to California, Doris and I attended Bell Friends Church, which supported us while we were in Bolivia. I even applied for ordination (Quakers call it "recording"), but I ran into a snag when I mentioned on the application form that I drank wine with my dinner. It then seemed wise to transfer our church membership to Lake Avenue Congregational Church (LACC) in Pasadena, which had informal historic ties with Fuller Seminary. It was Charles E. Fuller's church when he founded the seminary, and for some years the seminary classes had been held in LACC's educational unit. My first year at Fuller, in 1952, was the last year classes met at Lake Avenue. Many of the Fuller faculty were members of the church as well as a number of the Fuller trustees. This, then, became our church home for the next 25 years, and I was soon ordained by the Conservative Congregational Christian Conference (CCCC).

Chuck Miller, one of the LACC pastors, had been reading some of the church growth literature, including my book *Frontiers in Missionary Strategy*. He approached me and said that he would like to take some of my courses at SWM. I told him that he couldn't because of McGavran's rule that all students be experienced cross-cultural missionaries. But, correctly perceiving that I was in favor of contextualizing church growth for American churches, Chuck was persistent. So we prayed and strategized. It occurred to me that I might be able to teach a special course geared specifically to American church leaders. The obvious key would be to get McGavran to change his mind. So I sat down for a heart-to-heart talk with McGavran. After laying the foundation, I said, "Look, Dean, why don't we at least invite Chuck Miller in to explain his concern to an SWM faculty meeting? Then the whole faculty can talk about it." McGavran was favorable, and we did it. The upshot was that the faculty thought it would be a good idea. Not only that, but I asked McGavran if he would team-teach the course with me and, will wonders never cease, he agreed! This was the tipping point!

We taught the course, with 18 pastors and Christian workers from the Los Angeles area, at 7:00 A.M. to 9:00 A.M. every Tuesday morning at LACC for the fall quarter of 1972. The response was extraordinary, and McGavran enjoyed every minute of it. Two important things happened as a result of that course. First, we now agreed that church growth principles could indeed be contextualized into the American scene. Second, one of the students happened to be Win Arn, then Director of Christian Education for the California Conference of the Evangelical Covenant Church of America.

Win Arn was, by nature, an entrepreneur. He immediately perceived the huge potential for marketing church growth across the spectrum of American churches. He established a close, personal friendship with McGavran and persuaded him that his church growth ideas could permeate and transform churches in all 50 states. Arn resigned from his position with the Evangelical Covenant Church and founded the Institute for American Church Growth in 1974, which became his family-owned business for the next 25 years. McGavran worked closely with him in producing books and films and seminars and growth resources for congregations. Just as I see Vergil Gerber as the chief popularizer of church growth in more than 50 nations of the world, I see Win Arn as the chief popularizer of church growth in America. Both provided great satisfaction to me through the years because at least I had a small slice of the action to help move them into their destiny.

Fuller Institute for Evangelism and Church Growth

This is not to say that I was a mere spectator in this process. I did my part as well. By the mid-1970s, the financial resources for funding mission projects in Fuller Evangelistic Association were diminishing, and it became obvious that some changes needed to be made. Now that American church growth was becoming popular, and I was in growing demand for teaching church growth to pastors and denominational leaders across the country, I decided to cast a new vision for FEA, and the board agreed. We changed the name to the Charles E. Fuller Institute of Evangelism and Church Growth (CEFI) and developed a program offering national conferences on various aspects of church growth, as well as consultation services for denominations.

Meanwhile, the Fuller School of Theology decided to open a new Doctor of Ministry (D.Min.) program for experienced pastors and church leaders, and they invited me to be a part of the initial planning process. We agreed that church growth should be offered as part of the curriculum, and by then, I had logged considerable experience in teaching the principles to leaders of several different denominations. I processed this through the SWM faculty and they agreed to allow me to teach in this new School of Theology program. The D.Min. Church Growth Concentration became a success beyond our expectations. I introduced a basic two-week course involving 60 contact hours of teaching; soon I needed to add an advanced course requiring another two weeks. I would usually have 50 to 60 students or even more from every Protestant denomination imaginable signed 'up for each course. When combined with my regular SWM courses, I ended up teaching more students per year than any other Fuller professor. For a long time, doctoral dissertations related to church growth outnumbered all other FTS/SWM doctoral dissertations combined. Church growth was catching on in America!

John Wimber Appears

In 1975, a student named John Wimber appeared in one of my D.Min. classes. I had not previously met him, but I had heard a number of reports of his dynamic ministry in a Friends church in nearby Orange County. I managed to arrange several conversations with him over the two-week class period. During the first week, he said, "Peter, everything you are teaching I have already known. I just didn't know the terminology and how all the pieces fit together." By the end of the second week, I realized that John was as sharp a practitioner of church growth as anyone I had ever met. As I have mentioned, FEA was then developing professional church growth consultation services, but I had discovered that I was not a good consultant. I was a good theoretician all right, but I needed to team up with a bona fide practitioner. John appeared to me to fit the bill as that practitioner, so I took him to the FEA offices to meet Doris and some others. Doris agreed that we should hire him, and I suggested to John that he leave the pastorate and come full-time to FEA as a consultant, which he did.

Wimber and I became a very effective team for many years. I brought him in as a visiting professor in my D.Min. courses, especially the advanced session. He spoke in all of our CEFI church growth seminars and conferences, and he was key in putting CEFI on the map. He soon was in constant demand nationwide as a trainer and consultant. Later on we will see other major contributions that John made to my life and ministry to the extent that I am naming an entire chapter for him. Meanwhile, I felt that,

In my office in Cochabamba, Bolivia. At the time, I was involved in writing my first two books, both missionary biographies: *The Condor of the Jungle* and *Defeat of the Bird God*.

I admired Donald McGavran so much that I decided to grow a goatee like his. This is my first, fairly rough attempt as I am typing a book manuscript on my IBM Selectric typewriter.

Doris joined me when I was installed as the first incumbent of the Donald A. McGavran Chair of Church Growth at Fuller Theological Seminary.

along with Win Arn's Institute of American Church Growth, we at CEFI had developed the second barrel of a double-barreled church growth shotgun for our nation. At that point, my missiological task of contextualizing church growth, at least in my mind, was all but complete.

American Society of Church Growth

The blossoming of American church growth was rooted primarily in academia, led (somewhat reluctantly) by Donald McGavran and his School of World Mission. A normal part of academia is the role of professional societies where theoreticians and researchers routinely present their current findings to peers in the field. In religious circles we frequent organizations such as the Evangelical Theological Society or the Society of Biblical Literature or the American Society of Missiology, and others. Since by then academia had become my personal working environment, I began feeling that American church growth should be legitimized by a professional society. Once again my intuitions as a horizontal apostle (although I didn't know the term in those days) began to churn within me.

I was pleased to observe that several who had taken my Doctor of Ministry courses had chosen church growth as their professional career. Some had been appointed to their positions by their denominational leadership, while others had launched out independently with their own church growth teaching and consultation ministries across the board. At that time, John Wimber had left CEFI in order to plant what eventually became Anaheim Vineyard, and I had invited Carl George of Gainesville, Florida, one of my Fuller church growth disciples, to take his place. I shared with Carl my vision for a professional society, and he agreed that we should take steps in that direction.

My sense of protocol told me that the first person I should approach would be Donald McGavran, which I did. A surprise was in store for me. I imagined that McGavran would be very enthusiastic, because a professional church growth society would presumably advance the cause of church growth principles and practice to a new level throughout America. I thought he would be delighted to know that his ideas were spreading so rapidly. But McGavran's response to the idea turned out to be lukewarm at best. He gave me little encouragement to move ahead with the idea. I should have known by then that whatever I did with American church growth, as contrasted to foreign missions, would please him little.

So I went to Win Arn, and I was disappointed to find a similar response. This surprised me as well. In retrospect, I could surmise two things. First, McGavran probably got to Arn first and expressed his misgivings. Second, Arn, as a true entrepreneur, had a tendency to regard others active in the arena of American church growth as competitors rather than colleagues. Nevertheless, I moved ahead with the encouragement of many other church growth professionals such as Kent Hunter and Dan Reeves and George Hunter III and Carl George and John Vaughan and Elmer Towns and Bill Sullivan. As a result, I became the founding president in 1986. I first called the organization the North American Society of Church Growth, but eventually it became clear that the Canadians preferred having their own professional society rather than being mere footnotes to their U.S. counterparts. We then changed the name to the American Society of Church Growth (ASCG) and it thrives today under the able leadership of Gary McIntosh of Talbot Theological Seminary, who also edits the quarterly *ASCG Journal*. By the way, McIntosh has undertaken the enormous task of researching and writing the definitive biography of Donald McGavran.

I did manage to get Win Arn partially involved by establishing an annual Donald A. McGavran Church Growth Award and naming Arn as the first recipient. Both he and McGavran were in attendance for the presentation ceremony, and McGavran addressed the group. We were able to maintain McGavran's support by inviting him to keynote the annual meeting for a few years, but eventually both McGavran and Arn lost interest and dropped out.

Shifting Paradigms

It has regularly fallen to my lot to help introduce new ideas or paradigms into groups with which I have been associated. For example, back in high school our athletic teams had no mascot, so I helped them become the "Suffield Wildcats." The school had no Hi-Y Club, so I organized that. Hi-Y Clubs gather high school boys for developing an excellent standard of character, and they are affiliated with the YMCA. Such things continued through my days in Bolivia, as I described in the last chapter. Now, as Donald McGavran's understudy, I began to gain a voice in the field of church growth, so I was able to help move the Body of Christ into a number of new paradigms, some of them quite radical at the time. I now see this as a function of the spiritual gift of apostle that God had given me, although I did not know it then.

During what I am calling "The McGavran Era," five of these paradigm shifts stand out in my mind as worthy of mention: (1) employing strategy for church growth, (2) pragmatism and the use of numbers, (3) making disciples as the definition of evangelism, (4) third world missions, and (5) the people approach to world evangelization, or the "homogeneous unit principle." Let's conclude the chapter by looking at these one at a time.

1. Employing Strategy for Church Growth

Most historians date the beginning of the modern missionary movement to 1792, the year that William Carey left England and became a missionary to India. When I arrived on the mission field in the 1950s, the movement was a little more than 150 years old. Because of their dedication and their willingness to sacrifice, missionaries were often considered to be among the most heroic people in the Body of Christ.

Be that as it may, missionaries might have been *heroic*, but very few of them were *strategic*. They were called to the mission field and they were usually assigned to places perceived as having the most need. They knew that their job description was to evangelize the area they were sent to. They had received little training in how to evangelize properly and effectively, so they were taught to pray and leave the outcome to God. God was sovereign and He would see that they got their job done if they stayed prayed up. Why not? They were invariably regarded as doing good missionary work, no matter what the measurable outcome!

In none of my 16 years on the mission field can I recall a session of any kind where the leadership of a mission with which I was connected cast a vision for developing a strategy that might help us be more successful in the task of evangelizing our area. In fact, when I myself became the leader, I held no such session simply because it would not have occurred to me. That is, until I studied under Donald McGavran in 1967 and 1968. McGavran's courses in church growth principles and practice were pure strategy, and that is when my paradigm shift began. It made so much sense to me that when I returned to Bolivia, I imagined that all the missionaries I knew would welcome the idea of strategy planning with open arms as soon as I explained it to them. Such, however, did not turn out to be the case. In fact, in the two years I was there, I was able to persuade very few others that intentional planning could help us all to be better missionaries.

When I returned to America, I began teaching and writing with a passion on mission strategy. I found that I could pretty well persuade the missionaries I taught in the School of World Mission over a 10-week period, especially since my students were also taking classes with McGavran. But it was a struggle to change the paradigms of the wider missionary community. Most missionaries were so bound to the theology that God was sovereign and that He would show them everything they needed to do that many of them felt like efforts to plan strategy were essentially ungodly. I was criticized for attempting to apply sociology to spiritual things. I had done a good bit in sociology of religion during my PhD studies at the University of Southern California, so I could easily see the benefits of that approach. However, using tools like statistics and graphs and charts was still considered by many as carnal rather than spiritual. Strategy planning was seen as quenching the Holy Spirit. Books I wrote such as *Frontiers in Missionary Strategy, Strategies for Church Growth* and *Church Planting for a Greater Harvest* helped some, but in those days, changing this paradigm was not easy. However, I do think it was worthwhile at the end of the day because now strategy planning is widely accepted and practiced in missionary work.

2. Using Numbers: Pragmatism

One of the reasons behind much of the opposition to strategy planning was the pervasive aversion to measuring tangible results on the part of many church and missionary leaders. I can't think of any more comfortable profession than that of missionaries and evangelists who can get away with the simple and pious-sounding phrase, "We leave the results up to God." Think of this: It levels the playing field so much that it becomes impossible and even unspiritual to attempt to distinguish between excellent missionaries on the one hand and mediocre missionaries on the other. Some say, "Judge me on who I am, not what I do." With this mindset, donors are encouraged to support missionaries simply because they faithfully serve God, since "numbers are not important." Missionaries who raise the most funds are not necessarily the most efficient missionaries in accomplishing their task, but most frequently the ones who have magnetic personalities and who can tell the most tear-jerking stories with precision timing.

Having said this, I am not comparing missionaries who work with highly resistant peoples such as Muslims to those who might work with receptive animistic African tribespeople, for example. I am talking about productive and unproductive missionaries working among the same peoples in the same geographical region. How can we tell the difference? Numbers are an excellent measuring device. An evangelistic missionary who plants 250 churches in 10 years is probably a better missionary than one who might plant one or two in the same region over the same time period.

One of Donald McGavran's most notable breakthroughs in missiological theory was that production should be accurately measured. I recall him lamenting that book after book about missions carries not even a hint of what might have helped or hindered the growth of churches. The premise in such books is usually that the missionaries, no matter what, have been faithful to God, and if souls are not saved and churches have not been multiplied, it only means that God's timing has not yet arrived. McGavran would speak out against such nonsense every time he had the opportunity. He would make disturbing statements such as, "If our methods are not producing desired results, stop making excuses and discard the ineffective methods. Substitute methods that will work! Now!"

I don't think that McGavran ever described this kind of radical thinking as "pragmatism," although that is exactly what it was. One reason could have been that in religious circles pragmatism was generally considered a transgression. I, however, was a bit more audacious. Back in the mid-1970s, in my most popular book on American church growth, *Your Church Can Grow*, I labeled my approach as "consecrated pragmatism." In fact, I was so bold as to disagree with the common religious saying, "the end does not justify the means." If there are no issues of character, ethics or morality involved, what else could possibly justify the means except the end? If, for example, I need to dig a hole for the foundation of a new garage, some of the means available to do it would be using a teaspoon, a shovel or a backhoe. If I chose anything but the backhoe, I would be considered foolish. The end, in that case, justified my choice of means.

Predictably, my suggestions that we measure the results of our Christian initiatives by using numbers, and that we select or reject methods (or "means") on the basis of what works or what doesn't work, provoked considerable backlash. In fact, John MacArthur, a Christian leader whom I highly respect to this day, wrote a whole book scolding me, along with George Barna, Elmer Towns and others for our worldly pragmatism. The book's title *Ashamed of the Gospel* implied that we were just the opposite of the apostle Paul, who wrote, "I am *not* ashamed of the gospel" (Rom. 1:16, emphasis added). MacArthur's paradigm obviously was not ready to shift!

3. Evangelism = Making Disciples
One of the drawbacks hindering evangelists and evangelistic missionaries from agreeing that the results of their ministry should be measured and

Donald McGavran and I are chatting with David Wang from China. David studied under us in the early 1980s, and since then David has been my chief apostolic bridge to Hong Kong and China.

Donald McGavran and I pose in my office in Fuller Seminary with two of our most notable students: Elmer L. Towns (left) and John Vaugham (right), the international expert on megachurches.

their methods analyzed has been a failure to arrive at a consensus across the board as to what the product of evangelization really is. Should we measure evangelistic efforts by the number of those who have heard or otherwise been exposed to the gospel? Is our goal to count "decisions for Christ"? Or are unbelievers evangelized (past tense) only when they become true disciples of Jesus?

A major reason why I became concerned with saturation evangelism programs like Evangelism in Depth in Latin America is that I began reading reports of huge numbers of "decisions" or "conversions," but with little or no change in the number of ongoing disciples in a certain territory as a result. For example, I did careful research on Evangelism in Depth in Bolivia in 1965 and found that, despite 20,000 public professions of faith, the church membership in the nation actually declined during and after the initiative. Following that, I researched citywide evangelistic efforts in the United States by such as Billy Graham and Campus Crusade and found that a high of 16 percent and a low of 3 percent to 5 percent who signed decision cards eventually became church members. This rather shocking information helped me understand the roots of the popular phrase "evangelistically speaking," which means to most that undue exaggeration of numbers is being employed by the parties involved.

In order to help remedy this unfortunate situation, I made a strong attempt to use the version of the Great Commission found in Matthew 28:19 as a template. Jesus told us there to "make disciples." The word "disciple" (in the Greek *mathetes*) is the most frequent term in the New Testament used for believers in Christ. Simply put, "disciples" denotes adherents of Jesus. If evangelism is intended to make disciples, as over against mere decisions for Christ, how can we know when a disciple has really been made? My argument was that the best measurement (although admittedly not a perfect one) was that the person who made the decision would then become a responsible member of a local church. I taught this in my classes at Fuller. I published articles on it. I argued my point in books like *Stop the World, I Want to Get On; Your Church Can Grow; On the Crest of the Wave;* and *Strategies for Church Growth.* I spoke about it at conferences. However, with all this effort, I must admit that I was not as successful as I wished I had been in changing the paradigm of the great majority of church leaders.

My strongest opponent in this debate was none other than David B. Barrett, arguably the number-one researcher of the church in our generation, perhaps in all of history. He is widely known and respected as the editor of both the first and second editions of the massive *World Christian Encyclopedia*. David and I are personal friends and we admire one another, even if we don't agree. We have discussed the definition of evangelism personally more than once. In Barrett's elaborate scheme for calculating what he calls "missiometrics," he tells us that 72 percent of the world's population is now "evangelized." What does he mean by that? He means, not that 72 percent have necessarily even made a "decision" for Christ, but that they have had some sort of access or exposure to the message of Christianity. In the same statistical table he also reports that only 33 percent of the world is Christian. As you can readily see, there is no essential relationship in Barrett's mind between being evangelized and becoming a disciple.

Because of Barrett's enormous integrity and influence as a researcher, he won the argument. I still think I'm right, but I have since decided to fight other battles!

4. Third World Missions

When I joined Donald McGavran on the School of World Mission faculty in the early 1970s, the assumption among missiologists and the missionary community in general was that missionary sending nations were essentially limited to North America, Europe, and Australia/New Zealand. Missionaries were supposed to be sent from the Western world to the Third World. Today I find it appalling that most of us who had given our lives to foreign missions somehow lacked a vision for imparting to the people to whom we were ministering our own passion for cross-cultural missions. Yes, we trained our converts to evangelize those around them, but most of us never even suggested that they consider leaving their homeland to go to another people group with the gospel, as we had done. I say "us" because the seminary and the Bible school in Bolivia over which I had strong influence offered no courses at all in missions.

A distinct advantage of teaching in the School of World Mission at Fuller was the constant exposure we had to our students, all of whom were experienced and respected leaders from virtually every country in the world. Some were missionaries and some were national leaders. We happened to be the largest school of its kind at that time. We had a close-knit faculty of up to 14 missiologists, all of whom traveled internationally on a regular basis. As we interacted with our students and personally observed what was happening in other parts of the world, we eventually began hearing that some of the churches in the Third World had begun to send missionaries to other countries. This attracted my attention.

In 1971, a major consultation of IFMA and EFMA executives was called in order to discuss relationships between missions and national churches. Four hundred top leaders met in Green Lake, Wisconsin, for a week, wrestling with the problems that faced them all. Although the program did not include the topics of missions from Third World churches, David Cho (not to be confused with David Yonggi Cho) and Samuel Kim from Korea surfaced the issue in a persuasive way, exposing the ignorance of most Western mission leaders. I edited a follow-up book, *Church/Mission Tensions Today,* in which I was able to introduce three chapters on national churches sending their own missionaries. However, I knew that much more work still needed to be done.

A graduate school like SWM inevitably becomes a research center. Many students are ready and willing to undertake directed studies for credit toward their degrees. It was not difficult for me to find three students who had previously developed an interest in what we began to call "Third World Missions," namely, James Wong from Singapore; Edward Pentecost from Mexico and Dallas Seminary; and Peter Larson from Argentina. I organized them into a team, and they were able to research and produce a notable book, a first of its kind: *Missions from the Third World.* They found that by 1972, no fewer than 256 mission agencies could be located in Third World nations, sending out 3,369 missionaries. This began to open a whole new concept in the missions community of the day.

5. The People Approach to World Evangelization

Without question, the most controversial and strenuously debated paradigm shift in which I have been involved to date is known as the "homogeneous unit principle." I have been annoyingly puzzled as to why large numbers of church leaders reject this idea vociferously even though probably 90 percent of them actually practice it. The bulk of the opposition has consistently arisen among church leaders in the United States, not so much among missionaries or Third World leaders. This undoubtedly is due to the fact that we Americans have become so self-conscious about our embarrassing history of slavery and racism that we tend to be in denial of the positive aspects of race, ethnicity and culture. Even mentioning such a thing as I have just done would clearly appear to some as politically incorrect.

What is the homogeneous unit principle? Donald McGavran was the first to make the homogeneous unit principle a central feature in his missiological model. In his seminal book *Bridges of God,* and later in his classic textbook *Understanding Church Growth*, McGavran would repeat words to this effect: "People like to become Christians without crossing racial, linguistic, or class barriers." This observation is as much a law of sociology as gravity is a law of physics.

For example, most Korean unbelievers would naturally be more attracted to Korean churches than to Japanese churches. Most Spaniards would be more attracted to Spanish churches than to French churches. Most Paraguayans would be more attracted to Paraguayan churches than to Argentine churches. For example, I recall one sociological study of all the Presbyterian churches in Southern California in the 1980s that attempted to discover which were the most unifying factors among members of Presbyterian congregations across the board. I was amazed when they found out that the number-one unifying factor was Scottish ancestry! For those who might wonder, the Presbyterian Church was first founded back in the 1500s as the official Church of Scotland. Which also brings to mind the persistence of the homogeneous unit principle among Lutheran churches of the North Central states in America. Even though English is now the language of choice among all those churches, no informed person would make the mistake of confusing German Lutheran churches with Swedish Lutheran churches or with Norwegian Lutheran churches!

The ICOWE Seal of Approval

What many would consider the official missiological seal of approval on the homogeneous unit principle occurred at the International Congress on World Evangelization (ICOWE) sponsored by the Billy Graham Evangelistic Association (BGEA) in Lausanne, Switzerland, in 1974. No fewer than 4,500 handpicked evangelical leaders from 200 nations were invited to participate with their expenses paid by the BGEA. This became the largest and most influential missions event in the last part of the twentieth century, possibly of all time. Several of us on the SWM faculty were among the participants, with Donald McGavran, Ralph Winter and me on the roster of speakers.

Arguably the most influential address of ICOWE 1974 was Ralph Winter's plenary session on "The Highest Priority: Cross-Cultural Evangelism." Winter succeeded in persuading almost every delegate present that we need to shift our thinking about the goals of missions from evangelizing geographical territories such as nations or cities or regions to "people groups," as McGavran had been advocating since publishing *Bridges of God*. People groups, sometimes referred to as "peoples," are to be defined ethnically rather than geographically. In Jesus' command to make disciples of "all nations," the Greek for that is *panta ta ethne*, the word from which we get our English phrase "ethnic groups." Winter, whose doctorate is in anthropology, urged cross-cultural workers to minister to each people group on its own cultural terms and to avoid superimposing a foreign culture on them as many untrained missionaries had tended to do in the past. He also suggested that for the foreseeable future we agree to give top priority to those people groups in the world among whom the gospel has yet to be introduced, known as "unreached peoples."

At the conclusion of ICOWE, a Lausanne Committee for World Evangelization (LCWE) of 48 members was named, and I happened to be one of the 48. Soon after it began to function, two influential units were formed and officially commissioned. One was the Theology Working Group headed up by John Stott of the U.K., and the other the Strategy Working Group (SWG), which I headed up. I immediately approached Ed Dayton who was in charge of the research division of World Vision International, and he agreed to partner with me in the functional operations of the SWG. We worked together for many years in helping to change the paradigm of the Body of Christ in general and the missionary community in particular toward what we began to call "the people approach to world evangelization." Notice, by the way, that "the people approach to world evangelization" is a synonym for "the homogeneous unit principle."

Following Ralph Winter's lead, the SWG launched out on a serious research project aimed at identifying as many of the world's unreached peoples as we could. One result was the publication of the first three volumes of the Unreached Peoples Series, which Dayton and I coauthored. Within a relatively short period of time, the paradigm shift had taken place, and by and large, a critical mass of evangelical missions began to do their strategy planning around the homogeneous unit principle.

An Uphill Battle in the United States

Meanwhile, I continued to be heavily involved in promoting American church growth, and I soon found it was an uphill battle to expect leaders here in our society to agree with the homogeneous unit principle. Many of the objections seemed to be ethical, based on the supposition that all godly congregations should include members of all the ethnic groups found in their particular geographical location. The response to my suggestion that such might not actually prove to be a valid Christian principle was to label me politically incorrect at best and racist at worst. I became so involved in this controversy that the title of my PhD dissertation at the University of Southern California was "The Ethical Implications of the Homogeneous Unit Principle of Church Growth." John Knox Press later published it as *Our Kind of People.*

While the homogeneous unit principle made sense to cross-cultural missionaries, our U.S. monocultural pastors and denominational executives never were able to affirm it to any significant extent. This disappointed me, because it is a valid principle practiced by Jesus and the early church, throughout Christian history and even today in the United States. I could not convince many that this was not Christian doctrine; it was simply sound sociology. For example, a study reported in a recent issue of the sociological *Journal for the Scientific Study of Religion* affirmed that "the vast majority of U.S. congregations [are] virtually homogeneous [with] few possessing even modest representation by two or more racial groups."[3] To suggest that such a state of affairs might displease God is, in my opinion, absurd.

Let me give two up-to-date examples of how the homogeneous unit principle has actually played out, much to the dismay of its earlier opponents.

First, I was extremely fascinated by observing the homogeneous unit principle surfacing in Barack Obama's run for the presidency in 2008. While most people on both sides were sincerely striving to be politically correct and keep racial issues off the agenda, Obama's church membership could not be ignored. For 20 years he had been a committed member of Trinity United Church of Christ on the South Side of Chicago, one of America's more notably liberal churches. Not only was Trinity a typically American nonintegrated church, but its image of choice was "unashamedly black." When its current pastor, Otis Moss III (not to be confused with the former pastor, Jeremiah Wright, who has become notorious for anti-American remarks), was asked to explain this self-characterization, he responded, "I would begin by suggesting that a church that is 'unashamedly black and unapologetically Christian' is no different from a Korean Presbyterian church or a Greek Orthodox church or a German Baptist church at which an ethnic or national identity is paired with a Christian identity. Unfortunately, in America, we have this idea that 'black' is just a color, unconnected to culture or nation."[4] Political or theological issues aside, I love Otis Moss's anthropological intuitions and his implicit affirmation of the homogeneous unit principle!

Second, *Outreach* magazine does a highly respected annual survey of the 100 largest and fastest-growing churches in the United States. Their report in 2008 listed a number of success factors common to these top 100 churches. One of them was "monocultural congregation." The experts stated, "Churches on the lists tend to focus their attention and efforts on a specific demographic. There were few multicultural congregations."[5] Some may dislike this phenomenon, but it cannot be wished away.

Conclusion

As you have seen, the McGavran era was a stimulating, enlightening, highly energetic period of my life. I feel that Donald McGavran was one of the major positive influences on my person and on my ministry career. God used him to help steer my ship toward the destiny that God had for me. One of the more notable honors of my pilgrimage was to be named as the first incumbent of the Donald A. McGavran Chair of Church Growth in Fuller Seminary. This was to me what a Nobel Prize or a Pulitzer Prize might be to an international dignitary. When I was officially inaugurated, I felt I had reached the top of my field. Some frosting on the cake was McGavran's subsequent invitation to edit and revise the third edition of his classic textbook in the field, *Understanding Church Growth*, which I finalized in 1990. It is still in print.

When I arrived on the faculty of Fuller Seminary in 1971, McGavran had grown a Colonel Sanders type of white goatee. As a physical sign of my commitment to him as my church growth mentor, I started my own goatee in 1972. It was brown at first, but now it is as white as McGavran's. The legacy lives on!

Notes

1. See C. Peter Wagner, *Dominion!* (Grand Rapids MI: Chosen Books, 2008), p. 50.
2. See C. Peter Wagner, *Strategies for Church Growth* (Ventura, CA: Regal Books, 1987), p. 142, note 13.
3. Kevin D. Dougherty and Kimberly R. Huyser, "Racially Diverse Congregations: Organizational Identity and the Accommodation of Differences," *Journal for the Scientific Study of Religion*, 2008, 47(1), p. 31.
4. "Beloved Community," an interview with Otis Moss III, *Christian Century*, April 8, 2008, p. 10.
5. The "Outreach 100 Largest and Fastest-Growing Churches in America," 2008 Special Issue (www.OutreachMagazine.com), p. 26.

6

The Wimber Era

(1982–1989)

I don't cry much. I mean, hardly at all. When I was about 12, my father taught me that big boys don't cry, and I believed him.

That is why this unforgettable story belongs in these memoirs. In November 1997, I parked my car in my garage here in the Black Forest Park area of Colorado Springs, which I had been doing routinely for over a year. I can't remember where I had been. When I walked into the kitchen of our home, I saw on the island a note that someone had jotted down from a telephone message. It said, "John Wimber has died. Details to come." It wasn't 30 seconds until the whole thing sank in and suddenly I began to weep. I don't mean a tear or two coursing down my cheek, but loud sobs! And for a long time!

I was embarrassed at myself. Fortunately, I was alone. After I had used a substantial supply of Kleenex, I began to think. The truth is that I hadn't cried when my mother died, nor had I cried when my father died. I can't recall any episode of tears after hearing about anyone else's death, as far as that goes. What was happening? I knew that John Wimber had influenced my life as few others had, but this grieving must have meant that he had influenced it even far beyond what I had realized.

I'm sure this incident will help you understand why I am naming a chapter in my memoirs "The Wimber Era."

A Convinced Cessationist

When I went to Bolivia as a missionary, I was a convinced cessationist. Let me explain.

As I have mentioned, I grew up with no church or religious or theological background. After Doris led me to Christ, I knew that I should probably go to church, but what church? The only church I had become familiar with was Doris's family church, Christ Lutheran Church of Little Falls, New

York. Not only was it Lutheran, but it was also thoroughly German. Regular services were held in the German language, along with other English services, and I found it was to my advantage to have a German surname. I liked the church and we got married there, but I knew there was nothing like it around Rutgers University in New Brunswick, New Jersey, where I lived at the time. So the question remained: What church should I attend?

In chapter 2, I told the story of how I became a member of the small InterVarsity Christian Fellowship group on the Rutgers campus. One of the members was Doug Smith whose family lived in nearby Princeton. He told me that his grandmother attended the Methodist church right near the campus, so that was good enough for me. When we married, Doris and I routinely attended that Methodist church. This lasted until one Sunday when the pastor held up a copy of Karl Marx's *Das Kapital* in one hand and the Bible in the other and told us that the two were equally inspired. We didn't know much theology at the time, but we strongly suspected that this was not what we believed, so we met with the pastor and excused ourselves from the church.

Independent Fundamental Churches of America

Doug Smith's father, who led a Plymouth Brethren house assembly in nearby Princeton, took us under his wing and began to teach us the difference between liberalism (aka, modernism) and evangelicalism (aka, fundamentalism). Our choice then became a local fundamental church, New Brunswick Bible Church, and there we began to feel at home. For two years this is where we received our basic grounding in the Bible. We were sternly instructed to use the Scofield Reference edition of the *King James Version*, which we obediently did. In fact, if you remember in chapter 2, where I mentioned that for no good reason of my own I bought a Bible before I first went off to college, it happened to be a Scofield Bible. We knew that Scofield's notes weren't inspired, but nevertheless we believed them almost on the level of the biblical text. We were warmly accepted into the church family, especially since we intended to be missionaries. We eventually found that the church was affiliated with the Independent Fundamental Churches of America (IFCA).

Why do I mention this? Because all churches in the IFCA were cessationist. As you can see, this comes from the word "cease," and the general idea is that the more supernatural spiritual gifts (such as those the Pentecostals had been using) actually *ceased* at the end of the apostolic age and were not supposed to be in use today. That sounded reasonable enough to us, and we learned the Bible verses to prove it. This mindset was reinforced when we went to California to train for the mission field. Both Biola and Fuller were cessationist. The two missions under which we served in Bolivia, the South America Mission (SAM) and the Andes Evangelical Mission (AEM), were cessationist as well. Neither mission would accept any new missionary candidates who were not cessationist.

Fuller Seminary identified itself as teaching "Reformed Theology." This is theology that goes back to John Calvin of Geneva who arguably was the strongest progenitor of cessationism back in the sixteenth century. My Fuller professors relied, more than anyone else, on renowned Princeton Seminary professor Benjamin Breckenridge Warfield who taught:

> My conclusion then is, that the power of working miracles was not extended beyond the disciples upon whom the Apostles conferred it by the imposition of their hands. As the number of these disciples gradually diminished, the instances of the exercise of miraculous powers became continually less frequent, and ceased entirely at the death of the last individual on whom the hands of the Apostles had been laid.[1]

Needless to say, I believed what my professors taught me. When I returned to New Brunswick Bible Church for ordination after graduating from seminary, my committee needed assurance that I had no inclination toward Pentecostalism, where counterfeit gifts (according to Warfield) were being displayed. Under cross-examination, I flawlessly defended cessationism. I agreed that Pentecostals found themselves on what my teachers would call "the lunatic fringe!" So off I went to Bolivia, a convinced cessationist.

I have taken this time to explain my cessationist background so that the paradigm-shifting influence that John Wimber later had on my life can be better understood.

Working Cessationism Out

Cessationism was a nonissue during our five years in the jungle. All the other missionaries there were also cessationists, and we all simply operated under that unquestioned paradigm. When we moved to Cochabamba, however, the situation was more complex, because some Pentecostals, mainly Assemblies of God, had become deeply entrenched there. I developed my defenses, however, and I was able to keep my theological distance from them, even though I inevitably became aquainted with some of their leaders.

Over the years, I had been developing a measure of expertise in two subjects that I was currently teaching in seminary, First Corinthians and Spiritual Gifts. In 1967 and 1968, I did a series of nine monthly articles on First Corinthians in *Eternity* magazine published in Philadelphia. I eventually expanded it into a book, *A Turned-On Church in an Uptight World*, later released as *Our Corinthian Contemporaries*. First Corinthians has more detail on spiritual gifts than any other book of the Bible. Looking back, I find it significant that somehow I never made a case in my teaching or writing that controversial spiritual gifts such as tongues or healings or miracles or the office of apostle or the rest were not to be used today. I simply managed to avoid the issue.

An Experiment with Tongues

However, the plot thickens. One morning in 1966, I was alone in my study preparing a lesson I was going to teach the next day on 1 Corinthians 14. I had taught it many times before, so this was not strange territory. For some reason, my attention was attracted, probably for the first time, to verse 18: "I thank my God I speak with tongues more than you all." So I began to meditate. Paul by then had become my biblical role model. He mentioned speaking in tongues almost in passing. He seemed to treat it as a normal thing to do, no big deal. So I said to myself, *If Paul could do it, why couldn't I?*

All of this made a lot of sense to me. So I decided to do an experiment. I got down on my knees and before I knew it I was praying in tongues. It was real easy. I didn't understand a thing, but I knew that I wasn't supposed to understand it. There were no bright lights or rushing mighty winds. I wondered how long it would last, and it lasted a long time. In fact, I eventually thought it was lasting too long, so I just decided to quit. I probably could have gone on forever if I'd chosen to.

Now I had a real problem. I belonged to a cessationist mission agency that had dismissed missionaries who had spoken in tongues. Our AEM (Andes Evangelical Mission) belonged to the IFMA (Interdenominational Foreign Missions Association), which had a written policy that all members "will maintain a non-charismatic orientation." This was a battle that I did not want to fight. So my decision was a no-brainer. I kept quiet. I didn't pray in tongues again while I was in the mission. I didn't even tell

Doris that I had spoken in tongues. I lived for many years as a closet tongues-speaker. You would think I had committed a secret sin! All I did was experiment, and my experiment happened to work!

Our Enemies, the Pentecostals

You might suspect that this would have cured me of my cessationism. It may have made a dent, but only a small one. By this time, my cessationism had crystallized into anti-Pentecostalism. The Assemblies of God, led by Italian-American missionary Bruno Frigoli, had become firmly entrenched in Cochabamba, and I considered them enemies of those of us who perceived ourselves as the true, Bible-believing evangelicals. I preached against them. I wrote articles against them. I warned my people that what Pentecostals called divine healing was nothing but fraud. Nowadays, I would have said, God cures diseases with injections and capsules and operations, not with some oil on the forehead.

I was appalled that right in the midst of our high-visibility, energetic nationwide Evangelism in Depth program in 1965, Bruno Frigoli had the audacity to invite one of the best-known Pentecostal healing evangelists, Raimundo Jiménez of Puerto Rico, to do a healing crusade in Cochabamba. I took it almost as a declaration of war when posters advertising the crusade were pasted on telephone poles all over the city. The meetings were scheduled to be held in a vacant lot in the northern part of the city. A vacant lot? That was the time that, as I explained in chapter 4, I was pastoring the largest congregation in Cochabamba. I told my people not to go because respectable Christians met in buildings, not vacant lots! I told them that claims of healing were false and that their true faith in God would be severely damaged if they dared to show up at one of those disreputable gatherings.

My first disappointment, as you might have guessed, was that my people went to the healing services anyway. The second one was even worse—some of them were healed! But strange as it may seem now, I had a number of rational arguments that I felt were sufficient to explain away such claims to supernatural healing. In retrospect, I now see what a thorough spell the spirit of religion had cast over me and my cessationist colleagues at the time. I will explain more about this demonic principality later. But one of its most effective tactics is to convince those under its influence that what they are doing to quench the Holy Spirit is the will of God. This is exactly what I thought. I felt that I was serving God by denouncing Pentecostals!

E. Stanley Jones

One of the most unlikely persons that God used to help prepare me for the John Wimber days was the renowned Methodist missionary to India, E. Stanley Jones.

In order to understand the scenario, it is important to know that not only was I a convinced *cessationist*, but I was also a convinced *separatist*. What do I mean? I just mentioned that my New Brunswick Bible Church was affiliated with Independent Fundamental Churches of America. A strict rule in IFCA churches was to separate in every possible way from those who might be tinged in the slightest by such biblical deviations as liberalism on one hand or Pentecostalism on the other. That was commonly labeled "first-degree separatism." "Second-degree separatism" required separation even from all who might agree with you theologically, but who still might fraternize with those with whom they disagreed. I found myself somewhat between the two positions.

In Cochabamba, I had become influential in organizing and leading what we called *Iglesias Unidas* (United Churches). This was a relational group of missionaries and national church leaders designed essentially to keep us in touch with one another. The Methodists were members of *Iglesias Unidas*, and they were the most liberal or ecumenical of all the missions in Cochabamba. They belonged to the notorious World Council of Churches. At one meeting of *Iglesias Unidas* the Methodists announced that they had invited E. Stanley Jones to speak at a series of meetings in their school. They invited *Iglesias Unidas* to co-sponsor the event. My separatist instincts quickly moved front and center. E. Stanley Jones was a liberal in the opinion of those with whom I associated. Consequently I used my influence in *Iglesias Unidas* to turn down the invitation to co-sponsor his visit to Cochabamba. The Methodists had to go it alone.

The Gospel of Salvation

E. Stanley Jones's meetings in the Methodist school building started on a Tuesday night. Every Wednesday morning all the missionaries in the AEM who happened to be in Cochabamba at the time would gather for a prayer meeting, which I ordinarily led. I could not believe what I heard the morning after Jones's first meeting. Verne Roberts, well into his eighties, was Director Emeritus of the mission. He had preceded Joe McCullough who had preceded me. Mr. Roberts was a saintly veteran missionary from the old school. You can imagine my surprise when he told us that he had attended the Methodist meeting the night before! I thought he was more separatist than I was. Be that as it may, he reported that E. Stanley Jones preached a straightforward message of the gospel of salvation, gave an invitation and that many unbelievers were saved. This caught my attention.

By the end of that day my curiosity got the better of me. Doris and I decided to go to the Methodist school that night to find out firsthand what was happening. We felt like Nicodemus because we intentionally arrived late and unobtrusively sat toward the back of the room so that no one would notice us. The meeting, surprisingly enough, turned out to be an old-fashioned healing service, to my recollection the first one of its kind I had ever attended. Jones preached on biblical healing and then gave an invitation for all who needed healing to come forward and he would pray for them.

As I was sitting there, my thoughts went to a serious problem on my neck. I had developed a cyst on my neck that had required surgery. It so happened that after the procedure, I went into serious shock; I lost my vital signs and I passed out. The surgeon later told me that I had a very close call and that they almost lost me. To make matters worse, the incision would not heal. For weeks it had been a runny, pus-filled sore. Just a couple of days before this meeting, the doctor had told me that he would need to schedule another surgery. That was the last thing I wanted to hear!

So there I was, a cessationist listening to E. Stanley Jones's invitation for divine healing. The preaching, coming from a Methodist, had allowed me to bypass some of my anti-Pentecostal biases and had imparted to me a degree of faith in God's power to heal today. However, I was the mission director and I wasn't even supposed to be in the meeting, so I didn't move. Then, after several had gone forward for ministry, Jones did a wonderful thing. He said, "I know that there are others who need healing, but for one reason or another you have not come forward. Just relax, because I am going to pray for you also." I took that personally, and as he prayed, I had the faith to trust God to heal that wound on my neck.

When we got home, I removed the bandage. The sore was still open and runny, but I decided to go to bed that night without the bandage. The next morning, it was completely healed over, and it has been ever since! My paradigm began to shift a little more!

Where Does the Blessing of God Rest?

When I enrolled in the Fuller School of World Mission in 1967, to study under Donald McGavran, I was still anti-Pentecostal. However, a process of change began when I learned the basic principles of church growth research methodology. If you want to find out why churches are growing in a certain region at a certain time, you go to the field and ask these four questions: (1) Why does the blessing of God rest where it does? (2) Churches are not equal. Why are some churches more blessed than others at certain times? (3) Can any pattern of divine blessing be discerned? (4) If so, what are the common characteristics of those churches?

I returned to Bolivia in 1968, and I immediately began applying what I had learned. I wanted to find out why churches in Bolivia and in Latin America in general were growing. I asked the four questions, so I carefully looked around to find the churches where the blessing of God was resting the most. Much to my dismay, I found that the fastest-growing churches— not only in Cochabama, but also in all of Latin America—were the Pentecostal churches. For example, in 1950, only around 20 percent of churches in Latin America were Pentecostal. However, by 1970, the figure had mushroomed to 70 percent! Obviously, something important was happening there, and I became determined to find out what it was.

I knew I had to look into Pentecostal churches firsthand, but unfortunately, I had made enemies of the Pentecostal leaders in Bolivia. I could not embarrass myself by showing any interest in Pentecostal churches there! But I realized that just across the Andes Mountains in Chile, one of the world's most notable Pentecostal movements was flourishing. No one there would know that I had been anti-Pentecostal, so I got on a plane and went to Santiago, Chile.

A Pentecostal Adventure

My first step was to attend some Pentecostal services. I began seeing things I had never seen before. Dancing in the Spirit! Speaking messages in tongues! Interpretation of tongues! Prophecies! Clapping hands in church! Arms up in the air during worship! Rowdiness and joy! Lame people walking! All that was exciting to me, but I was suspicious that such behavior would have little grounding in the Word of God. At the same time, I had to admit that these people behaved like true born-again Christians. I observed the fruit of the Spirit in their lives. All of this dissonance caused numbers of theological questions to spin around in my head.

I was able to make personal appointments with some of the Pentecostal leaders, even including Javier Vásquez, pastor of the legendary

Jotabeche Methodist Pentecostal Church, which was one of the world's first megachurches and one of the largest churches in Latin America at the time. Vásquez and I immediately liked each other! I started asking him very tough theological questions. He amazed me when he not only answered my questions thoroughly and astutely, but he also kept drawing me to Scriptures that I, along with Scofield, had been ignoring. This man was quite a biblical theologian! I began to think that possibly the miraculous gifts had not gone out with the first apostles after all!

Back in Bolivia, I knew that some changes were in order. So I decided that instead of being a *convinced* cessationist, I would switch to being an *open* cessationist. I went to Bruno Frigoli and apologized for my bad attitude toward him and toward Pentecostals in general. That is when I found, to my relief, that Bruno not only had the *gifts* of the Spirit, but he also had the *fruit* of the Spirit, and he forgave me. In fact, Doris and I ended up being good personal friends with Bruno and Frances. My anti-Pentecostal days were over!

Look Out! The Pentecostals Are Coming

As usual, I soon put my newest thoughts into print. The first book I wrote after returning to the United States and joining the Fuller faculty was *Look Out! The Pentecostals Are Coming*. Throughout the book, I argued that the Pentecostals had rapidly become the largest movement in Latin America because they had been using classic church growth principles much better than the rest of us. I also mentioned that they probably experienced more of the power of the Holy Spirit than we did. While I addressed the book to my fellow evangelicals, not surprisingly, my most avid readers were Pentecostal leaders. I inadvertently became one of their heroes!

One of the outcomes of this was that I began getting invitations to teach church growth principles to leaders of Pentecostal denominations in America, such as Assemblies of God, Pentecostal Holiness and Church of God (Cleveland, Tennessee). Especially with the Church of God, I began learning as much from them as they were learning from me. Every time I visited them I came home spiritually refreshed. I remember that one time I brought home a tape recording of a message in tongues with interpretation, and I played it in one of our School of World Mission faculty meetings. The professors were fascinated because, probably for all of them, it was the first time they had ever heard such a thing, and I gave it at least a grain of credibility. On occasion, I began secretly wondering why I wasn't a Pentecostal.

John Wimber (left) made an unforgettable impression on Fuller Seminary when he started teaching the MC510 course "Signs, Wonders and Church Growth." Among the theology faculty the impression was largely negative, while the missions faculty embraced him and the students considered him at or near the top of their list of favorite professors.

During the early 1980s, I was trying to work my way through the transition from a cessationist to an advocate and spokesperson of the Third Wave, primarily under the influence of John Wimber. It is notable that "Third Wave" has gained the status of a theological technical term, appearing in one of the latest dictionaries of theology.

One of my responsibilities was to counsel students at Fuller Seminary. This individual wanted guidance as to how to move forward in a ministry of healing the sick as a result of taking John Wimber's course.

It was just then that John Wimber came on the scene. In the last chapter, I told how he had enrolled in one of my church growth courses and subsequently came to work for me as a church growth consultant with Charles E. Fuller Institute of Evangelism and Church Growth (CEFI). As we consulted with Pentecostal leaders, I found that John, who was a cessationist as well, began opening up to the idea of experiencing more of the Holy Spirit. I actually later discovered that John, again like me, had personally experienced one tongues-speaking incident soon after he was saved, but when he was told by his Quaker mentors that he shouldn't do it anymore, he obeyed. Neither of us, however, even thought of advocating that spiritual power could have a direct causal effect on church growth. But at least at this point we were not against it. It was just that we knew little or nothing about it.

Anaheim Vineyard

A dramatic change came when John left CEFI in 1978 in order to pastor what eventually became Anaheim Vineyard. It began with a home group, and then quickly reached around 100 people, at which time John constituted it a church. God spoke to John at the beginning and told him to preach exclusively from the Gospel of Luke, which John proceeded to do. The more he preached from Luke, the more he saw the hand of God operating back in biblical days in ways to which we were not accustomed in our evangelical churches. Being more of a practitioner than a theoretician, John decided that in his church they should begin "doin' the stuff!" This phrase eventually became a classic Vineyard motivational motto. It meant that Wimber wanted to see the operation of the supernatural phenomena, reported by Luke, become standard practice in his church today. So John began praying for sick people to be healed as a regular part of the church services, which were held at first on Sunday nights.

I became very interested because this was so different from the way that John and I had operated in the field with CEFI. We stayed in regular contact with each other as he launched into this experiment, so I was keeping track. I needed to see if what he was trying really would work for us non-Pentecostals. Unbelievably, Wimber prayed for the sick for a full 10 months before the first person was healed! From then on healings increased exponentially. Doris and I started visiting the services in Canyon High School in Placentia, California, occasionally to see "doin' the stuff" with our own eyes.

One of the things that impressed me greatly was Wimber's aversion to the role of the classic faith healer or healing televangelist who monopolizes the healing ministry in a given event. His desire was to equip the saints in his congregation so that all would pray for the sick and see God's hand of healing operate through them.

I will long remember my deep dismay when I found myself in an unfamiliar situation one Sunday night at Canyon High School. After his message, John did not call out words of knowledge for healing as he frequently did, but instead he said that he wanted the whole congregation to do the healing. He invited all those who needed physical healing to stand where they were. A man right behind Doris and me stood. Then John told those who were around the ones standing to lay on hands and pray for their healing. Doris and I obediently stood up and laid on hands. A young woman, maybe around 20, also laid her hands on the man. Probably because I was the most mature one of the group, and a seminary professor, I would be the natural choice to pray. So I started praying a very bumbling, weak, insecure traditional prayer. Obviously nothing was happening. Before I knew it, the young woman interrupted me, gently nudged me to one side and started to pray a fluent, powerful healing prayer!

I forget what happened to the man. All I could remember was that I ended up so embarrassed that I really didn't know how to pray for the sick! That was another wake-up call! Somehow I needed to go to a new level.

1982

The year 1982 was pivotal. Four important things happened that year: (1) John Wimber established the Vineyard Christian Fellowship of Anaheim, (2) Wimber took leadership of the whole Vineyard movement, (3) Wimber taught the first MC510 course at Fuller, and (4) I started the 120 Fellowship Sunday School class at Lake Avenue Church. Let me explain each of these four things.

The home church meeting that Wimber was pastoring became a Calvary Chapel affiliate under Chuck Smith in 1977, but the relationship between the two leaders was strained from the beginning. By 1982, the two agreed that they should go in different directions. Meanwhile, John had connected with Kenn Gulliksen, who had also left Calvary Chapel a few years earlier and planted a new church in Los Angeles that he named Vineyard. At the time, five other churches had affiliated with Gulliksen. John eventually took his church into the Vineyard movement as well. In the same year, 1982, Kenn decided to step back and ask John to take the reins of the whole Vineyard movement, then consisting of seven churches. As soon as John did, 30 other Calvary Chapels switched affiliation to Vineyard!

Launching MC510

Please remember that soon after John Wimber came on board with me in CEFI, I began using him to teach a segment of my annual advanced Doctor of Ministry course in church growth. He would teach Tuesday, Wednesday, Thursday and Friday mornings of the second week. Incidentally, the first year that he taught he got very poor student evaluations. The second year, they were so bad that the head of the D.Min. program called me in and suggested that I discontinue having John teach. But I knew very well that his pastoral intuitions, his experience and his astute analysis of church growth principles could not be matched. I knew that John was a winner. So I kept mentoring him, and before he finished a few years later, he was regularly receiving higher evaluations than mine! I was elated!

Every year I would call John ahead of time to talk over what subjects he should be planning to teach in the year's course. When I called him in 1981, he suggested that he use the final Friday morning to teach on how signs and wonders can affect the growth of churches. By then I had visited Anaheim Vineyard many times and I greatly admired John's integrity of praying for the sick and also his success in teaching his people how to do it as well. Furthermore, his church had by then become one of the fastest-growing churches in Southern California. So I approved the idea and scheduled the class. No harm in trying something new!

A few days before the time came, I met with our School of World Mission dean, Paul Pierson, and gave him a heads-up about what was to happen in Friday's D.Min. course (which, by the way, was under the School of Theology). Pierson had served as a Presbyterian missionary in Brazil, interestingly enough stationed in the same jungle area and at the same time as Doris and me, but on the other side of the Bolivia-Brazil border. Paul was always open to new ideas, so I invited him to attend the class with me, and he accepted.

It is important to keep in mind what a radical departure this was from anything that had ever happened in the history of Fuller Seminary. Fuller's classical Reformed theology was cessationist. Those who practiced faith healing at the time were at best ignored and at worst scorned by the theologians. Almost all of the 50 or so pastors and church leaders in my course were from non-Pentecostal and non-charismatic denominations. However, they trusted me and they trusted John, so I rightly anticipated that they would receive John's teaching well. In fact, a number of them had visited Anaheim Vineyard during the times they had come to Pasadena for courses.

Neither Paul Pierson nor I had ever heard classroom teaching on signs and wonders like we did that morning. We thought it was excellent, and the class agreed. John's material was biblical, it was moderate, it was honed with practical experience and it was presented in an authentically humble manner. The students naturally raised numerous questions, and John addressed them in an understanding and nondefensive tone.

After class, Doris brought a lunch into my office and the four of us ate together. As the conversation progressed, John detected that Paul and I were favorably impressed by what he had taught. At one point, he casually said, "I have enough material on the subject to teach a whole course." It is hard to exaggerate how that suggestion began burning in my heart and my mind. The Holy Spirit had me well prepared for it.

Paul, Doris and I talked it over later, and Paul gave me permission to present the idea of a whole course to our SWM faculty. Before I go on, let me pause to say a few words about our faculty.

The SWM Faculty

I should remind you that Fuller Seminary has three separate but interrelated schools: the School of Theology, the School of Psychology and the School of World Mission (now the School of Intercultural Studies). This will become important when I describe later developments with MC510.

When the events I am describing took place, there would be no disagreement with the statement that the SWM faculty was the premier missiological faculty in the world. With 14 professional missiologists, each of whom not only had the necessary academic credentials but who also had served as field missionaries in a second culture, no similar faculty approached even half that size. More unusual was the fact that we all respected, appreciated and loved one another. That is not the typical description of academic colleagues anywhere. The major contributing factor to that, in my opinion, was the weekly two-hour luncheon and prayer meeting we shared together and highly valued. I had the privilege of leading that meeting from 1980 to 1990, and it was one of my most rewarding endeavors. We genuinely felt like family.

By then we had SWM graduates all over the world, and while Arthur Glasser was still dean, he assigned Doris and me to edit an SWM newsletter, which we called "Forwarding the Missionary Task." We sent this out quarterly from 1978 to 1990. The newsletter circulated widely and built a strong constituency for SWM. Speaking of Doris, she was serving as my assistant and as SWM research librarian, meaning that she needed to give final approval to all graduate theses and dissertations. Needless to say, the students all courted her favor. At one point, Bobby Clinton was my teaching assistant, and Doris observed that his wife, Marilyn, had some outstanding skills that we badly needed on our staff. Doris persuaded the current dean, Paul Pierson, to hire Marilyn as his personal assistant. In his authorized history of the school, Chuck Kraft says, "Doris Wagner . . . ably carried administrative responsibilities. She started by serving Peter's expanding responsibilities but soon added to her responsibilities such areas as publicity and alumni matters. . . . She knew almost everyone who had been at the school and knew where to go to get anything at Fuller. Arguably, the office has never been run as well as under the duo of Marilyn Clinton and Doris Wagner."[2]

I was also in charge of the annual Church Growth Lectures, which had been originally instituted by Donald McGavran. I greatly enjoyed scouring my list of contacts in the United States and around the world and choosing the most outstanding individuals to visit the seminary for seminary-wide lectures each day for two days. The whole student body as well as the faculty from all three schools were invited and expected to attend. I was able to bring in such leaders as Harvie Conn, Leighton Ford, David Yonggi Cho, William Kumuyi, Eva Burrows, George G. Hunter III, and many more. On the evening of the first day of lectures, Doris and I would host a dinner and discussion with the lecturer and our SWM faculty, the seminary president, the provost and all of our spouses. It was always an outstanding social event.

All this is to help us understand how I could bring an idea as radical as a course in supernatural healing to the faculty and eventually gain unanimous approval. Remarkably, we had come from very diverse backgrounds: United Presbyterian, Mennonite, Brethren, United Methodist, Reformed Presbyterian, Congregational, Disciples of Christ, and Bible Church. We had ministered in different parts of the world: Brazil, India, Nigeria, Bolivia, China, Jamaica, Portugal and Singapore. As we shared, we found that most of us had similar experiences during our years as field missionaries. We were aware of demons and supernatural powers to one degree or another, but our ministries had never really intersected with them. We had been rightly criticized by some who felt that our emphasis on the behavioral sciences in missiology had eclipsed any significant emphasis on the spiritual dimension or the work of the Holy Spirit in missions. Many of our students, who had come from 70 nations of the world, yearned for more insight into God's supernatural power that would help them confront the demonic forces in their animistic cultures. Unfortunately, however, none of the 14 of us was equipped to meet the needs of those students.

It took some months for us to fully discuss the possibility of a new course among ourselves and then work through the tedious seminary joint faculty processes necessary to introduce any new course into the curriculum. We called it "MC510: Signs, Wonders and Church Growth." I was the official professor of record. This would give me the freedom to invite any outsiders I desired for "course enrichment," such as John Wimber. By taking this route, we bypassed any necessity of having John officially approved as adjunct faculty, which would have been virtually impossible because he did not have the necessary academic credentials. We scheduled the first MC510 for every Monday night during the 10 weeks of the winter quarter of 1982, beginning in January.

The "Famous" Course

Robert Meye, the Dean of the School of Theology, some time later made a classic and frequently quoted statement: "I know of only two seminary courses which have been truly famous. One was the course on dogmatics taught by Karl Barth in Switzerland and the other is MC510 taught by John Wimber here at Fuller."

Please notice that when Meye referenced MC510 he did not mention my name. That was because John immediately became much more than "course enrichment." MC510 became known as John Wimber's course. He was the de facto professor, even though seminary regulations would not allow him to have the title. My role was to introduce each three-hour class, take attendance, make any necessary announcements, call on someone for an opening prayer and turn the rest over to John. I would see that the students' papers were graded and submit the grades to the registrar after the course. My name appeared on the transcripts as professor of record, however there was no question that it was Wimber's course.

"Doin' the Stuff"

We met at 7:00 P.M. in one of the larger classrooms, which seated around 85. The room was packed. When I turned the class over to John, he would teach for about two hours. Then, at around 9:30, he would close his notebook and say, "It's time to do the stuff." This began what John called "the clinic." He would invite the presence of the Holy Spirit and then pause to receive "words of knowledge." These were specific prophetic revelations concerning the physical needs of certain ones in the room.

Usually John or members of the ministry team he brought from Vineyard would receive the words from the Lord and call them out. One might be, "Someone tore a finger in a bicycle accident and needs healing" or "A recent mammogram showed a tumor in the left breast" or "You have chronic asthma and it has been flaring up in the last couple of weeks." Those described, maybe up to 10 per night, would almost invariably respond immediately, come forward, be prayed for and, as far as I remember, every one of them was healed.

All of the SWM faculty were invited to attend the course, but only Doris and I, along with Chuck and Meg Kraft, did so. A few others may have dropped in for a night or so. A member of our staff, Alvin Martin, who had been a missionary to Israel, came one night and responded to a word of knowledge about a hiatal hernia. For years Alvin had been sleeping on an inclined bed to prevent the stomach acid from entering his throat. John prayed for him, he was completely healed and ever since he has slept on a normal bed.

Word about the course got out, and numbers of Christian leaders from different parts of the country dropped in to visit. At that time, the "Evangelism Explosion" program promoted by James Kennedy of Fort Lauderdale, Florida, was sweeping churches of all denominations. The person who actually developed the program for him, Archie Parrish, visited us one Monday. He had suffered a severe chronic back pain for 17 years, and he was completely healed that night. Weeks later, he wrote us saying that the pain had not returned.

Without question our most significant visitor was Robert Walker of Wheaton, Illinois, editor of *Christian Life* magazine, one of the most widely circulated periodicals of the day throughout the evangelical community. A skilled and experienced investigative journalist, Walker did a thorough job of researching what was happening at Fuller, publishing his findings in the entire October 1982 issue of *Christian Life*. The issue broke all publication records for the magazine, and it had to be reprinted several times. For a number of years it continued to sell in booklet form, with a study guide, called *Signs & Wonders Today*. I later did an expanded edition in book form under the same title. For good or for bad, this sparked a wave of media attention focused on MC510. Much to the dismay of some long-term theology faculty, John Wimber became the best-known Fuller "professor" in churches throughout the nation.

Completing the Paradigm Shift

In this chapter I have tried to highlight various incidents that contributed to my paradigm shift from a cessationist to my present position of openness to all the power of the Holy Spirit. You may recall my experiment with tongues, the healing under E. Stanley Jones, my visit to the Chilean Pentecostals, the influence of the Church of God and attending Vineyard services. All this, however, was preliminary to the 10 weeks in MC510, which completed the paradigm shift.

It began slowly for me. My initial role in the class was much more of a spectator than a participant. I recall my discomfort when, about the third Monday night into the course, instead of asking for words of knowledge, Wimber announced that he was going to have members of the class pray for each other during the clinic. The incident in the Vineyard service when the young woman nudged me aside and prayed for the sick man flashed into my mind. I did not want a repeat of that. So I pulled my rank as "professor of record." While the rest of the class was standing in groups praying for different people, I simply walked around observing and making sure that everything was being done decently and in order! That was one of the smoothest cop-outs I ever devised.

It worked until one night, when the clinic began, John simply started off by saying, "Who needs healing?" Without any premeditation, I suddenly found my hand in the air! So John said, "Peter, come up here," and he had me sit on a stool facing the class. I told him and the class that I had been diagnosed with high blood pressure for two years and that the doctor had put me on three medications to control it. When John started praying, I felt a warm blanket of power come over me and I felt like my mind was partially disconnected. I could hear most of what was going on, but I didn't care.

To describe it in words that I learned later, I now know that I was slain in the Spirit, but I didn't fall, because I was on the stool. John was describing my physical reactions to the class like a sports announcer giving a play-by-play account of what was happening to me. "See the eyelids fluttering?" "There's some flushing on the sides of his face!" "Watch the lips—they're quivering!" "Thank You, Lord! More power!" A few days later, I went back to the doctor and he took me off one of the medications. Soon afterward, he took me off the second, and then the third. My blood pressure was fine.

This was a turning point. From then on, instead of inspecting what other people were doing, I started praying for the sick as well. I found myself "doin' the stuff!" By the time the course was over, I was no longer a spectator; I was a participant. And I have been a participant ever since.

The 120 Fellowship

The expectation at Lake Avenue Church was that members would set aside two hours for church on Sunday mornings, not just one hour as was the custom of most other churches. One hour was the normal worship service, and the other hour was Sunday School. Doris and I followed that pattern from the time we joined in 1972. After some years, however, my gift of teaching began to assert itself. Instead of attending someone else's class, I wanted to do some teaching.

By 1982, the door opened to start a new adult class, which we called "The 120 Fellowship," named after the group that had gathered together in the upper room on the day of Pentecost. I ended up teaching and leading that class for 13 years. I would routinely turn down invitations to speak at other churches on Sundays because I felt that my place was with the 120 Fellowship. We normally gathered around 100 adults of all ages.

When the class first started, I had no vision beyond another normal adult Sunday School class, which would teach the Bible and offer a group of Lake Avenue members the weekly opportunity they desired to be part of a smaller group where they knew others and where they were known. This could not happen in the LAC worship services with attendance of 3,000 or more.

I chose the book of Acts for our initial Bible study focus. Little did I know that I would end up teaching Acts for all 13 years and that the class would begin *living* the book of Acts instead of only *studying* it.

Charging Up at Vineyard

Four years previously, John Wimber had begun ministering to the small church that, in the same year of 1982, became Anaheim Vineyard. Healings, signs and wonders and miracles had begun. As I have mentioned, Doris and I had been visiting the Vineyard on Sunday evenings from time to time. But also in 1982, MC510 began and, as I just explained, my paradigm shift in the direction of spiritual power was completed. That substantially changed our teaching and ministry time in 120 Fellowship. In fact, a large number of us would go to Vineyard on Sunday night to get charged up, and then come back and discharge in our Congregational church on Sunday mornings. We began to see healings and deliverances on a regular basis during our class times.

This provoked a very interesting situation. Lake Avenue Church was clearly in the tradition of the Benjamin Warfield and C. I. Scofield cessationist theology. The leaders did whatever was necessary to distance themselves from Pentecostals and charismatics. Most people in the community considered it a safe evangelical church. With more than 3,000 members, it was considered a very large and influential church in those days (it now has 5,000 members). It was strongly evangelistic and missionary minded. In fact, it was the first church in the United States to go above $1 million per year in their missionary budget. It is the only church I know of that, when it celebrated its 100-year anniversary, had grown in membership during each of its 10 decades! It was Charles E. Fuller's church. Fuller Seminary held their classes at LAC for the first six years of its existence. These were strong and deeply rooted traditions to maintain.

Then came 120 Fellowship, which, even though I strongly resisted it, soon gained the reputation of "the charismatic class." Some of the other adult Sunday School classes at LAC were made up of disciples of John MacArthur, one of the most outspoken and persuasive cessationists of the day. What did this do to the church?

Paul Cedar's Open Mind

I believe the hand of God was on these developments, and in His sovereignty He had raised up Paul Cedar to become the senior pastor in Lake Avenue Church. I may be wrong, but I do not believe that either the anchor pastor of 35 years, James Henry Hutchins, or his successor for 20 years, Ray Ortlund, could have handled this potentially explosive situation the way Cedar did. Several favorable things entered the equation. Paul and I had established a very good personal relationship. I was a respected professor at Fuller, and by then I had gained a solid reputation as a spokesperson for the church growth movement across denominational lines and on a national scope. My book How to Grow a Church was in the library of most evangelical pastors. I led the Fuller Evangelistic Association, which had its roots in LAC. I enjoyed quite a high level of trust and respect among Christian leaders who knew me, including Paul Cedar.

While Cedar positioned himself clearly as a traditional evangelical, he was open to new things as well. In one of his sermons, he had preached on spiritual gifts and had said words to this effect: "I want every one of God's spiritual gifts to be active on some level in the church that I pastor." Although he didn't mention any specific controversial gifts such as tongues or prophecy or miracles, at the time it was rightly interpreted by all as a statement that he was not a cessationist. The church must have been ready for this, because I am not aware of any notable backlash from his somewhat non-conventional statement.

Public Tongues

This gave us the green light to move ahead with Vineyard-type ministry in 120 Fellowship. I did talk to Paul personally, however, and I asked him what he would do if someone stood up in a worship service and began to give a message in tongues. He said that he would interrupt the person and tell him or her that while the message they have might be from God, it is the policy of this church not to allow public tongues in the worship services. He would not permit it to go on. So we talked about what might happen in 120 Fellowship. He generously said that it would be up to me and that he would trust me to do the right thing. But I responded that since we were a part of LAC, which did not permit public tongues in the services, I would follow that lead and not permit public tongues in 120 Fellowship.

Please note the adjective "public." Neither Cedar nor I had any problem with those who had the gift to use tongues, sometimes called a "prayer language," in their private devotions. Occasionally in class, when prayer for a sick person or a spiritual warfare issue became intense, someone would pray for a few moments in tongues. But this was different from a *message* in tongues, which would require interpretation, according to 1 Corinthians 14. This policy of no public tongues would probably have been the most prominent deviation of 120 Fellowship from the normal behavior patterns of Vineyard. The other would have been that 120 maintained its status of a sub-set of Lake Avenue Church, traditionally non-charismatic.

Because 120 Fellowship was so different from anything else seen in LAC for the last century, I knew it would be important to keep communication channels open, especially with the church staff. I felt that I was under an imperative from the Holy Spirit to avoid anything that might split the church, not necessarily outwardly but under the surface as well. I believe that my solid evangelical credentials and my academic mindset were determining factors in helping me to avoid this. With the help of class members such as Lil Walker, Sandra Gilbreath, Jane Rumph and others, we initiated a class newsletter we called *Body Life*. It turned into a monthly 24- to 36-page document, well written, well edited, well formatted and well printed. In *Body Life*, we were very transparent as to all that was happening in the class, and we made sure that all the LAC staff members, including Paul Cedar, received a copy. We didn't want to do anything that would surprise, embarrass or blindside any of the staff.

The Third Wave

My primary sphere of influence at the time embraced evangelical churches like LAC and the churches represented by my Fuller D.Min. students, who totaled 2,500 before I was done. With a few exceptions, they would have been by and large non-Pentecostal, non-charismatic. But their exposure to John Wimber and me, a Quaker and a Congregationalist, who both ministered in the power of the Holy Spirit, helped to broaden their perspectives. I suddenly found myself in the position of a role model attempting to demonstrate how the supernatural gifts of the Spirit could be used in traditional church settings in a nonthreatening way.

All of these events, which some characterized as a movement, were drawing their share of attention from the Christian media. In fact, the name "Third Wave" emerged during a telephone interview with *Pastoral Renewal* magazine in 1983. After I had described what was going on in Fuller and in 120 Fellowship, the editor asked me what the name of this movement was. I believe the Lord prompted me to respond, "Let's call it the Third Wave," and the term stuck.

What is the Third Wave? Here is my formal definition: "The term *third wave* is used to designate a movement that is similar to the Pentecostal movement (first wave) and charismatic movement (second wave), but has what its constituents perceive as some fairly important differences. It is composed largely of evangelical Christians who, while applauding and supporting the work of the Holy Spirit in the first two waves, have chosen not to be identified with either. The desire of those in the Third Wave is to experience the power of the Holy Spirit in healing the sick, casting out demons, receiving prophecies, and

Although Fuller Seminary had a policy against hiring husband-wife teams, they made an exception for Doris and me. Doris had her office right outside my office door, and she served as my executive assistant. She was also the research librarian for the School of World Mission, meaning she had to give final approval to the technical format for all the theses and dissertations of the graduating students. Needless to say, many of the students wanted to be her best friend.

David Yonggi Cho, pastor of the world's largest church in Seoul, Korea, was a strong influence in my life. I deeply respected his leadership ability and his integrity to public ministry. I considered it an honor to serve on his Church Growth International Board through the years.

participating in other charismatic-type manifestations without disturbing the current philosophy of ministry governing their congregations."[3]

The major differences from the other two waves would include the belief that the *baptism* of the Holy Spirit comes at conversion, that notable experiences after conversion are *fillings* of the Holy Spirit, that tongues is not a necessary initial evidence of a filling or baptism but is rather a spiritual gift used by some for ministry or prayer language, and willingness to be flexible in any areas that might cause divisiveness in the church.

I did my best to communicate the move of God through the Third Wave to the whole Body of Christ. I wrote 23 monthly columns, "The Third Wave," in *Christian Life* magazine from 1984 to 1986. The editor of the magazine, Bob Walker, was the one who visited the first MC510 class and publicized it nationally. In 1988, I published a book, *The Third Wave of the Holy Spirit*.

Useful, Then Not So Useful

The concept of a "third wave" was extremely useful in the 1980s. It provided a relatively safe way for traditional evangelicals to begin moving in the power of the Holy Spirit without upsetting their friends and colleagues who were not choosing to go in that direction. However, the term began to lose its usefulness as we moved through the 1990s. John Wimber very perceptively saw this coming. In the mid-1980s, Wimber wrote, "I believe Dr. Wagner's 'third wave' is not so much another wave as the next stage of development in the charismatic renewal. Perhaps both the Pentecostal and charismatic movements are part of one great movement of the Holy Spirit in this century. In this perspective the similarities between the movements outweigh their differences."[4]

Meanwhile, with all its caveats, the Third Wave still ruffled the feathers of many of the more outspoken cessationists of the time. John MacArthur was one of the most prominent. He was so provoked that he wrote a whole book called *Charismatic Chaos*. After he reluctantly admitted the "astonishing success" of the Third Wave, he then declared: "The Third Wave is now rolling like a destructive tsunami, leaving chaos and confusion in its wake."[5]

Moving in the Power

Up to now I have not said much about my own personal involvement in signs and wonders. Most of the focus has been on how new ideas were formed and paradigms were shifted. Let me now take a few moments to switch from ideas to implementation. How did I move forward in the Wimber Era in receiving and practicing healing? When this season started, I had no thought whatsoever that I might have or ever would have a gift of healing. Before it ended, I knew I had the gift.

Omar Cabrera of Argentina

One of the most life-changing experiences that Doris and I enjoyed was a trip to Argentina soon after MC510 began. A by-product of the amazing growth of the Anaheim Vineyard was the rather abundant cash flow that John Wimber had at his disposal. The church was governed apostolically (although we wouldn't have used that language back then). Unlike old wineskin churches, John, as the senior pastor, was the leader of the church. He was not under the supervision of a church board or the congregation. One implication of that is that he decided how the money was to be spent. He set his own salary as a starter. I mention that to say that at one point John thought that Doris and I should do some fieldwork in healing under Omar Cabrera in Argentina, so he sent us there and covered all the expenses.

Since the mid-1970s, Cabrera had been the highest-profile healing evangelist in Argentina. Unfortunately, he was so radical in his modus operandi that the mainstream evangelicals, even including the Pentecostals, refused to endorse him. One of their issues was that he dressed in a clerical collar because he knew that in a Catholic country, most people would regard him as a spiritual authority if he did. His healings were numerous and many were spectacular. For example, one woman's lung had been surgically removed, but when Omar prayed for her, a new lung grew in its place. This was medically recorded. But the traditional believers shrugged it off. Attendance at his meetings would run from 3,000 to 10,000 or more. With all its branches, his church, Vision of the Future, had 145,000 regular attenders, the largest in Latin America. In one city the Catholics had him arrested and jailed for "practicing medicine without a license." No one from the other Protestant churches would step up to the plate and come to his defense!

Doris and I had met Omar and his wife, Marfa, when they dropped in to Fuller to see us on one of their trips to the United States. We had not heard of them previously, but as we had lunch together we were immediately attracted to them. When later we heard that others, some of our friends included, were *opposing* the Cabreras, we did not feel free to agree with them.

Consequently, when we arrived in Argentina, the Cabreras welcomed us warmly. We ended up driving several thousand miles with them around the country and attending a number of their meetings. Night after night we saw numerous, verified physical healings. That was the first time we saw, firsthand, teeth being supernaturally filled. One of Omar's staff had been frightened of going to the dentist all her life; consequently, her mouth was filled with horribly decayed teeth. Then God's power touched her one night. She invited us to inspect her mouth. It had perfectly straight rows of teeth with no defects whatsoever!

Speaking of teeth, this miracle of decayed teeth being filled, new teeth growing where there had been extractions and even old bridges physically falling out and being replaced with healthy teeth became so much a part of the subsequent Argentina revival, which lasted through the 1990s, that one could hardly find a congregation in the whole nation in which one or more members had not experienced dental miracles.

As I began to publicize this in America, John MacArthur once again became upset with me. In his book *Charismatic Chaos* he mentions my stories of dental miracles and then says, "Frankly, I find all those accounts preposterous. It is difficult to resist the conclusion that they are either utter fabrications or yarns that have grown with the telling."[6] He doesn't quite do it, but he comes very close to calling me a liar!

I knew that what I was seeing was no fabrication, and Omar Cabrera's ministry had a great impact on my personal future.

A Headache Demon?

In 1973, I began getting migraine headaches. They increased in intensity through the years until I recorded one of them that lasted 70 days and 70 nights without stopping.

I did everything I knew to get relief. I underwent extensive treatments by one of Southern California's most renowned chiropractors. I changed my diet. I revised my exercise routine. I learned about acupressure points. I began getting more rest by sleeping later in the mornings (previously my farmer's routine had been to arise at 4:30 every morning). I read books on headaches and their treatment. I took vitamins. I tried painkillers of all kinds. But nothing seemed to help.

Finally, I discovered a Canadian drug called "222" which, if I exceeded the recommended dosage, would give me some relief. It was not unusual for me to have a headache five out of seven days. Fortunately, the headaches were not entirely debilitating like some migraines are. If I took enough 222 and applied enough courage and persistence, I usually could move through my daily routine and many people would not even know I was in pain. I had many people pray for me, even David Yonggi Cho of Korea, who laid hands on me after I preached for him one Sunday morning.

Things began to change when, on a Sunday night in Anaheim Vineyard, someone had a word of knowledge for migraine headaches. Even though I did not happen to have a headache that night, I responded, and a group gathered around me to pray. After the meeting, John Wimber came up and said, "Peter, one of the people ministering to you discerned that your headaches are caused by a spirit." I thanked him, went home and the headaches continued as usual. I'm not sure I was ready for the idea that a demon could be causing my incurable headache. Still, when MC510 started up the next time, I asked John to pray for my headache again. He remembered and said, "Don't forget about that spirit!" "Okay," I replied, "but what am I supposed to do about it?" His answer? "Treat it like a cat on the back porch! Yell at it and tell it to go away!"

By then, after 10 years of pain, I was willing to try anything short of amputation, but John's suggestion was definitely pulling me out of my comfort zone. I was used to speaking to God, whom I couldn't see, but yelling at a demon? Only crazy people do things like that! Besides, how would a demon get in? I surmised that it might have been during one of my tours of pagan temples in other nations, which I frequently took. (Just for the record, I no longer do that, nor do I recommend it.) But mostly, I kept quiet. I didn't even tell Doris.

One morning, I was in the shower when the unmistakable symptoms of another headache began. My thought was to take a dose of 222 as soon as I got out of the shower. Then I believe the Lord prompted me to realize that I was all alone. Doris was still in bed. The shower was making plenty of noise, so no one would hear me and think I was crazy. So I did what Wimber told me and treated that demon like a cat on the back porch. I yelled at it, rebuked it in the name of Jesus and told it to get out once and for all!

By the time I finished the shower I was thinking about something else, and I actually forgot about the episode. Around 10:30 that morning, I suddenly realized that the headache that began in the shower had not materialized! That was the end of the headaches. In the more than 20 years since then, the migraine headaches have never returned! This was one of my first practical lessons in spiritual warfare.

Spiritual Housecleaning

A second lesson came around a year later. For 17 years, Doris and I had lived in a 60-year-old Spanish colonial house in Altadena, California. We knew nothing about the early history of the house.

From time to time, we would host a group from 120 Fellowship for an evening of intercession. On one of those nights, two class members who have the gift of discernment of spirits sensed something wrong in the house, especially in our bedroom. They went upstairs and rebuked the spirits they felt were there. We assumed they had been successful.

But no. Not long afterward, in the middle of one night when I was away, Doris suddenly woke up with a terrible fear. Her heart was pounding. She opened her eyes to see a luminous green outline of some being in the corner of the room. She could see a pair of eyes, also luminous green. She instantly realized that she was face to face with an evil spirit, and she rebuked it in the name of Jesus. She commanded it to leave the house. It moved around for a few moments, and then disappeared. Doris slept soundly for the rest of the night.

A couple of months later, Doris woke up in the middle of the night with a piercing cramp in her foot. She tried to work it out, but it wouldn't leave, so she woke me up and asked me to pray for it. I laid my hand on her foot and prayed for healing, but nothing happened. The pain persisted. Soon she said, "I think it's a spirit!" So, as Wimber taught me, I treated it like a cat on the back porch and commanded it to leave, in the name of Jesus. The pain immediately subsided and did not come back. The intercessors were right. There was obviously something wrong in our house!

The word got around 120 Fellowship, so two members of the class volunteered to do some serious frontline spiritual warfare in our house. For starters, when they got out of their car they came up against a powerful physical force that would literally not allow them to enter the small courtyard in front of the house. So they entered the garage instead. As soon as they did they felt strange energy and actually smelled the evil that was there. They soon located the offending demonic spirit and cast it out. One of them saw an ax hanging on the wall and knew that it symbolized some sort of violence from the past, possibly even a murder in the garage.

Once they had dealt with the spirit in the garage, they could easily enter the courtyard and the house. The Lord had told one of them previous to coming that they would find an idol shaped like an animal. Sure enough, in the living room was a stone puma that we had brought home from Bolivia. They confronted the spirit that was in the puma until it left the house. Needless to say, when Doris and I returned home that evening, we took the puma as well as two pagan ceremonial masks that we also foolishly had brought with us and smashed them to bits.

They found nothing else downstairs, but when they went upstairs to our bedroom they sensed a demonic presence as strong as that in the garage. At that moment, in the exact spot where Doris had seen the evil spirit, God showed them a vision that a man with an ax, like the one in the garage, had committed an act of terrible violence against a woman who, in the vision, was screaming. Whether there had been a murder, as they suspected, they couldn't be sure, but they dealt with whatever was there and successfully evicted it, or them, from the house. I say "successfully" because from that time on we never had another indication that there was anything unclean in our house.

The Gift of Healing

Those familiar with my teaching on spiritual gifts know that I feel it is important to distinguish between Christian roles and spiritual gifts. I explain this very useful distinction in *Your Spiritual Gifts Can Help Your Church Grow*, as well as in *Discovering Your Spiritual Gifts*. Briefly, it means that there are certain roles for every believer, like witnessing and leading people to Christ, without necessarily having the gift of evangelist. We all don't have to be a Billy Graham to win souls. The same would apply to casting out demons, which every believer should do when the situation demands it. I just told the story of how I cast a demon out of Doris's foot. But that did not mean that I have the gift of deliverance, which I do not. Doris, by the way, does have the gift and uses it.

When John Wimber taught me how to pray for the sick, I started doing it on occasion and did see some people healed. In my mind, that was my role, as it is for every believer. I did not suspect that I had a gift of healing like John had, nor did I particularly desire it. I felt that I had enough other gifts that God was already using through me.

This began to change in 1983, when I happened to be teaching a two-week Fuller D.Min. course in church growth near Cleveland, Ohio. One of my students was a Lutheran pastor named Fred Luthy. Because of him it became the most unusual course I had ever taught. Fred's own powerful spiritual gift of healing became evident to all from the first day of the two-week event. With my encouragement, Fred conducted an impromptu, informal healing seminar during the breaks and after class. We saw many, many miraculous works of God before it was over.

The following year, Fred came to Pasadena for Church Growth II. While he was there, I invited him to dinner in my home with leaders of my 120 Fellowship prayer team. As the group was about to break up and go home, Fred asked if anyone needed prayer for healing. One of them had a leg a bit shorter than the other. I was watching with great interest as he carefully measured the legs and prepared to ask God to lengthen them. But he suddenly turned to me and said, "Peter, I think God wants you to pray for this leg." I did, and it was instantly healed. Before the evening was over, God used me to heal two other cases of short legs and back pains.

I don't believe an experience like that proves that one has a gift of healing, but it did plant a seed in my mind. In fact, I found myself asking God to give some clear evidence during the four remaining months of 1984 if He had truly given me a gift of healing. He answered yes through two dramatic events.

The first came when I was invited to address a banquet meeting in a hotel where John Wimber was holding a training conference for about 1,000 pastors and spouses. During the worship session, I felt an overpowering presence of the Holy Spirit telling me to conduct a mass healing. I had never even thought of such a thing previously, but I knew that I must obey God. As a result, more than 50 people who had short legs, back pains and other skeletal problems were healed before I began my talk on church growth. John confirmed the healings in the conference session the following morning.

The second extraordinary confirmation happened when I invited David Yonggi Cho to deliver the 1984 annual Church Growth Lectures at Fuller Seminary. Before I tell this story, I must fill in a bit of background concerning Cho.

David Yonggi Cho

David Yonggi Cho of Seoul, Korea, was a legend to those of us who were professors of church growth. Why? Simply because he had grown the largest church in the world—the Yoido Full Gospel Church, then around 500,000 members. He would arguably have been the highest visibility church leader of the day. I traveled to Korea from time to time, and not only did I attend Yoido Church, but soon God gave me the distinct privilege of becoming personal friends with Cho. In fact, Cho invited me to be a member of the board of his Church Growth International organization, and I have served him in that capacity to this day. Doris and I visited Korea every year for many years. I spoke at his church from time to time and did occasional conferences with him in different countries.

As I have previously indicated, one of my responsibilities as the Mc-Gavran Professor of Church Growth at Fuller was to organize the annual seminary-wide Church Growth Lectures. The lectures were for two days, beginning at 10:00 A.M. each day. When the speaker arrived, I would have him or her come over to my office at 9:30 for a cup of coffee, prayer and instructions about the logistics of the lecture each morning.

As Cho and I were chatting in my office the first day, he said, "Peter, I'm jealous of you!" When I asked him why, he said, "Because God has given you the gift of healing and He hasn't given it to me!" As we talked, he said, "I hear you lengthen legs." How he heard that I don't know, but apparently the word gets around. He continued, "I've never seen a leg lengthen," which I thought was unusual for a Pentecostal leader. So I was bold enough to reply, "Maybe God will give us a short leg before you go back!"

Sure enough! That afternoon I received a phone call from a member of 120 Fellowship, where I had been lengthening legs for some time. He said, "Peter, I need your help. An Egyptian Coptic priest just moved into the apartment next to mine, and he has a short leg. He wants you to pray for him." I was elated. I said, "Can you have that priest over to my office at 9:30 tomorrow morning?" "No problem," he replied.

So when Cho and I were having coffee the next morning, the priest arrived. I couldn't believe what I saw. He walked with an unbelievably grotesque limp. When I sat him down to pray for him, he insisted on showing us his right leg. He had been run over by a train when he was 17, and his leg from the knee down was one solid scar! I suppose his leg was six inches shorter than normal. I became inwardly terrified! I had dealt with legs maybe an inch shorter, or a little more, but never anything like this. However, there was no turning back. As I held his feet out and started to pray, in the front of my mind was the vivid thought: *The pastor of the world's largest church is sitting here watching me! How did I ever get myself into this one?*

You guessed it—nothing happened! Please understand that until then every short leg that I had prayed for had been lengthened! Why did my streak have to be broken with no one less than Yonggi Cho sitting there watching me? So I had the priest stand up, walk across the room and back and sit down once again. I had him repeat after me a Lutheran liturgical declaration that I had learned from Fred Luthy: "I renounce the devil and all his works and all his ways. I believe that Jesus can heal me!"

I wish I could brag that my faith was stronger than ever, but such was far from the case. Nevertheless, when I prayed for him the second time, the leg grew even with the other one! Cho looked at me and smiled. "Peter," he said, "I have a confession to make. The first time you prayed, I didn't want that leg to come out. Then the Holy Spirit convicted me, and the second time, I was praying with you!"

Fair enough. Before he left, the priest was standing like a crane on one leg. I asked him why he was standing like that and he said it was the first time he had been able to do it in 15 years!

Deaconess Park Arrives from Korea

I thought that was all there was to it until the next week when I got a call from Kim Young Gil, the pastor of Cho's branch church in Los Angeles. He said, "Dr. Wagner, I'm going to come to your office tomorrow. A woman named Deaconess Park is coming from Korea to have you pray for her." I informed him that she had no appointment so I could not see her. "You don't understand," he said. "Dr. Cho has sent her and she's already on the Korea Airlines plane." Then I looked at my schedule and told him that I would be in a faculty meeting. His answer was that someone could call me out of the faculty meeting. I checked with Doris and she agreed.

What had happened was that Cho had returned to his pulpit the next Sunday and told the story of the Coptic priest. Afterward, Deaconess Park, whose hip bones had been deteriorating, came up and asked Pastor Cho if I would pray for her. He assured her that I (his good friend!) would, so she booked the next possible flight to America and let Kim Young Gil know she was coming. By then it was obvious that she was a person of considerable wealth and influence.

The next afternoon, Deaconess Park, Pastor Kim and another Assemblies of God couple arrived. Park was walking painfully with one crutch. Doris called me out of the faculty meeting and we went into my office. After the usual formalities, I had her sit down, and sure enough, one leg was shorter. When I prayed, it came right out, and then I prayed for the hips. In a few minutes, Deaconess Park was dancing around the room, praising God. In fact, when she left she had forgotten her crutch, and Doris had to run after her to give it back!

But it didn't end there. The next week, Kim Young Gil called me and said that Deaconess Park needed one more prayer before she returned to Korea. I said I couldn't do it because I was going to be home. Characteristically, he told me that that was no problem, because Deaconess Park would come to my home. I relented, gave him my home address, and, surprisingly, Deaconess Park showed up in a taxi. She came into my home office with a large manila envelope under her arm. After we greeted each other, she opened the envelope, which contained X-rays that showed distinct white areas where, incredibly, new bone structure had grown into the hips!

That was the confirmation that I had asked from the Lord to show me that I had a gift of healing. By the way, it is quite a specialized gift, such as we might find in the medical profession. Orthopedists, for example, are different from gynecologists, and they are different from dentists. When I look back at 1 Corinthians 12, I read that the plural "gifts of healings" is used, and I think that indicates specializations such as I have. If someone needs prayer for diabetes or hepatitis or cancer or Down syndrome or kidney problems, they need to see someone else. But backs and legs and other skeletal problems, I can usually handle!

Keeping Track

Even though I might have had a gift of healing, my scientific intuition told me to keep as accurate a record as possible of my successes and failures. I attempted to do this by handing a report form in a self-addressed envelope to everyone I prayed for over a five-year period. I asked them to wait two weeks, and then return the forms. Granted, not everyone sent them back, but a surprisingly large number did. The report form asked them if they were "completely well" or "considerably improved" or "some improvement" or "no healing" after two weeks or more.

Over a period of five years, the percentage of people who had received no healing varied from 17 percent to 29 percent per year. The percentage of those who were completely well varied from 22 percent to 44 percent per year. Significantly enough, I later discovered that John Wimber's Vineyard had also been keeping track, and that their figures were more or less identical to mine. I thought it was encouraging that some 75 percent to 80 percent of those prayed for received some healing and that around 25 percent to 30 percent were completely symptom-free!

The Demise of MC510

I dislike ending this chapter on the Wimber Era with a sad story, but it is an unfortunate part of history. As I have indicated, I am trying to relate the bad as well as the good in this book, and I must say that my three most difficult "wilderness" years of ministry happened in the aftermath of MC510.

One of my known weaknesses is my gullibility. To me, the glass is not only half full; it is more often about 90 percent full! Doris does her best to help me compensate for this, but she is not always successful. In this case, I was so excited about what God was doing with John Wimber and MC510 that I was largely oblivious of the dark side.

Fuller Seminary, as I will remind you, has three separate but interrelated schools: Missions (now Intercultural Studies), Theology and Psychology. MC510 was a missions course, which students from theology or psychology could take for elective credit if their schedules permitted. However, MC510 was not just another elective. For several years it became the elective *du jour*. Fuller had no classroom space large enough to accommodate it, so we had to hold our Monday night classes in the nearby Presbyterian Church, then the Methodist Church and finally the Congregational Church basement where we ended up with a record-breaking class of 250!

In fact, so many were attracted to MC510 that we had to post administrative guards at the door to keep those who were not officially registered from coming in. Doris and others on the staff would stand at the entrance checking off the ones who had paid tuition, and turning away those who had not. Amusingly, on one night, a young School of Theology faculty member on crutches with a broken ankle showed up, hoping for healing. Doris, who had not previously met him, actually turned him away! She later regretted it and apologized.

Another thing we eventually discovered was the ingenious technique that some of those who had not registered had developed in order to get into the class. They would quietly wait outside until the evening break, and then join the crowd as they returned to class when Doris and the others were no longer at the door checking the attendance list! They knew this would allow them to be present when John started "Doin' the stuff!" We took our hats off to them for their creativity!

The Theology Faculty Steps In

I should have guessed what might be happening among the School of Theology faculty, but somehow my optimistic nature and its accompanying gullibility prevented me from doing so until it was too late. Keep in mind that most of Fuller's theologians, following John Calvin and Benjamin Warfield, were cessationists. They were only reluctantly tolerant of Pentecostals and charismatics, which they saw John Wimber personifying and even importing into their educational domain. The majority of the students in MC510 were theology students who, not surprisingly, began to raise bold and uncomfortable questions in their theology classes. Never before had the theologians experienced such widespread discord concerning aspects of traditional Reformed theology in their Fuller classes.

The one person most responsible for this disconcerting turn of events, of course, was Peter Wagner! Because the nature of academicians is to display courtesy to those with whom they disagree, I did not pick up their increasing hostility toward MC510 right away. It finally surfaced, however, in a School of Theology faculty meeting in the spring of 1985. One of the most upset faculty members had picked up the fact that John Wimber's publicity department had allowed some people who were promoting him on the outside to label him as a Fuller Seminary Adjunct Professor. This, of course, was technically incorrect. Because John did not have the proper academic credentials for graduate school teaching, I carefully avoided suggesting adjunct status, knowing it could turn out to be an insurmountable roadblock. Instead, I had brought him into my classroom as "course enrichment," which operates only at the discretion of the professor of record.

Nevertheless, after someone brought up John's national media image of being a Fuller professor, the School of Theology faculty meeting erupted like a volcano. All the previously suppressed feelings about Wimber and the invasion of the charismatic movement and healing people on the Fuller campus surfaced as if a pressure valve had been opened. The outcome was a ruling unprecedented in Fuller's history. From then on, no theology student would be awarded academic credit for taking MC510!

The School of World Missions faculty was shocked! We immediately realized that there was nothing we could do to change Theology's decision. After talking to the president and the provost, both of whom had approved MC510, we realized that we now had been placed in a tenuous position that, for the good of the seminary as a whole, would cause us to cancel MC510. I was personally devastated, but it was nothing compared to John Wimber's reaction. Here is what his widow, Carol Wimber, says in her biography of John: "He was experiencing heartache, literally. Heartache in his soul and body . . . it was beginning to show in his health."[7] It was reported that one of his closest associates, Ken Blue, "thinks John never fully recovered from the hurt."[8] I wouldn't be surprised if that were the case!

Picking Up the Pieces

Where do we go from here? I was very fortunate to have the continued backing of my colleagues in the School of World Mission, especially from Chuck Kraft who taught anthropology. Chuck and I were the two faculty members who actually underwent paradigm shifts and became disciples of Wimber during the first MC510. So it was up to us to do what was necessary to keep signs, wonders and the miraculous works of God in the Fuller curriculum.

First of all, I had to endure a long, painful process of academic dialogue. By then a new provost had come in who, unlike his predecessor who had died unexpectedly, was strongly opinionated against anything that touched on charismatic types of ministry. He clearly did not like me, whom he considered a major troublemaker. One of his first moves was to name a study commission of 12 faculty members who would meet once a week for three months and produce a report setting forth what they thought Fuller's position should be. The provost skillfully designed the committee so that I would be the only member who would defend Wimber's ministry. I was upset when he bypassed Chuck Kraft in order to name another anthropologist, Paul Hiebert, to the committee. Of all the SWM faculty, Hiebert was the one who had kept MC510 most at an arm's length. What a miserable ordeal for me! For 12 weeks it was 11 against 1. To make things worse, almost everyone else on the committee clearly had a higher IQ than I did!

The report, *Ministry and the Miraculous*, was a disjointed compilation of everyone's opinions. It was an attempt to position Fuller as being open to new ideas, but it was far from an approval of power ministries, especially actually praying for and healing the sick in seminary classrooms. Bill Jackson astutely comments: "Not far below the surface was a clear bias against Wimber's thesis that the church is called to move in the miraculous as a part of everyday life."[9] When the report came out, it was clear that any attempts that Kraft and I were to make in order to perpetuate power ministries in the Fuller curriculum would be an uphill struggle.

The New Courses? Awful!

One of the seminary's long-standing rules was that every new course in any of the three schools needed to be approved first by the school's faculty, and then by the joint faculty. Up until then, the approval was a routine rubber stamp, including MC510 when it first started, because no one anticipated that it would produce such fuss. Once the School of Theology faculty blew up, the protocol changed. Any similar course would undergo severe scrutiny and would have to please all involved.

The student body then entered the picture. They wanted the training, so they petitioned the provost for permission to organize their own course for no credit. The provost agreed and even contributed some money to help them pay honoraria to the speakers they would invite. They invited Chuck Kraft and me, as well as several others. Surprisingly, around 135 students enrolled.

Meanwhile, Chuck Kraft happened to be a member of the Faculty Senate, and I began to meet with them to design a course that would keep power ministries in the curriculum. My feelings were very complicated at the time. I took the cancelation of MC510 as a personal defeat, so my Plan B was to keep something like it for which the School of Theology would allow credit. The Faculty Senate agreed to allow Kraft and me to organize a course, which we would label MC550. However, the condition was that we would invite speakers over the 10 nights who would represent the whole spectrum of opinions. This was definitely a compromise, but we at least had a course in the curriculum.

We ran MC550 for two years, and it was awful. Some of the visiting professors had theologies that explained things like why God was pleased with sickness and why pain was beneficial to the human body. Chuck Kraft, John Wimber and I presented the case for power ministries; but by the time the 10 weeks were over, confusion reigned. I received the worst course evaluations in my 30 years at Fuller. After two dismal years, neither Chuck nor I was willing to continue MC550.

During this time, Kraft and I had begun to specialize in different facets of power ministries. I began specializing in physical healing and in the role of healing in world evangelization. Chuck began specializing in inner healing and deliverance. Our desire was to initiate two new courses, one in each field. However, feelings were extremely high. Theology faculty colleagues had become adversaries! I haven't written this before, but I had endured enough of this academic nonsense. I was ready to go to the next Faculty Senate meeting with my guns loaded. I was ready to announce that if I wasn't given permission to organize a new course in healing and the miraculous, for which I would determine the content and invite outside speakers that I wished, I would retain an attorney who specializes in academic freedom and take Fuller Seminary to court!

By this time, I had begun to organize a team of personal intercessors, and they were praying fervently for a solution to this serious problem. I believe that God answered their prayers in a very unexpected way. The seminary president, David Hubbard, who appropriately had maintained a neutral position in the whole affair, did something that had never happened before. He invited a group of about 15 faculty, including Kraft and me, over to his home one evening for "pie and coffee." I was very apprehensive about this meeting. I thought it might end up being a battle scene! I kept asking the Lord if this would be the time for me to pull out my loaded guns regarding academic freedom and possible litigation.

I can only attribute what happened to my intercessors opening heaven's door for God's hand to come down in a mighty way. When the discussion began, the first Theology faculty member to take the floor gave a personal testimony of miraculous divine healing! It went uphill from there! The discussion was friendly and mutually supportive. By the end of the night, we were friends once again. Although people had opinions that differed from Kraft's and mine, the classic academic attitude of flexibility on controversial issues prevailed. From that point on, the door was open for me to organize my new class and for Chuck to organize his.

Power ministries and teaching on the miraculous, and hands-on ministry in class, had become an accepted part of Fuller Seminary's curriculum. I love personal intercessors!

Notes

1. Benjamin Breckenridge Warfield, *Miracles Yesterday and Today: Real and Counterfeit* (Grand Rapids, MI: William B. Eerdmans Publishing Company, 1965), pp. 23-24.
2. Charles H. Kraft, *SWM/SIS at Forty* (Pasadena, CA: William Carey Library, 2005), p. 153.
3. C. Peter Wagner, "Third Wave," *The New International Dictionary of Pentecostal and Charismatic Movements*, Stanley M. Burgess, editor (Grand Rapids, MI: Zondervan, 2002), p. 1141.
4. John Wimber with Kevin Springer, *Power Evangelism* (San Francisco, CA: Harper & Row Publishers, 1986), p. 122.
5. John F. MacArthur, Jr., *Charismatic Chaos* (Grand Rapids, MI: Zondervan Publishing House, 1992), p. 131.
6. Ibid., p. 132.
7. Carol Wimber, *John Wimber: The Way It Was* (London, UK: Hodder & Stoughton, 1999), p. 168.
8. Bill Jackson, *The Quest for the Radical Middle: A History of the Vineyard* (Cape Town, South Africa: Vineyard International Publishing, 1999), p. 125.
9. Ibid., p. 124.

The Jacobs Era
(1989–1996)

Paradigm shifts can become challenging. They involve a change of mind that causes a person to see, interpret and understand certain phenomena in a new and different way. They tend to pull people out of their comfort zones. Romans 12:2 tells us that we must be transformed by the renewing of our mind. Somehow, I always seemed to be open to this. New thoughts to me were something like moving from place to place while I was a kid growing up—changes were and are an exciting part of life!

I thought that the shift from being a convinced cessationist to a practitioner of supernatural signs and wonders within the walls of a traditional seminary was paradigm shift enough. It certainly was exciting. But, not surprisingly, that one was not going to be the last. Another shift, almost as radical as the one under John Wimber, was yet in store. I was about to move into the uncharted waters, at least for me, of serious spiritual warfare. The chief instigator of this new phase of my life was an unpretentious woman the age of my daughters, ensconced in Weatherford, Texas, named Cindy Jacobs. She will come into the picture a bit later, but you will soon see why I have named this chapter "The Jacobs Era."

Does Prayer Influence Church Growth?

First, back to the paradigm shift with John Wimber. The most fundamental renewing of my mind during the Wimber Era was the realization that spiritual dimensions of church growth could be as important, or even more important, as the anthropological, sociological, methodological, technical, ecclesiological and empirical dimensions that we had largely been dealing with up to then. While acknowledging, of course, that Jesus is the one who builds His church, I had been teaching that the growth of all churches was determined by a combination of institutional factors and contextual factors. I now began to realize that I needed to add a third category, namely, *spiritual factors,* to the equation as well. If this were the case, the next step would be to identify, research and analyze whatever spiritual factors could be discovered. Once that was done, we would then be able to concentrate on the proper ways and means to maximize their application to missions and church growth. My assignment for the new season was becoming clear.

Wimber helped enable me to do all of the above, especially with regard to signs and wonders—mostly physical healing, but also demonic deliverance. Actually my wife, Doris, eventually became an accomplished deliverance minister and a noted teacher and author in the field. I began to see very clearly how these power ministries not only *could*, but *had* affected the growth of churches, mainly in the Global South, but also to a lesser extent here in the United States. My book *How to Have a Healing Ministry in Any Church* summed up a great deal of what I was learning.

If signs and wonders could affect the growth of the church, what could prayer do? It could only have been the Holy Spirit who prompted me to begin raising questions about prayer, around 1980, because at that time prayer had been occupying a dismally low position on my personal priority list. I hate to admit it, but sometime in the 1970s, I entered a prayerless period of my life. Through the years up until then, I had practiced a daily quiet time the first thing in the morning. I was taught that a good Christian should read the Bible and pray every day, and I did it. However, possibly because I was going through some sort of a mid-life crisis, at one point I concluded that my quiet time had become exceedingly boring. I personally wasn't getting anything out of it that I could discern, and I suspected that God had also become quite disinterested in my routine. So what did I do? I decided to quit the quiet time! Yes, it was a poor decision, but my prayerlessness ended up lasting for a number of years.

Overcoming Prayerlessness

Even so, God, with gentle persistence, soon began speaking to me about prayer. I began improving in 1982, when I started the 120 Fellowship Sunday School class I told you about in the last chapter. Among what turned out to be the faithful core of class members, God had placed several gifted intercessors to stand alongside me. It took time, but mostly through their influence prayer gradually rose higher and higher on my personal priority list. Finally, I began feeling guilty and uncomfortable that I had unwisely ceased my daily devotions, but at the same time, I had little inclination to reinstate my boring practice.

Then one Sunday morning, Pastor Paul Cedar preached what I fondly remember as his "Reader's Digest Sermon." He apologized to the congregation that instead of preaching his normal message he was simply going to read us an article from *Reader's Digest*. Then he began sharing an article on, you guessed it, the necessity of having a quiet time! As I listened, I became more and more persuaded that he had chosen the article specifically for me, although I'm sure that he knew nothing about my prayerlessness. By the time he finished, I was under full-blown conviction, and I knew for sure that I needed to change my ways. To this day I am thankful for his concluding remarks to the congregation. Cedar said words to this effect, "I know that the Lord has spoken to some of you who are not having a quiet time. Here's what I'm going to ask you to do. Starting tomorrow, I want you to promise to give five minutes a day to the Lord!"

Five minutes? I'm thinking, *All right! What a relief! I can do that!* So I followed his instructions and began 5 minutes a day. As Paul undoubtedly suspected it would, the 5 minutes eventually became 10, and then 20, and I found myself praying anything but boring prayers, up to 30 minutes a day. I thought I was doing pretty well, but then Larry Lea came on the scene with his book, *Could You Not Tarry One Hour?* According to Lea, my 30 minutes were not enough, and he was right. Through his book, and through a subsequent personal relationship with him, God used Larry as a major influence in helping me get my personal prayer life and my understanding of prayer on the right track. It would launch me into a fascinating future in which I would eventually write more on prayer than even the famous E. M. Bounds, although I must be clear that I am referencing only *quantity*, not *quality*. Bounds' books will still be in print long after mine are forgotten.

Researching Prayer

In 1987, I put on my professorial hat and seriously began researching the field of prayer. My first step was to build a substantial personal library on prayer and to read as many of the books as I could. Because it was a new field for me, I wanted to begin by finding out what people of some expertise had been saying about prayer, and then identify key areas in which not much had yet been said in print. My desire would be to concentrate my research and writing and teaching on those somewhat neglected areas. As time went by, I was able to identify three such areas: (1) intercession for Christian leaders, (2) strategic-level intercession, and (3) the relationship

Cindy Jacobs in action. Cindy was one of the key leaders for the prayer movement of the 1990s, and she now heads up the Reformation Prayer Network. Many of her prophecies enabled me to turn certain corners in my life by the direction of God.

Life ain't all work and no play! Here, in Nashville, Tennessee, in the mid-1990s, I am pretending to sing in a country music quartet with my friends (from left to right) Sharon White (Ricky Skagg's wife), Connie Smith and Barbara Fairchild. The three were involved with us in one of our first spiritual warfare conferences. Since our childhood, Doris and I have been country music aficionados.

of prayer to missions and church growth. I began to give considerable time and effort to each of the three.

Power Evangelism Gains Influence

Meanwhile, the interest sparked by having John Wimber teach at Fuller had begun to spread throughout evangelical academia, particularly among missions professors. Although there was some ongoing opposition, it was clearly diminishing. Several institutions like Fuller had begun to introduce courses, sections of courses and lectures dealing with power ministries, despite predictable irritation on the part of some of the more traditional theologians on their faculties. Although MC510 had been terminated, Wimber continued to teach at Fuller in several of my courses as a visiting lecturer. His first book, *Power Evangelism,* had been released and it became the most commonly used textbook in the new courses that had been springing up in schools around the United States and Canada.

As I watched this development, my apostolic intuitions began to stir. Why not get these professors together? Why not allow them to talk to each other? Why not connect evangelicals and charismatics? Why not do it here at Fuller where some of the theology professors might take note that power evangelism had been gaining academic respectability? I presented the idea to our School of World Mission faculty and they agreed to sponsor it. We would call the meeting "Academic Symposium on Power Evangelism," and I would be the facilitator.

Forty scholars from Christian institutions came together in Pasadena in December 1988. Fittingly, John Wimber was the keynote speaker. The format allowed a large number of those who attended to make presentations or formally respond to what others were saying. My friend Douglas Pennoyer, then from Seattle Pacific University, agreed to help me by undertaking the lion's share of editorial work on compiling the presentations and responses into a book. The title we decided on was *Wrestling with Dark Angels.* I found it interesting because, under the broad topic of power ministries, the title highlighted dealing with the demonic instead of highlighting the more accustomed area of physically healing the sick. It turned out to be prophetic. My address to the symposium introduced the subject of territorial spirits. Sure enough, the next major area to which God would assign me would be strategic-level intercession, which deals, among other things, with confronting territorial demonic spirits. This was one of the three topics within the field of prayer that I felt had been neglected in the previous literature.

Personal Intercessors

Another of the three areas of prayer that I thought could use more attention was intercession for Christian leaders. One of the most notable growing churches in Southern California at the time was Skyline Wesleyan Church in San Diego, pastored by John Maxwell. Its dynamic growth would naturally attract the attention of a church growth professor, but I soon learned something else. Maxwell had gained the reputation of gathering around him one of the most admired teams of pastors' prayer partners. I soon got to know John personally, and he did more than anyone else to help me lay the groundwork for understanding and analyzing the phenomenon of intercession for Christian leaders. His book *Partners in Prayer* helped me immensely.

I have mentioned that some of the core members of my 120 Fellowship class turned out to be gifted and experienced intercessors. Without any prodding on my part, they took the initiative to begin praying for me personally. Around the time they did, I could not help but notice a measurable improvement in my teaching and in the other ministries in which I was involved. It didn't take long to connect the dots and realize that the new prayer was actually making a difference. It was the first time I ever enjoyed that kind of focused prayer on my behalf, and we began talking about it with one another.

The 120 Fellowship then became my field laboratory for experimenting with the idea of personal intercession for leaders. Among other things, I began to discern that I had three concentric circles of intercessors who prayed for me, which I called I-1 ("I" standing for "intercessors"), I-2 and I-3. I began with one I-1 intercessor and a half dozen or so I-2s. The I-2 group eventually grew to around 20, and I still keep in close touch with I-1s and I-2s. I recruited maybe 100 or more I-3 intercessors to whom I began sending periodic information to help them know what to pray for.

Over a period of time, I gradually began to compile my experiences and my understandings about personal intercession into teaching notes, which I shared and discussed especially with my Doctor of Ministry students at Fuller, who were mostly pastors. With this refining, I was able to write my book *Prayer Shield*. If I were asked, I would nominate *Prayer Shield* as the most important and most helpful book I have written for pastors. Through the years, I have received numerous ongoing testimonies of how recruiting and organizing teams of personal intercessors has lifted the ministry of pastors everywhere to unprecedented new levels.

Cindy Jacobs Appears

Soon after Doris and I began getting more and more involved in the area of prayer, we felt that we needed to become aquainted firsthand with some of the recognized national prayer leaders who habitually gathered each year for the U.S. National Day of Prayer. So we flew to Washington, D.C., to attend the May 1989 meetings. One desire was to network with as many of our nation's seasoned prayer leaders as possible in order to learn what we could from them. Among other things, we registered for a day-long seminar on prayer taught by Joy Dawson of Youth With A Mission (YWAM).

During the lunch break, the group was to meet in a nearby restaurant. It so happened that Mike and Cindy Jacobs of Generals of Intercession in Weatherford, Texas, ended up in the same automobile that was taking Doris and me to lunch. After we introduced ourselves, I asked what Generals of Intercession did. Cindy replied, "We pray for the healing of nations!" I had never heard of anything like that before! However, "healing nations" instantly sounded very missiological to me. Could this be one of the links I had been seeking between prayer and missions? I asked her to explain what she meant, and Cindy, who is never at a loss for words, talked until we arrived at the restaurant. Because she hadn't finished her explanation, we invited the Jacobses to sit with us at lunch, which they did. It was a history-making lunch for us!

By the time we returned to the seminar that afternoon, I had turned a corner in my career. Cindy had initiated a notable paradigm shift. We didn't have the terminology at the time, but this was my introduction to strategic-level spiritual warfare, which became a driving force in what we did throughout the 1990s and beyond. Before the day was out, I was able to connect Cindy to Jane Campbell of Chosen Books, and the result of that meeting was the book that launched Cindy into the public eye, *Possessing the Gates of the Enemy.*

Up to then, we had assumed that our prayers for missions would be focused mostly on individuals. Jesus told us that we should pray that the Lord would send laborers into His harvest fields, so we prayed for missionaries and evangelists and pastors and others who were spreading the gospel. Then we prayed for unsaved individuals so that they would become ripened fruit and respond positively to the message and be saved. But Cindy Jacobs convinced us that we should not only pray for individuals, but we should also pray for whole social units like nations or cities to be healed and saved. We must begin taking *corporate* prayer seriously. I didn't comprehend all that she was telling us at the moment, but the implications of this concept have since become enormous, and they have continued to escalate throughout the years in my life and ministry.

Lausanne II in Manila

You may remember that in chapter 5, I mentioned my involvement with the International Congress on World Evangelization held in Lausanne, Switzerland, in 1974, and that I was subsequently named to the 48-member central Lausanne Committee for World Evangelization (LCWE) that would continue to guide the movement. I was then asked to chair the new Strategy Working Group, so I teamed up with Ed Dayton of World Vision, and I dedicated a great deal of time and energy to this assignment over the years. By 1989, we on LCWE had decided that the time had come, after 15 years, to convene a Lausanne II Congress, this time in Manila.

As I was working through the ripple effects of MC510 and the different spiritual factors that might play a role in world missions and church growth, dealing with demonic forces began to take on a vivid reality. In MC510, we taught and practiced casting demons out of individuals, even some as actual demonstrations while the whole class looked on. As time went by, Chuck Kraft, as well as my wife, Doris, began to minister deliverance, write books on the subject, and both have since become widely recognized for their expertise in the field. Once I became convinced of the objective reality of demonic beings in our real world, my thoughts began to escalate.

I began to wonder if demons could not only affect *people*, but also possibly even whole people *groups*. As I have said, I expressed some ideas about territorial spirits in the Symposium on Power Evangelism that I just told about, but even before then some related thoughts had been forming. A year earlier, when I was writing my book *How to Have a Healing Ministry,* I had been entertaining the notion, spurred significantly through my experiences in Argentina, that some spirits, such as principalities and powers, might possibly exercise their evil assignments over certain geographical regions. Consequently, I included a short section under the title "Territorial Spirits" in that book. I raised the intriguing question: "Church growth theory has long ago recognized the phenomenon of resistant peoples. Could it be that at least some of the resistance may be caused by the direct working of demonic forces?"[1]

The more I researched, taught and discussed this hypothesis in forums like our symposium, the more convinced I became that we were on to a valid missiological principle that should be thoroughly researched and applied in the field. I didn't immediately see how Lausanne II in Manila would become the history-making vehicle it ultimately did for diffusing the concept of territorial spirits.

Barriers Are Lowering

The 15 years between Lausanne I and Lausanne II recorded a significant lowering of the barriers between traditional evangelicals and Pentecostal/charismatics. I'm sure that the publicity surrounding MC510 helped the process, but many other factors were at work as well. One of them was the influence of Thomas F. Zimmerman, then General Superintendent of the Assemblies of God, one of my close colleagues on the Lausanne Committee. Zimmerman had been waging a largely successful campaign to make classical Pentecostals more "respectable" in the eyes of evangelicals in general.

The upshot was that the program of Lausanne II, unlike Lausanne I, included an intentional emphasis on the person and work of the Holy Spirit in world evangelization. Strongly symbolic of this was the appearance of prominent Pentecostal leader, Jack Hayford, on the platform in two of the plenary sessions, plus a plenary video presentation of the work of David Yonggi Cho of Korea. Perhaps equally symbolic was the fact that up to one-half of those who attended plenary sessions raised their hands during worship, whereas similar body language was virtually absent from Lausanne I.

The afternoon program over the 10 days included 40 or 50 electives or "tracks" on a wide variety of subjects of interest. Each track would have nine one-hour sessions. Significantly, the three electives that ended up attracting the most interest in terms of attendance were the Holy Spirit Track, the Spiritual Warfare Track and the Prayer Track, in that order. That was especially satisfying to me, because those were the three that I directly participated in organizing. Obviously, the spiritual dimensions of world evangelization were now rising rapidly on our collective missiological agenda.

It so happened that Ed Dayton, my good friend and partner in developing the Strategy Working Group, was appointed program chairperson for Lausanne II. Because we were closely connected, Ed asked my help in introducing tracks that would reflect some of the new concepts related to the spiritual dimensions of world evangelization that I had been working on.

We agreed that we should incorporate the three tracks I just mentioned, and Ed's assistant, Gary Clark, would help facilitate them. It turned out that Jack Hayford would lead the Holy Spirit Track, Glenn Shepherd would lead the Prayer Track, and Chuck Kraft would lead the Spiritual Warfare Track. I was invited to speak in all three.

On-Site Intercession

During the time that I was giving a good bit of my attention to Lausanne II in Manila, the Lord spoke clearly to me. He said words to the effect that if I was benefiting so much personally from the ministry of my newly recruited personal intercessors, it might be well to recruit a team of seasoned, competent intercessors to provide on-site intercession for Lausanne II. I took this as an urgent challenge. Where would I find such a team? I felt that my own intercessors in 120 Fellowship did not as yet have the experience or the necessary national and international exposure to rise to such an occasion.

The one person on the Lausanne Committee who most strongly and persistently had been focusing our attention on prayer was Vonette Bright of Campus Crusade, so I called Vonette. She was thrilled with the idea, and she suggested that I contact the leader of the whole Campus Crusade prayer ministry, Ben Jennings. She promised to lay the groundwork and let Ben know that I would be calling.

When I presented the concept to Ben, he quickly comprehended that this would not be a trivial assignment. He knew that it would be something that would demand huge inputs of time and energy as well as fervent intercession on his part. Nothing like this that we knew of had ever been attempted previously. My initial suggestion was to recruit 20 to 25 recognized intercessors, none of whom would be official delegates to Lausanne II. They would agree to go to Manila at their own expense (Billy Graham was paying the expenses of the delegates), contract a prayer room in a nearby hotel, and pray 24 hours a day throughout the whole event. Jennings prayed about it, consulted others, received the backing of Campus Crusade through Bill and Vonette Bright and told me that he would step up to the plate and do what he could. I was thrilled! We ended up with 39 fervent intercessors working four-hour shifts in the Philippine Plaza Hotel right across the street from the congress. Ironically, the suite that became the official intercession room ended up right across the hall from Bill and Vonette's hotel room!

We had met Cindy Jacobs in May, and Lausanne II was scheduled for July, only two months later. I believe it had to be the Lord Himself who prompted Doris and me to spontaneously invite Cindy to Manila. She had known little or nothing about LCWE; we had very few mutual friends, but we knew that she was a winner and that there would never be another chance like this for us to help draw her into the circles of worldwide evangelization in which we moved. I was influential enough in LCWE leadership so that I could pull whatever strings were necessary to open the doors for her to participate. Cindy had the time available, so she came to Manila as our guest.

Shortly after we arrived, Cindy introduced us to her friend, Barbara Byerly, who had come to Manila as an official delegate. Because Barbara and Cindy were both intercessors, they wanted to be included on the prayer team as soon as they heard about it. I suggested it to Ben Jennings, and he welcomed them.

A fringe benefit for Doris and me was that both of them soon became invaluable personal I-2 intercessors for us from then on. Their work began immediately. First, Doris happened to harbor a demon who found a way to attach itself to her and cause foggy depression for around 24 hours before Cindy helped set her free. Then a practicing witch somehow found her way into one of the sessions I was teaching, and her curses were strong enough actually to cause me to lose my train of thought for several minutes. However, in the spiritual realm, Cindy, who was physically present in the session, astutely discerned the spiritual battle that was going on in the invisible world, quickly bound the witchcraft spirits, broke the spell in the name of Jesus, and I was able to continue teaching as usual. Needless to say, we were very glad we had brought her to Manila!

Three Tracks

The timing of all this was right, and the three afternoon tracks that I helped initiate became a highlight of the congress. In the Holy Spirit Track, I spoke on "The Holy Spirit in World Evangelization"; in the Prayer Track, I spoke on "Intercession for Christian Leaders"; and in the Spiritual Warfare Track, I spoke on "Territorial Spirits." Of the three, I was personally most attracted to the Spiritual Warfare Track. Much to my amazement, four of the other speakers in that track also addressed the subject of territorial spirits! I have no knowledge that up to that point the subject of territorial spirits had ever been dealt with in a public session except for my talk in our

Fuller Power Evangelism Symposium a few months earlier. It was a brand-new topic, and it seemed to fit all the new paradigms I had been considering, including Cindy Jacobs' concept of healing nations.

At this stage of my life, I was just getting used to the idea that God at times speaks to us directly, not just by putting desires in our hearts or opening the right doors or giving us ideas or leading us to do certain things, but actually in words that can be quoted. It was during the Spiritual Warfare Track that this happened to me, perhaps for the first time. It was not an audible voice, but I distinctly heard God say in my spirit, "I want you to take leadership in the area of territorial spirits!" This, then, was clearly my assignment for the next season of my life. Little did I know that it would once again get me in serious trouble with the Fuller Seminary theologians and cause a crisis comparable to the MC510 blow-up!

The Spiritual Warfare Network

Although I knew I was supposed to take leadership, it was a boost from John Robb of World Vision that prompted me to convene a meeting of whatever leaders we could find who knew something about strategic-level spiritual warfare. I first asked Chuck Kraft, Cindy Jacobs and Gary Clark to join me as conveners of the group, which met in a Sunday School classroom at Lake Avenue Church in Pasadena, on February 12, 1990. Some of the more recognizable ones among the 30 who met with us were Jack Hayford, John Dawson, Ed Silvoso, Gwen Shaw, Frank Hammond, Joy Dawson, Ed Murphy, Tom White, and many others. Barbara Byerly led an intercession group, which prayed fervently in the room next door throughout the entire meeting.

Theological Fireworks

This is where I got into trouble again with the Fuller Seminary theologians. Because I felt it was newsworthy that leaders representing both the traditional evangelical stream and the Pentecostal/charismatic stream, coming out of Lausanne II, could sit down and discuss such cutting-edge issues as confronting demonic powers on all levels, I called my friend John Dart, then religion editor of the *Los Angeles Times,* and I let him know that we were meeting. Much to my surprise, he himself came and personally covered the event with what I considered a well-presented article. However, the article touched off serious fireworks among the Fuller theologians.

They were furious! Some of them were still smarting from dealing with John Wimber and MC510. Most decidedly, I was not one of their theological folk heroes. I had been teaching about demons and territorial spirits in my classes, which were well attended by theology students, and the professors had been getting unwelcome questions in their classrooms. Many of them had been seething under the surface, but the newspaper article took the lid off and the fireworks exploded. In their minds, the general public would now know that Fuller was teaching about demons, while some of the theologians were still wrestling with whether they really even believed in them. On the administrative level, there was a fear that this new development might possibly even alienate some financial supporters.

Not surprisingly, I was soon invited to the president's office for a heart-to-heart talk with David Hubbard. By then, a full factual report of the February 12 meeting had been written by our friend Jane Rumph, and that helped greatly to balance the journalistic approach of John Dart. Hubbard disclosed to me a good deal about the unrest that I had been causing in the seminary by advocating strategic-level spiritual warfare, and he asked me to attend the March meeting of the Faculty Senate to discuss the issues I had raised.

I wrote what I thought was a very reasonable presentation of my point of view, and I read it when the Faculty Senate meeting began. I soon found out, however, that some members of the theology faculty were not in the mood for reasonable presentations. They had come with their personal agendas and grievances and they were out to take me down if they possibly could. They cross-examined me for two hours in what soon turned into a volatile environment. The only thing that kept it from becoming an outright heresy trial was the comforting fact that the official Fuller statement of faith had nothing to say about the demonic and, consequently, there was no way for them to find me in violation.

Coming to Terms

After I left, the Senate made three resolutions: (1) They would not form a faculty study commission such as they did with MC510, (2) They would not "censure" me at this time, and (3) A letter of concern from the Faculty Senate would be sent to me and go on my record. The three-page letter arrived two months later, signed by the president and the provost, stating that they felt I had not yet grasped the intensity of the concern of the Faculty Senate over the matters in question and that more discussion would be necessary.

As I read the letter, I realized that the feeling was mutual, and I contended that the Faculty Senate had not sufficiently grasped *my* concerns, especially as related to the field of *missiology* as over against the field of *theology*. In my response, I wrote this paragraph:

> It seems to me that the most fundamental issue we have before us relates to research methodology. Much of our failure to hear each other stems from this. What is the relationship between theology and experience? Between the exegetical and the phenomenological? Between philosophy and social science? Between the ought and the is? Between library research and field research? Between systematic theology and contextualized theology? Between orthodoxy and orthopraxy? Between static theology and dynamic theology? Between concern for the ethical and concern for the pragmatic? Between Western worldviews and Third World worldviews? What are the underlying values of our respective schools?

Looking back, I think that these questions served to defuse a good bit of the hostility. The "further discussion" turned out to be an evening gathering of 8 to 10 professors in David Hubbard's home. Hubbard had given each one a copy of Chuck Kraft's book *Christianity with Power*, which they all obediently had read. Chuck started off with a brief summary of his book, and that, happily for me, effectively shifted the agenda from my controversial spiritual warfare issues to the broader topics of Chuck's book. The conversation was extremely cordial, and I said as little as possible. The surprising conclusion was that we missiologists admitted that we needed the theologians to keep us from falling into "dualism," and the theologians admitted that they needed us missiologists to keep them from falling into "deism." We ended up friends!

I think the seminary then held out an olive branch to me when in the following school year they instituted a new Alumnus of the Year award and presented it to me at the commencement service. No more controversy over signs and wonders, demons, spiritual warfare, territorial spirits, and the like! A year or so later, I introduced a new course on strategic-level spiritual warfare called "Spiritual Issues in Church Growth" with no opposition from the theology faculty. It actually became the favorite course that I had ever taught.

Back to the SWN

Back to our post-Lausanne II meeting of February 12, 1990. We spent a
good amount of time in that initial meeting, held in the Lake Avenue
Church, building personal relationships and sharing a bit of what each
of us had previously learned about spiritual warfare. We agreed that a useful terminology would be to distinguish between three levels of warfare:
(1) Ground-level spiritual warfare, which is casting out demons from individuals, (2) Occult-level spiritual warfare, which is dealing with more organized demonic forces, such as witchcraft, New Age, Freemasonry, voodoo,
Eastern religions, magic, and the like, and (3) Strategic-level spiritual warfare, which is confronting the higher-level principalities and powers, including territorial spirits. We decided to call our group the "Spiritual Warfare
Network" (SWN), and we agreed to meet again in November.

The SWN continued to meet privately throughout 1991 and 1992, and
then we decided to go public with a "Gideon's Army" event, inviting 300
people from around the world to the Kwang Lim Methodist Church Prayer
Mountain in Korea for several days in 1993. I'll tell more about that later.

Through this whole process I was researching and building what library I could consisting of books making some references to strategic-level
spiritual warfare and specifically to territorial spirits. Before long, I had
enough material to compile a book of my own on the subject, citing the
works of 18 authors, including such dignitaries as Jack Hayford, David
Yonggi Cho, Ed Silvoso, John Dawson and even the noted theologian Os-
car Cullmann. I was surprised to find that so many had made reference to
the phenomenon. The title of the book was *Engaging the Enemy: How to Fight
and Defeat Territorial Spirits.* It helped begin an exciting new paradigm shift
for many.

The new paradigm that Cindy Jacobs had introduced us to at lunch,
in Washington, D.C., had just begun to unfold, as we will see in the next
chapter.

Note

1. C. Peter Wagner, *How to Have a Healing Ministry in Any Church* (Ventura, CA: Regal, 1988), p. 197.

8

The Bush Era
(1991–1999)

I knew *of* Luis Bush long before I *knew* him.

Today, many more career missionaries are being sent out to other countries by nations in the Global South than by the traditional missionary-sending nations of the West. It wasn't always like that. In chapter 5, by way of reminder, I told how, back in the early 1970s, I had recruited three of my students in the School of World Mission to launch pioneer research on missionaries being sent out from churches located in the Third World. Their resulting book, *Missions from the Third World*, was a rather startling eye-opener to mission leaders far and wide. For many, the concept that churches on "the mission field" could raise money and send out missionaries themselves had not so much as entered their minds!

However, 10 years later, around the mid 1980s, the idea had become generally accepted. Although what we called "Third World missions" never did become an ongoing specialty of mine, I nevertheless remained very much in touch with the phenomenon. That is when I began hearing of Luis Bush. The word was getting out that Bush, a foreign missionary to El Salvador, was not only pastoring a sizable church, as well as pioneering a Bible institute, but he also had become one of the chief advocates and practitioners of Third World missions.

When I say that Bush was a "foreign missionary," I must add that he had a leg up on most of us who have gone through the challenging experience of launching out cross-culturally. He was born in Argentina of a family that spoke English, so both English and Spanish were first languages, and then his family moved to Brazil where he added fluency in Portuguese to his language repertoire. As early as 1984, he founded the Salvadoran Evangelical Mission, which began sending out career missionaries, one of the first such initiatives in Latin America. He planted seven other churches, and his anchor church in San Salvador, *Iglesia Nazaret,* gave no less than 40 percent of its budget to missions!

With this, it will be easy to see why Luis Bush became one of my missiological heroes even though I had never met him personally. When I eventually did meet him, he ended up playing a major role in expanding the scope of my ministry during the 1990s throughout the world. This became so important to me that I have decided to name this chapter "The Bush Era."

By necessity, the Jacobs Era had to precede the Bush Era. The reason for this is that I needed to explain in detail the context of the Spiritual Warfare Network (SWN) before Bush's role could be properly understood. You will see how the two are tied together as we move along. Keep in mind that the formation of the SWN took place in 1990, only the beginning of the decade in question.

Luis Bush starts to assume a significant role in shaping the direction of my future through his admirable leadership in the AD2000 Movement. I think I should take some time at this point to explain what was behind my transition from LCWE to AD2000.

The Big Picture

I consider the 1974 Lausanne Congress on World Evangelization the most important single event for missions in the twentieth century. It highlighted cross-cultural evangelism, the people approach to world evangelization, and it helped us missiologists to focus on the unreached peoples of the world. It was also a major international sounding board for the Church Growth Movement. I was honored to be included in the 48-member follow-up Lausanne Committee for World Evangelization (LCWE), chairing its Strategy Working Group, and serving on its Executive Committee. This became a top-level priority for me in my off-campus ministries through the 1970s and most of the 1980s.

However, around 1985 or 1986, I began to detect, slowly at first, that the Lausanne Movement appeared to be losing steam. I felt that things were becoming a bit routinized and that the earlier cutting-edge zeal had been diminishing. I didn't have the language for it then, but now I know that I was detecting that LCWE was becoming an old wineskin. I could not yet imagine what the new wineskin might be; nevertheless, I started pulling back from LCWE so that I would be as available as possible to move into the new when it did come. I turned the Strategy Working Group over to Ed Dayton, and I moved off of the LCWE Executive Committee. I remained a member of LCWE, but I let it be known that I would be completing that task as well after the 1989 Lausanne II Congress in Manila.

Meanwhile, Thomas Wang had become the International Director of LCWE under chairman Leighton Ford (Billy Graham's brother-in-law) as well as the Congress Director for Lausanne II in Manila. As he was executing these functions, God began to give Thomas an overwhelming vision for focusing world evangelization on the year AD 2000. He pushed this as much as he could within LCWE, but I will now only surmise what must have been happening. By then I was no longer an LCWE insider, so I have no direct knowledge of this. However, I would guess that Wang was also perceiving that LCWE had been showing symptoms of an old wineskin. The other LCWE leaders could not seem to embrace his new concept with sufficient enthusiasm. While his Asian courtesy would not allow such a thing to surface, I suspect that Wang was concluding that the new wineskin would definitely have something to do with the year AD 2000 and that it would not happen within LCWE.

As this vision was forming and becoming more concrete, Wang connected with Luis Bush. By then Bush had left El Salvador and had become president of Partners International, headquartered in San Jose, California. Bush fully shared Wang's desire for a new wineskin that would focus world missions on AD 2000. Both of them cast this vision in plenary sessions of Lausanne II. Then Wang resigned from LCWE after Lausanne II, turning his position over to Tom Houston of the United Kingdom. He and Bush went on to form what became known as the AD2000 Movement. Thomas Wang became the chairperson of the AD2000 board, and Luis Bush became the international director. Although it was *officially* denied, those who had eyes to see would realize that a new AD2000 wineskin was now, to all intents and purposes, replacing the old LCWE wineskin in the arena of world missions.

One of Bush's first contributions to the AD2000 Movement, and a brilliant one at that, was to coin a term that has since become a household word, namely, "The 10/40 Window." He saw some research by David Barrett of *The World Christian Encyclopedia*, whose statistics showed that an area encompassing North Africa, the Middle East and sections of Asia to Japan contained at least 95 percent of the world's unreached peoples. As Bush studied this on a map, he observed that this area was situated between the latitudes of 10 degrees and 40 degrees north and called it the 10/40 Window. This became the most crucial focus of world missions throughout the 1990s.

The AD2000 Movement

I came into the AD2000 Movement, oddly enough, through my role as international coordinator of the Spiritual Warfare Network. That explains why I needed to chronicle the background of the founding of SWN before moving on to this next step.

Luis Bush had structured the AD2000 Movement around 13 semi-autonomous tracks. Each track would have a chairperson who would be more or less a public figurehead. However, the formation, the vision and the operation of each track would be in the hands of a coordinator. The coordinator, then, would be the de facto leader of the track. The role of the international director was to appoint the track chairpersons and coordinators, monitor the progress they were making in fulfilling their specific assignments, connect them with each other through regular meetings, and assure that all the activities were woven together into the whole of the AD2000 Movement. No one else that I know of could have matched Luis Bush's masterful leadership throughout the decade.

This organizational structure was an amazing development. I noticed it then, but I see it much more clearly now; and I have language to describe it that I did not have at the time. Almost every similar organization that I had been involved in up to then was based on religious democratic principles, so that *groups* of people rather than *individuals* had the final authority. LCWE had clearly been organized on that premise. Luis Bush and AD2000, however, were thoroughly *apostolic,* although we were not using the term at that time. Bush was, and still is, what I term in my book *Apostles Today,* a "functional apostle." He unquestionably had the final decision-making authority in AD2000, but he was wise enough not only to consult with his board, but also to allow the track coordinators, who constituted the middle level of management, all the freedom necessary for them to use their creativity and to guide their tracks along the pathway on which they felt God was leading them. Please note that the tracks were not run by committees or boards, as they would have been in the old wineskin; they were run by apostolic coordinators. I am convinced that the notable success of the AD2000 Movement in the decade of the 1990s was primarily due to this creative apostolic leadership structure.

The United Prayer Track

One of Luis Bush's 13 tracks happened to be a Spiritual Mapping Track. When I first heard about this it came as a total surprise. I was amazed! Let me explain.

First, spiritual mapping was a notable development connected to the whole introduction of spiritual principles related to world evangelization, which, as I have detailed, received a large boost in Lausanne II. Spiritual mapping involves doing the necessary historical, geographical and spiritual research to identify, as much as possible, the specific demonic entities and forces that are active in keeping a territory or a people group in darkness. This opens the way for more effective and targeted intercession and spiritual warfare. The first individual to rise to the top of this profession, so to speak, was George Otis, Jr., who was a member of SWN. Otis likes to call spiritual mapping "informed intercession."

Second, Luis Bush was a graduate of Dallas Theological Seminary, at the time one of the most outspoken cessationist educational institutions in our nation. Even though some modifications have recently taken place, Dallas then was uncompromisingly anti-Pentecostal and anti-charismatic. However, one of the most positive character traits of Bush was that he was his own man. He himself was neither Pentecostal nor charismatic nor even Third Wave, but he kept himself open to whatever the Holy Spirit happened to be saying to the churches. He refused to follow the Dallas separatist party line, and he became fully open to working with all evangelical leaders, even those who were charismatic, as were the members of SWN.

Luis, appropriately, had recruited George Otis, Jr., to be the coordinator of the Spiritual Mapping Track. Subsequently, they both approached me and asked me to be the chairperson of the track. I told them that I would be inclined to accept that role, but that I would not finalize my decision without first checking with my colleagues in the Spiritual Warfare Network. We discussed the matter considerably at the next SWN meeting, and the consensus was that the SWN would probably fit the AD2000 Movement better under the United Prayer Track than under the Spiritual Mapping Track. Consequently, I did not feel free to join the Spiritual Mapping Track.

Meanwhile, Luis had invited David Bryant of Concerts of Prayer International to serve as the coordinator of the United Prayer Track. He then approached me to be the chairperson. I checked it out with David, whom I knew well, and we agreed that we could work together, so I accepted. Then a very surprising, but defining, event took place. Bryant's board concluded that they were not in a position to encourage David to undertake this new responsibility! So what did Bush do? He asked me that, instead of serving as the *chairperson* (a figurehead), I would consider serving as the *coordinator* of the United Prayer Track. If so, he would name Kim Joon Gon of Korea as the chairperson. I told him that I would pray about it, but that a condition of acceptance would be that I could bring the entire SWN with me. Bush unhesitatingly agreed, which I considered more than remarkable from an alumnus of Dallas Seminary!

It took considerable time and serious prayer to come to a decision on that, since I realized from the start that a commitment to coordinate the United Prayer Track would initiate a major change in the direction of my ministry throughout the 1990s. As we prayed, Doris agreed that we should be open to the possibility. At that point, we had 18 I-1 and I-2 intercessors, so we sent an alert out to them. Before long, an unusual quantity of prophetic words began to pour in from the intercessors, all to the effect that God was saying that He had ordained the AD2000 Movement as a powerful new stream of His activity in the whole world for the 1990s, and that God had anointed me and assigned me to take a leadership role in it. As soon as I read the prophetic words, I rapidly concluded that I would actually risk *disobeying* God if I turned Bush's invitation down.

So Luis and I had breakfast on February 17, 1991, and I agreed to take the United Prayer Track. A later development was that George Otis, Jr., would no longer launch a separate Spiritual Mapping Track after all, but rather be incorporated as a division of the United Prayer Track. I recorded the date of our breakfast because, as you will see, this turned out to be one of the most important career decisions I had ever made.

Could It All Fit Together?

Over the next few months, the Lord confirmed my decision by showing me clearly that I would be leading a new movement that promised to produce the greatest combination of prayer and world evangelization that had ever been known. This would be my chief passion for years to come. But how about teaching at Fuller?

I met with Paul Pierson, my School of World Mission dean, and talked it over. We agreed that my base for operating the United Prayer Track would remain in Fuller Seminary, but that I would probably have to pull back some on the extra teaching load I had been carrying. My plan was to operate the United Prayer Track from my Fuller office, with Doris continuing as the SWM research librarian and assisting me with the other things as well.

With my new responsibility, I needed to take a closer look at my priorities and how I was to budget my use of time. One thing that had become clear to me over the years was that seminary joint faculty meetings were typically quite boring. I'm not speaking of our School of World Mission faculty meetings, which were always creative and exciting and cutting edge. Rather, I mean the meetings of the faculties of theology, psychology and missions all together. I could hardly remember one in which my presence made any difference at all, either to me or to the rest of the faculty. So I decided to stop going to joint faculty meetings!

A Cordial Talk with the President

I thought this was working out all right until the day I received an invitation to visit the president, David Hubbard, in his office. When I arrived, I saw that the provost, Richard Mouw, was there as well. The three of us had a heart-to-heart talk for quite some time. It turned out that they had become very concerned that I had taken on an off-campus ministry assignment with the scope of the United Prayer Track of the AD2000 Movement. They also had noticed my absence from joint faculty meetings, and this had disturbed them as well. I had suspected beforehand that this might be a critical meeting, similar to my two previous episodes with the Faculty Senate, so I had my intercessors praying fervently for it beforehand.

Fortunately, I had three strong points in my favor. First, involvement with the AD2000 Movement was clearly a missiological assignment. It would not conflict at all with my chief role as professor of missions and church growth. In fact, it would provide a new, broad, worldwide exposure to help me to remain on the cutting edge of my field. Furthermore, I had cleared it all previously with my dean, Paul Pierson. Second, at the time, I was actually teaching more than double the number of tuition-paying students in Fuller than any other faculty member, and I was publishing at least as many books. This was a distinct advantage. And third, President David Hubbard's and my personal friendship went back almost 40 years to when we were both Fuller students in the 1950s. Because of that, we didn't need to play verbal games, but rather we could talk directly and frankly to each other.

When things began coming to an end, I said words to the effect: "Tell me, Dave, do you really want me to be just another cog in your academic machinery, or do you want me to be as free and creative as I can be in order to fulfill my destiny?" True to his reasonable and generous nature, Hubbard admitted that it was a very good question. The conversation ended on a cordial note, and the issue never came up again. However, along with many other things, this helped seal my reputation as an academic maverick. Even though I ended up teaching in Fuller for 30 years, I am positive there will be no plans to name a future building on campus "Wagner Hall"!

Avoiding Fuller's Inner Circle

As a matter of fact, it had been my own choice, long before that, not to become a Fuller Seminary insider. This went back to 1979. You may recall that, even though I was a disciple of SWM founding dean, Donald McGavran, I did not finalize my decision to join the faculty until I was sure that his successor as dean would be Arthur Glasser. Due to age limitations, Glasser was expected to retire as dean in 1980, nine years after I had become a faculty member. Around a year before that, David Hubbard visited me in my office to talk to me about the possibility of considering taking Glasser's place as dean when he retired. My first thought related to how honored and humbled I was to be approached for such a position. After all, the Fuller School of World Mission was, at that time, the premier missiological institution in the world. As a professional missiologist, the position of dean of SWM would place me at the very top of my profession. Still, without a pause in the conversation, I told Dave that I was not interested.

Hubbard, quite naturally, was surprised, not to say taken aback, by my unexpected response. He asked, "Why would you turn something like this down?" I replied, "Because I don't have the spiritual gifts that the position requires." The puzzled look on Dave's face and the shaking of his head clearly told me that he was looking for a more satisfactory explanation.

Spiritual Gifts and Convergence

All right, let me explain. As I have mentioned, a major area of my teaching ministry, both on and off campus, has been the subject of spiritual gifts. My book *Your Spiritual Gifts Can Help Your Church Grow* has become my best-selling book, with over a quarter of a million copies in circulation. In it I argue that it is just as important to know what gifts you *don't* have as it is to know which ones you *do* have. Once this becomes clear, the door to what J. Robert (Bobby) Clinton, in his book *The Making of a Leader,* calls "convergence" begins to open. In convergence, you learn to concentrate on what you are good at and you avoid expending time and energy on what you don't like to do and what you are not good at. I had long since learned that I was a poor administrator, and furthermore, that I greatly disliked the task. At the same time, I loved teaching, and I was quite competent at it.

The job description for the dean of the School of World Mission was heavy on management and administration and light on teaching. Even when I explained this to David Hubbard, he was reluctant to accept my reasons at face value. It was then that I suddenly recalled that a few months previously I had taken the psychological PF16 test, just on a whim, and that the professional evaluation, which I had on file, specifically indicated that "[Wagner] is not suitable for academic administration." When I showed it to David, he then understood perfectly. Paul Pierson, much more suited than I in every way, ended up in the position.

Just for the record, Bobby Clinton began his distinguished career at Fuller as my teaching assistant from 1979 to 1981. During those two years he was gathering material for his teaching on leadership and his subsequent book *The Making of a Leader*. Much later he told me that I was one of the field leadership models he was carefully studying and analyzing as he was reaching his conclusions on convergence.

Paul Traxel and Global Harvest Ministries

Toward the end of the 1980s, a German missionary to Malawi, Paul Traxel, enrolled in the School of World Mission. Paul was attracted to my pragmatic approach to church growth and missions, and we became friends. Paul, I soon found out, was actually more of an entrepreneur than a normal missionary. His mission board, like mine, and most others of that day, had been strongly influenced by the spirit of poverty. That is why they became upset when they discovered that Paul had begun importing automobiles from South Africa into Malawi and, because of currency exchange rates, was making a substantial profit. It didn't matter that he was using his profit for missionary work. The rule was that missionaries should receive their money from donations through the home mission board, and not engage in worldly, profitable businesses on the side. The mission board eventually asked him to leave.

In Fuller, Traxel began taking courses, and he did well. I was able to award him a David Yonggi Cho scholarship to attend the annual convention at the world's largest church in Seoul, Korea. But as time went on, Traxel's entrepreneurial projects began overshadowing his academic pursuits. He was trilingual. Raised by a German family in Latvia, still behind the Iron Curtain, his first two languages were German and Russian, and

I was in the middle of teaching Acts in the 120 Fellowship, preparing the manuscript for what I consider my best book, *The Book of Acts: A Commentary*. It differs from other commentaries in that it interlaces insights from power ministries and missiology, two of my specialties.

Luis Bush, international director of the AD2000 and Beyond Movement.

Moments after our first and only plane crash. We were on our way to Almolonga, Guatemala, with Harold and Cecelia Caballeros (on the left). The landing gear failed to come down, so we crashed, splitting the belly of the airplane wide open and bending the propellers. We thanked God profusely for protecting us, ministered in Almolonga, and took the bus back to Guatemala City!

he had learned English as well. He had attended and graduated from Rees Howell's Bible School in England. Among other things, he started buying and selling fine art. He established an import-export business. He was sending American computers to Russia in exchange for Russian lumber. He landed the contract to provide the clothing and memorabilia for the Russian Olympic hockey team. He started a telephone company 10 years before MCI, which eventually failed. He got into the oil business in Siberia and at one point had to purchase a Swiss bank to handle the cash flow. He began a business of wholesale marketing of clothing and was the first to bring whole airplanes loaded with merchandise from Korea into Russia.

One day, Paul invited Doris and me out to dinner. The conversation soon turned to missions and missiology and especially our commitment to lead the AD2000 United Prayer Track. Paul was able to see the big picture before we could. He emphatically told us that we were foolish to think that we could run the Prayer Track just as a sideline to what we were doing in Fuller. The job was much bigger than we had imagined it would be, and it would continue to grow. He advised us to start our own ministry. Interestingly enough, Cindy Jacobs had suggested such a thing to us previously, and we had decisively rejected the idea. My response to Paul was that we couldn't start our own ministry, because we had no money. I was simply a seminary professor. Then Paul said, "If you start your own ministry, you will have enough money. I'll provide it for you!" I said, "How much?" He replied, "I'll cover your whole budget!" Doris and I were flabbergasted.

And that is how Global Harvest Ministries (GHM) was born!

Now we had to start making the necessary adjustments. We would need to incorporate as a 501(c)3, which we did in December 1991. Doris would have to resign from the seminary staff and become the COO/CFO of the new organization. We had to write a business plan and project a budget. Strategies were needed to build a long-term donor base. A mailing list would be essential. How about a staff?

Even before Doris resigned from Fuller, we knew that we would have to answer that last question about staff sooner rather than later. Our agreement with Fuller was that Doris would continue her duties as my personal assistant in her new position, but with her salary coming from GHM. However, with the added responsibilities of the Prayer Track she would then need an office manager, whom God provided in the person of Jean Van Engen, the wife of one of our SWM faculty colleagues. Their first office was the dining room of our home in Altadena. The whole transition was severely complicated by a very rough and painful replacement of Doris's right knee. Paul Traxel had volunteered to secure our permanent facility, and he chose an upscale modern office building four blocks from the seminary, which was occupied by a bank with most of the other tenants attorneys. Paul also furnished the office for us. The Doris and Jean team ably and efficiently carried the management and administration of Global Harvest Ministries until we moved from California to Colorado in 1996.

Professor of Church Growth

I fully agreed with David Hubbard that my main job was still serving Fuller Seminary as professor of church growth. At this time, more students in the School of World Mission and in the D.Min. program were coming to Fuller because of church growth than because of any other attraction. Church leaders across the country were very excited about church growth. Leaders of many denominations were using my textbook *Your Church Can Grow*. It ended up with 24 printings over the years.

When Donald McGavran retired, our dean, Paul Pierson, agreed that we should search for another church growth professor not only to help me with the load, but also as a possible successor when I finished. My choice, back in the 1980s, was Eddie Gibbs of London, England, who first came to Fuller as one of my D.Min. students. Gibbs, who had served as an Anglican missionary to Chile, was then working for the British and Foreign Bible Society. In class, I soon saw that he had a remarkably high aptitude for church growth, reminding me a bit of how I first noticed John Wimber in a similar class. We became friends, he accepted the invitation to come onto the faculty, but the costs of moving him and his family from England seemed to be an obstacle. Because I was partnering with the Billy Graham Association in my LCWE work, and since Eddie had helped with Billy Graham's London crusade, I felt free to ask Graham to help with the funding, and he agreed. Things worked out well, and Eddie did, indeed, become my successor in the Donald McGavran Chair of Church Growth.

Handling Snakes in Church!

One of the things I enjoyed most was interacting with missionaries from all over the world as well as with pastors from numerous denominations across the board. I was getting more requests for speaking engagements and consultation than I could handle. An unusual occasion worth mentioning was when I agreed to teach at the Pentecostal Holiness school in Georgia on the condition that the dean, my friend Garnet Pike, would help satisfy my curiosity and take me to a snake-handling church, since I had never been to one. He said that he had never been to one either, but that he would do what he could. It took a good bit of research on his part to locate the Church of Our Lord Jesus Christ in Kingston, Georgia, a small rural town in the mountains.

Garnet and I were more than apprehensive when we first entered the small wooden building on a Saturday evening. We sat in the back pew as close to the door as possible. We were ready to move out of that door on an instant's notice if necessary. However, we found that they only opened the black boxes and handled the serpents up front behind the altar rail. We were still tense, and wouldn't you know it? We didn't realize that we were sitting right in front of an old, rusty water cooler. Just as a snake was winding around someone's arm up on the platform, the cooler happened to turn on, and it rattled exactly like a rattlesnake! We definitely jumped, but fortunately recognized what it was and were able to calm down.

Which reminds me of a joke. A country singer was invited to one of these churches without knowing what it was. When he finished singing, he sat next to the pastor on the platform. Soon the boxes came out, and he was dumbfounded! He looked at the pastor and asked, "Where's the back door?" The pastor said, "We ain't got none!" So the panicked country singer looked back wide-eyed and said, "Where do you want it?"

Seriously, I ended up visiting that church five times over the years. They told me I could join if I wanted to, but I wasn't inclined to, because the church, not surprisingly, wasn't growing! Once, I took my whole Doctor of Ministry class of around 55 pastors there on a field trip. John Wimber and Eddie Gibbs were with me as well. I called the church ahead of time and they felt so honored that they invited their bishop to preach, and he drove more than 200 miles just to be with us. In bib overalls no less, he delivered a theological treatise on the biblical rationale behind handling serpents, and I must say he was quite convincing. When we debriefed that Monday, where our class was being held in Atlanta, a Presbyterian pastor said, "That was one of the most profound spiritual experiences I have had! I'll admit that I came real close to going forward and taking up one of those serpents!"

I had a chance to chronicle experiences like that for more than 10 years, from 1986 to 1996, in a regular column in *Ministries Today* magazine, which came out every other month. *Ministries Today*, published by Strang Communications, was aimed at the leadership of the charismatic/Pentecostal stream. I might mention that, since I was an ordained Congregational minister, I was reluctant to be labeled a "charismatic." As I said in the last chapter, I coined the term "Third Wave" to describe myself and others like me. However, in the minds of most people who knew me, I could no longer disguise my charismatic ideas and behavior. The title of my column was "Power Evangelism." These magazine articles helped greatly toward orienting the Body of Christ in general toward supernatural interventions of many different and unusual kinds, including snake handling!

Understanding Church Growth and Other Writings

The standard textbook for the worldwide church growth movement was *Understanding Church Growth* by Donald McGavran. I was constantly teaching from it, and I still marvel at the huge quantity of innovative, groundbreaking missiological insights that God gave to McGavran. He would easily be ranked as one of the top 10 missiologists of the twentieth century.

That is why I was so pleased when he agreed one day to sit down with me to talk about the future of *Understanding Church Growth*. The book was getting to be 20 years old. Its ideas were as fresh as ever, but obviously they were expressed in terms that were painfully out of date. For one thing, McGavran had used gender-specific language, which by that time, especially in academic circles, would automatically grade any author a B- or C. I was pleasantly surprised when McGavran wholeheartedly agreed that I should do a complete revision of the book. He gave me a free hand. I carefully avoided including any of my personal interpretations of McGavran's thoughts, but rather I focused only on bringing McGavran himself up to date. While he reviewed my revisions of each chapter, he made surprisingly few changes of his own. As frosting on the cake, he generously assigned me all literary rights to this Third Edition, and to this day, I continue receiving royalties from its sales.

When I inquired, I found that the School of Theology had never offered a course on planting new churches, so I began teaching one, focused mainly on the United States. It drew students from the School of Theology as well as from the School of World Mission. One of my signature axiomatic quotes eventually became: "The most effective evangelistic methodology under heaven is planting new churches!" This was not just a slogan; it was an empirically verified statistic worldwide. I compiled my thoughts in a widely circulated book, *Church Planting for a Greater Harvest.*

Other writings of the time included, first of all, *The Healthy Church.* I tried to make a case that one characteristic of healthy churches is that they grow numerically. I also developed a pathology of church growth in which I enumerated a number of growth-inhibiting diseases that could be diagnosed and, in most cases, cured. I optimistically thought that the names of these diseases, like "ethnikitis" or "St. John's syndrome" or "sociological strangulation" or "koinonitis" or "hyponeumia" would become technical terms used throughout the whole church world from then on, but sadly they never did!

Second, in the 120 Fellowship, I had been teaching from only one book of the Bible, the book of Acts. I had built an extensive personal library of commentaries on Acts, as well as historical and sociological works on the first century. I soon noticed that not much material appeared in the classical commentaries on (1) the missiological dimensions of Acts, or (2) the crucial role of power ministries. I worked strongly on this and wrote a commentary that has gone through several editions and now is published with the title *The Book of Acts: A Commentary.* If anyone asks me, I have to say that this is the best book I have ever written. It is certainly the longest—more than 500 pages!

Third, I had been analyzing the prayer ministries of several successful churches and I reported my findings in *Churches That Pray.* This was one of the books that highlighted some spiritual factors relating to church growth in addition to the more traditional institutional and contextual factors. One of my career disappointments was that I was never successful in getting my church growth colleagues, including Donald McGavran, on board with me. No matter how I tried to persuade them otherwise, they perceived that what I was doing with prayer and spiritual warfare and healing was, in fact, a field separate and distinct from church growth. In fact, some even criticized me for abandoning the field of church growth altogether because I had begun dealing so much with the spiritual factors!

Ed Silvoso Appears

Such criticism was bothersome enough to stir me to further action in order to try to verify empirically that my theories were correct. I knew that I needed a field laboratory to test the relationship of spiritual power to

church growth. God graciously met my need in a remarkable way by bringing Argentine Ed Silvoso to Fuller. His ministry, Harvest Evangelism, was
based both in Argentina and in San Jose, California. From our first en-
counter, I realized that Ed was one of the most brilliant leaders we had met,
and Doris and I became close friends with Ed and Ruth even until now. He
soaked up church growth principles like a sponge. Before he came, the
renowned Argentine revival had already started, but Silvoso had discovered
that it had seemed to bypass the city of Resistencia in northern Argentina.
As of the beginning of 1990, fewer than 6,000 of Resistencia's 400,000 population were evangelical believers, a mere 1.5 percent.

Silvoso took this as a challenge. In 1989, he went back to Argentina and
initiated a three-year *Plan Resistencia* (The Resistencia Plan) aimed at significant, measurable evangelism. He based it not only on the principles of church
growth that he had learned, but he also began incorporating some of the
principles of spiritual warfare that we were beginning to teach. He was able
to discern two major demonic strongholds over the small evangelical community in Resistencia, namely, a spirit of disunity and a spirit of apathy toward
the lost. With this in mind, his Harvest Evangelism team spent a year on site
laying a solid foundation of prayer, spiritual warfare and leadership training.

We now had our field laboratory in place. In 1990, Ed took Doris and me
to Resistencia, where we immediately felt at home because it reminded us so
much of nearby Bolivia. My assignment was to teach the leaders church
growth principles. But Doris was busy taking the spiritual temperature of
the city. What she discovered alarmed her. It became obvious that the believers had meager knowledge of intercession, strategic-level spiritual warfare
and warfare prayer. Unless this could be changed, the chances of a significant
evangelistic impact were slim. She sensed that God wanted to see it changed.

This was our opportunity to use Resistencia as an experiment to see if
spiritual factors could really make a difference for church growth. So we
started at the top and suggested to Ed that he bring Cindy Jacobs onto the
team. Ed had never heard of Cindy. We will not soon forget his first question:
"Can she preach?" When we finished chuckling and assured him that she
definitely could preach, he invited her to join us in *Plan Resistencia*. Doris and
Cindy made three more visits to Argentina in 1990 alone, introducing both
in theory and in practice the principles of strategic-level spiritual warfare.

My much-needed field laboratory experiment worked! Spiritual factors
made a huge difference. The evangelical population of Resistencia doubled in
1990 alone and continued after that! Silvoso says, "From the handful of 5,143

believers who were in the evangelical church population in 1988, the number has grown to over 100,000 in the entire city. The ominous control the devil exercised over the region has been replaced by open heavens, and the Church is impacting the city, the government, the media, and the schools."[1]

The Harvest Evangelism International Institute

Although I taught these things in Fuller, I knew that lasting paradigm shifts are more likely to take place on the field than in the classroom. So Silvoso and I got together in 1991 and launched the Harvest Evangelism International Institute (HEII), an annual training program for leaders that Ed would convene in Argentina. I served as the initial dean of HEII for five years. I offered credit to Fuller students who would attend, and many did. After I eventually dropped off, Cindy Jacobs stayed on as a faculty member for many more years, and at this writing, the institute continues. I summarized the many lessons I learned from HEII in my book *Warfare Prayer*.

This assignment tied me in very closely with the leaders of the Argentine Revival, one of the most outstanding revivals of our generation. Omar Cabrera had planted the seeds in the 1970s. I've already told about Doris's and my connection with Omar in chapter 6. Then Carlos Annacondia and many others came into the picture around the beginning of the 1980s. The revival, accompanied by extraordinary signs and wonders, demonic deliverances, strategic-level spiritual warfare, huge evangelistic harvests and the like lasted for 16 years, a very long shelf life for a revival. With the help of Pablo Deiros, whom I brought onto the School of World Missions faculty, we published a book, *The Rising Revival*, documenting the phenomenon firsthand.

Personal Spiritual Warfare

It's one thing to work on applying theories of spiritual warfare to church growth in the field, but it is another to face some of the battles personally. I know that it is difficult for many to understand that our enemy is a created personality absorbed with a passion for stealing, killing and destroying, a being with considerable intelligence and possessing supernatural powers that he employs for his evil tasks. He rules over an army of demonic spirits, which he uses extensively to accomplish his works of darkness.

Furthermore, he is known to focus his attention more on the servants of God who most directly threaten his efforts to maintain the dominion he usurped from Adam than on those who are either ignorant of his devices or who are indifferent to them. I believe that this is one reason why Doris and I found ourselves engaging the enemy in fairly close proximity throughout these years. As in any sustained warfare effort, those on the front lines inevitably experience some victories along with some hits. Let me give you a few examples.

As you might remember, I was not brought up in a religious home. We were a functional family, but for reasons I never understood, my parents would not even allow discussions about God or spiritual things. When I became a believer, naturally I began praying for my family to be saved. I found my sister, Margo, to be receptive, and she readily accepted Christ and was born again. However, we were not able to make any progress with my mother or father. My mother died unexpectedly, while we were in Bolivia, and my father remarried Phyllis. When we returned to America in 1971, we had good relationships, but still nothing about religious things. For years and years I prayed for my father daily, but I saw so little progress that at one point in time I actually reasoned that God knew my heart by then, and I dropped my father from my prayer list.

This could have had a sad ending, but it didn't. It turned out to be one of those victories. Only months before Dad died at age 87, when he was quite weak and undoubtedly knew that the end was coming, he let me bring up the subject, and without any hesitation he prayed the sinner's prayer and invited Jesus into his heart. My stepmother, Phyllis, said that she had wanted to be born again for years and she was more than ready. From then on, she regularly testified to her salvation until she died several years later.

Healing Through Deliverance

Paul Cedar believed that God heals in answer to prayer. That is why, when he designed the new sanctuary for Lake Avenue Church, he built a large, tastefully furnished prayer room located off the front of the worship center. At the end of each service, instead of giving an altar call for prayer in the auditorium itself, he would usually invite those who needed prayer for healing and other things to go to the prayer room where a team would be waiting to minister to them.

One Sunday morning, he surprised us all when he preached a whole sermon on supernatural healing, and he changed the ordinary pattern by stationing the ministry team in front of the church and inviting those who needed healing to come forward for prayer. The response was so overwhelming that

Cedar soon took the microphone and said, "We need some help here! Will others who pray for the sick, *like Peter and Doris Wagner*, please come forward?" So we quickly joined the ministry team.

I was excited when the first woman who asked me to pray fell right into my area of specialization—she had severe scoliosis in her back, which had pained her since her teens. The presence of God was so strong in that room that when I laid my hand on her back and began to pray, I could feel the crunch and the pop-pop-pop of the bones coming into place, straightening the curvature of the spine immediately! She was completely healed! As I was finishing, however, I noticed out of the corner of my eye that my friend Phyllis Bennett was waiting to be next.

Phyllis's husband, Dave Bennett, had served on the pastoral staff at LAC for a time. In fact, he performed my oldest daughter, Karen's, wedding. He was currently a PhD student in the Fuller School of Theology. As a part of his field research on leadership, he and Phyllis had recently spent a few months in India.

Phyllis told me she had been suffering from a terrible pain in her chest, which her doctor could not diagnose. Because it had symptoms similar to an ulcer, her doctor had put her on ulcer medication, even though an ulcer had not shown on the X-rays. But the pain persisted. Then she showed me an ugly rash on her left forearm where the flesh had actually begun to fall off in chunks.

As I prayed for Phyllis, I soon knew in my spirit that nothing was happening! So I began giving her some kind words of consolation and encouragement when I noticed that Doris had come up beside me. The next thing I knew, an intense look came on Doris's face, and she pushed me to one side. She said, "Let's take a different approach!" She told Phyllis to look into her eyes, and instantly Doris locked horns in the unseen world with a demonic spirit that she then knew Phyllis had picked up through a curse while in India. Because casting out demons was not the usual fare in our Congregational Church on Sunday mornings, Doris sternly commanded the spirit to be silent. After a minute or so, Phyllis's eyes suddenly opened wide with a look of terror, her body jerked for an instant, and then total peace. The evil spirit was gone! Paul Cedar walked up a moment or two later, and we said as nonchalantly as we could, "A demon just got cast out!" He seemed delighted.

The pain in Phyllis's chest was instantly healed! The doctor took her off the ulcer medication. Two weeks later she passed me in her car, rolled down the window and held out her left arm. The rash was well on its way to recovery—it had been caused by the medication she had been taking for the "ulcer"! What a wonderful victory this was!

The Ex-Priestess of San La Muerte

Since we are talking about warfare, I will include this other example of a victory, although it has a rather gruesome ending. When we began working with Ed Silvoso in *Plan Resistencia*, our spiritual mapping soon uncovered the fact that one of the territorial spirits that had Resistencia under its grip was San La Muerte, the spirit of death. Multitudes openly worshiped this spirit because, believe it or not, it promised them "a good death."

We were amazed at the desperation and hopelessness that must have been present in the hearts of those people who would be attracted to such a grotesque promise! "Death" was worshiped in no fewer than 13 shrines located around the city. Many people would take one of its idols, carved from human bone, and have it surgically implanted under their skin so that no matter where they went they would be assured of a good death!

A series of seminars on intercession, taught by Doris, Cindy Jacobs and others, sparked fervent aggressive prayer throughout the city. When the time came for the climactic evangelistic event, Doris and Cindy flew to Resistencia and were met with a startling piece of news. The week before they arrived, the high priestess of the cult of San La Muerte had been smoking in bed. She fell asleep, her bed caught on fire and only three things were consumed by the flames: her mattress, herself and her statue of San La Muerte, which was in another room! Nothing else in the adobe house was touched. The one who had promised others a good death, herself died a horrible death! The fear of God fell on the city!

This victory on the front lines of the battlefield for the kingdom of God helps explain in part the dramatic changes in Resistencia that I described previously.

Casualties of the War

Doris and I began going out to the front lines in Argentina in 1990. We soon found that spiritual warfare on this level has its casualties. Within months after the first trip, we had the worst family fight of now 59 years of marriage! We were hit with a severe problem concerning one of our close intercessors! Doris was incapacitated for almost five months with blown-out discs, back surgery and knee surgery! There is no question at all in our minds, or in the minds of our intercessors, that all of this and more was a direct backlash from the spirits who were so riled up by our invading their territory.

Our dining room in Altadena, California, was the first office when Global Harvest Ministries started in 1991. At the typewriter is Jean Van Engen, who was the wife of my School of World Mission faculty colleague, Chuck Van Engen. They were missionaries to Mexico.

In fact, right at that time, a number of our intercessors were staying in our home in Altadena, California. We all went out to dinner, and when we came home, our street was blocked with fire engines! Fortunately, it was not our house that was on fire, but it was the house right across the street, a house that we called the "drug store" because some kind of illicit drug activity had been going on there, not by the owners who were friends of ours, but by their adult children. The house was gutted, and we gave them some clothing and pieces of furniture to help them survive. When we regrouped, Alice Smith heard from the Lord. He told her that the fire had been intended for us through the spirit of death who had been infuriated by what Doris and Cindy had done in Argentina. The prayers of the intercessors in our home had diverted it across the street to the "drug store"!

It is not our nature to be cowardly. We got knocked down, but not out. We never were tempted to be deserters from the army of God, despite books that had been written in an attempt to cause us to be fearful of becoming needless casualties of war. We were constantly reminded that we were in the heat of the spiritual battle by some other near misses that the enemy sent our way, but we would not give the devil the satisfaction of our slowing down or backing up!

Near Misses

One of the near misses occurred when I was climbing a 12-foot stepladder into the loft in my garage where I had some important documents filed. I had done this on numerous occasions with no problem, but this time, while I was stepping from the ladder to the loft, something (I use this word advisedly!) pulled the ladder out from under me and I free-fell 12 feet onto the concrete floor, landing on the back of my head and neck. As I fell, I shouted so loudly that Doris came running out of the house and my next-door neighbor appeared also. They called 911, and the ambulance took me to the hospital. After a battery of X-rays and other tests, I was discharged with a clean slate of health!

What was going on? Twelve miles away, one of our intercessors was enjoying a Christian concert when she suddenly was interrupted by the Holy Spirit who told her that someone close to her, not one of her children, was in serious trouble and needed immediate intercession. She travailed fervently in tongues for 20 minutes at exactly the time I fell off the ladder! The power of her prayers, I am convinced, kept the enemy from taking me down, as he intended to do.

Another near miss came when Doris and I were flying in a private plane to Almolonga, Guatemala, with our friends Harold and Cecelia Caballeros of the El Shaddai Church in Guatemala City. Our intention was to do some spiritual espionage connected with the Spiritual Warfare Network in Central America. Almolonga was a city marvelously transformed by being delivered from bondage to the territorial spirit of the region, Maximón. Waiting for us on the ground near the dirt runway was Filiberto Lemus, an experienced warfare intercessor, spiritual mapper and member of the Spiritual Warfare Network. He began praying for us fervently when he saw the plane on the final approach with no landing gear exposed! Filiberto instantly sensed through the Holy Spirit that Maximón was attempting to kill the Wagners and the Caballeros as they entered his domain.

The airplane crashed into the runway before we knew what was happening. The belly ripped open and bushels of earth poured around us in the cabin like a waterfall! When the frightening jolts ended, cracking wings and twisting propellers, the plane was still upright, and we walked out, dirty but unharmed. We praised God for His protection, and we had no doubt that, once again, intercession had ruined the plans of the enemy!

Was it worth it? In chapter 5, I mentioned that our Lausanne Strategy Working Group had focused the attention of missiologists on the unreached peoples of the world. But we weren't sure how we should number them. By the time AD2000 started, some were suggesting there might be 16,000 of them or more. Doris and I knew that it would be next to impossible to mobilize people to pray for 16,000 people groups, so we urged Luis Bush to take the necessary steps to reduce the number to something more manageable, and he did. Through extensive research and consultation, AD2000 settled on 1,739 as the number of significantly large unreached peoples at the beginning of the decade of the 1990s.

What I am about to tell you may go down as one of the most amazing missiological reports of all time. Before the year 2000, all but 500 of the 1,739 unreached people groups had present at least an initial church planting movement, and many of the 500 remaining had a commitment from a sending agency poised to begin a pioneer work in that unreached people group. Was it worth withstanding the attacks of the enemy? No one with a heart for world evangelization would have doubted in the least that it was!

Territorial Spirits Turmoil

Controversies surrounding the theology and practice of strategic-level spiritual warfare or territorial spirits continued. The storms in Fuller Seminary had largely quieted, but not until one of our key School of World Mission faculty members, Paul Hiebert, resigned over his disagreements with the issue and went elsewhere to teach. However, many outside of Fuller continued to be upset with what we were doing in the AD2000 United Prayer Track. In fact, one outspoken critic wrote, "Wagner's wild and wacky ideas, doctrines and activities should be considered controversial and heretical!"

Whole books and sections of books were being written against me. One by Chuck Lowe, *Territorial Spirits and World Evangelization,* included no fewer than 167 quotes from my works, footnotes and all, with a refutation of each of my statements. After Lausanne II in Manila (at which time I resigned from LCWE), the ongoing Lausanne Committee had formed a new unit for the United States that began to raise issues about what I was doing. One leader wrote me and said, "There are concerns that

I have been picking up recently that the United Prayer Track is becoming a 'charismatic' track." Then, in 1993, the Intercession Working Group of LCWE found it necessary to release an official statement opposing the Spiritual Warfare Network (although not by name), warning of the dangers of such things as "a preoccupation with the demonic" and the "territorial spirits concept" and "warfare language" and "preoccupation with the powers of darkness," among other things.[2]

Crossroads with John Wimber

The most regrettable fallout of the turmoil, however, was a split between John Wimber and me over the issue. As you know, even after MC510 was cancelled in 1985, John and I continued working closely with each other. John's teaching in my D.Min. classes, including signs and wonders, was never interrupted. When I regrouped and began teaching new SWM courses on healing and spiritual power, I regularly invited John as a visiting lecturer. I was a frequent visitor to John's Vineyard Christian Fellowship. I knew he was somewhat uncomfortable with the concept of strategic-level spiritual warfare, but we both politely kept it under the surface as long as we could.

In December 1991, however, John finally surfaced the issue when he told my Fuller class that the two of us "seriously disagreed" with each other in our views of spiritual warfare. When I heard him say that, I immediately suspected that this might be the beginning of the end. I've said it before, but let me reiterate that I interpret my role as a seminary professor slightly differently from that of most academics. The norm in graduate schools of religion like Fuller is for the instructor to hold tentatively whatever views he or she might have in order to stimulate debates about varying points of view. This is called "critical thinking." Coming to a conclusion and acting on it is not usually characteristic of seminary professors, unless, of course, they are dealing with a clear boundary line between orthodoxy and heresy. Attempts to superimpose the professor's view on the students are frequently scorned as "indoctrination" rather than "education."

To the contrary, I see my role in a classroom as equipping the saints for the work of ministry (see Eph. 4:12). Students take my courses because they want me to impart to them what I have learned through research and experience. I invariably spark lively discussions on differing perspectives, but I do not allow my classes to become Socratic forums. By the time John

Wimber brought up our differences, I had gone through a careful process of formulating my conclusions regarding spiritual warfare, the SWN had been firmly established and I had no desire that my students be divided between two opinions on such a serious issue.

I wanted to confront the situation, but I wanted to do it with dignity and mutual respect. By this time, John and I had been working together and hanging out as friends through thick and thin for 20 years. So I initiated a serious, scholarly, written dialogue with John over strategic-level spiritual warfare, which ended up filling numerous pages of typewritten paper and lasting for almost two years. Working with John were a seminary professor, Jack Deere, and a prophet, John Paul Jackson. We did our best to change each other's minds, but to no avail. I consequently had to make the tough decision to discontinue John as a visiting lecturer in my courses, and we went different ways from then on. Fortunately, we enjoyed a very cordial personal meeting just a few months before he died.

Answering the Critics?

The more this turmoil continued, the more demands I had from many directions to refute my critics. Let me tell you why I didn't want to do this. Through most of my early years, I was fairly good at debating. During the years that I was a convinced cessationist and a separatist and anti-Pentecostal, I was quite polemical. By this I mean that I had strong inclinations to quote those who disagreed with me and formulate persuasive arguments to prove that they were wrong and I was right, at least to my satisfaction. Such pursuits had become a normal part of my professional lifestyle, which, by the way, was quite typical of academia in general. I labored under a felt need to preserve the "truth"!

For example, while I was leading the Strategy Working Group of the Lausanne Movement, I constantly found myself debating the priority of evangelism over social action. I had some staunch opponents, mainly the Latin American theologians who, as I explained in chapter 5, harshly criticized my book *Latin American Theology* back in 1970. After sparring with them and others for 10 years, I decided to write a definitive biblical, theological and ethical rationale defending my point of view, which I did in *Church Growth and the Whole Gospel*. I had a good library and a good filing system, so I was able to pull out accurate quotes from numerous opponents and present scholarly arguments on how wrong I thought they were. I was flattered when a prestigious, nonevangelical publisher like Harper & Row agreed to publish the book.

At that time, the Lord spoke clearly to me, and I have never forgotten the occasion. I had submitted my book to the publisher, but it had not yet been released. God first told me that He approved of what I had written, for which I was very grateful. But then He went on and said three words that I can quote: "No more polemics!" This was definitive as far as I was concerned. As we dialogued, God uncovered to me what I really had been doing behind the scenes in my writings. I had developed the terrible habit of making other people look bad so that I could look good! I repented of this selfish, arrogant, prideful attitude and—you can check out my writings—to the best of my recollection, I haven't done it since.

Still, all this did not relieve the pressure I was feeling to make a definitive, positive, non-polemical statement on strategic-level spiritual warfare. I had become a chief lightning rod for those who opposed what the SWN and the AD2000 United Prayer Track were doing worldwide, and many good people were hungry for answers. While I knew I couldn't be polemical, I still could write a straightforward theological apologetic, which I did. I wrote *Confronting the Powers*. In it, I did not quote or refute a single critic. However, I systematically compiled all the criticisms and dealt with each of the major ones by stating the essence of their objections and countering them with my point of view, chapter by chapter, as persuasively as I could. The book, unfortunately, did not have as great an impact as I had wished. For one thing, it was so theological that it appealed to a very limited audience. For another, those who had already formed contrary opinions, like John Wimber and his friends, were not at all open to possible change. And, ironically, some strongly criticized me for not taking on my opponents by name!

Adjusting to Prophecy

For us who have a cessationist background, the new element of the charismatic stream most difficult to accept is prophecy. We jokingly say that our Trinity was "Father, Son, and Holy Scripture!" Old Testament scholar Jack Deere, who was asked to leave the Dallas Theological Seminary faculty because he began attending a Vineyard church, has written undoubtedly the most persuasive scholarly book on the inadequacy of cessationism, *Surprised by the Power of the Spirit*. When he started writing it, he anticipated including a chapter on prophecy, but he soon realized that this was such a crucial subject that it required a whole book of its own, *Surprised by the Voice of God.* Deere said, "The most difficult transition for me in my pilgrimage was not in accepting that Scripture teaches that God heals and does miracles today through gifted believers. The thing I resisted the most, was most afraid of, and which took the most convincing was accepting that God still *speaks* today."[3] To expect that God might reveal anything to us outside the canon of Scripture was far beyond the boundaries of our theological comfort zone. We usually scorned it and rejected it as "extra-biblical revelation."

I might insert here that perhaps the most perplexing problem we cessationists had with that position was that our accepted biblical canon of 66 books, no more or no less, was never revealed to us in Scripture itself, even though we believed that the canon was given to us by the Holy Spirit. The canon itself, therefore, had to be a clear case of extra-biblical revelation. The Holy Spirit used human beings over a period of time to decide that the New Testament had 27 books and that the Apocrypha should not be included in the Protestant Old Testament. The Third Synod of Carthage in A.D. 397 decided on the New Testament's 27 books. The Old Testament of 39 books only (that Dallas Seminary accepts) was not finally established until the Protestant Reformation in the sixteenth century.

Be that as it may, during the Wimber years, with the focus on signs and wonders, prophecy played a subordinate role. Yes, Wimber believed in prophecy, and certain people routinely gave spontaneous "prophetic" words of encouragement or exhortation to the Vineyard congregation. However, it was only in late 1988 that John began connecting with some who were seriously recognizing the office of prophet. It began when Jack Deere arranged a phone conversation between Wimber and a prophet living in Texas, Paul Cain. Cain said that God had told him to go to California and visit Wimber. He added that, as a sign that this visit was truly from God, an earthquake would occur under Fuller Seminary the day he arrived! Wimber asked the normal Californian's question, "Will this be the 'big one'?" Cain said no, but the big one would occur the day after he left.

Sure enough, the day Cain arrived we had a 5.0 earthquake with the epicenter under Fuller, and I spent three days replacing the books on the shelves in my seminary office! Then the day after he left, a devastating world-class earthquake hit Armenia, killing tens of thousands of people. Even though I remained somewhat skeptical about prophecy, this was very impressive to me because not even the seismologists at Cal Tech could predict earthquakes.

A few months later, John invited Paul Cain to come and do the first Vineyard conference on prophecy in Anaheim. I was teaching a D.Min. course at the time, so the class decided to visit Anaheim Vineyard the first night of the conference to see for ourselves what this was all about. As it turned out, that was not one of Cain's better nights, and he did not perform well. He later explained that he was suffering from jet lag. We debriefed for some time in class the next morning, and we collectively agreed that prophecy may be all right for the Vineyard, but we didn't want very much to do with it at all.

Word of our class discussion got back to John, and he and Carol invited Doris and me to have dinner with them. I must confess that by the time that dinner was over, John had thoroughly convinced me that the new prophetic movement was real and that it needed to be an essential part of our ministry. However, I didn't have a clear understanding of what we were dealing with until I read Bill Hamon's *Prophets and Personal Prophecy*. Written from the charismatic perspective, Hamon's book frankly addresses both the strengths and weaknesses of the way prophecy has been taught and practiced for decades. It covers uses and abuses alike. It helped greatly to shift my paradigm.

From Theory to Practice

Now that I was comfortable with the theory of prophecy, I had little idea of how to put it into practice in ministry. However, it was just then that Doris and I had become aquainted with Cindy and Mike Jacobs, and we had discovered that Cindy knew a great deal about how prophecy works in real life. So I invited Cindy to be the speaker at our annual 120 Fellowship weekend retreat and teach us about prophecy.

Cindy not only taught us prophecy, but she suddenly announced to us the second day that she was actually going to prophesy! This was something different and slightly risky to us Congregationalists, most of whom may have heard about personal prophecy but had never been up close to it in this way. As I observed Cindy, however, I noticed that she was following all the rules that Bill Hamon had spelled out in his book. For one thing, she insisted on having all her prophecies tape-recorded so there would be no question later on about what she sensed God was saying through her.

The resulting ministry was truly remarkable, and to this day many attendees date important changes in their lives to that retreat. We transcribed and published the prophecies in our *Body Life* newsletter; and in

subsequent newsletters, many class members shared testimonies of healing in their lives. One prophecy that Doris and I will long remember was
the healing of some secret chronic addictions in our own nephew, Jonathan Mueller. A major consequence of his getting set free is the fact that
he now heads up the deliverance ministry in his church in Texas.

Gideon's Army

While we were getting things in order, like spiritual warfare and prophecy, the global prayer movement was mushrooming. As you will recall,
the Spiritual Warfare Network (SWN) was the largest initial component of
the AD2000 United Prayer Track. Over our first three years, 1990 to 1992,
about two dozen of us met privately several times. As we matured in our
understanding of strategic-level spiritual warfare, we decided to open SWN
to a wider audience with two events. The first would be an invitation-only
"International Spiritual Warfare Consultation" held in Korea, in 1993; the
second would be a "National Conference on Prayer and Spiritual Warfare"
open to the public in California.

Through the years, I had become friends with Sundo Kim, pastor of
the Kwang Lim Methodist Church in Seoul, actually the largest Methodist
church in the world. He invited me to speak to his congregation from time
to time, and on one occasion, he took me to tour his prayer mountain retreat center. I was very impressed with the quality of the prayer mountain.
I had been to David Yonggi Cho's prayer mountain several times, and I
couldn't help but compare the two. Cho's was the Greyhound bus while
Kim's was the Mercedes stretch limo, smaller but very high class. So I asked
Kim what it would take to use his prayer mountain for our international
SWN meeting. With characteristic Korean hospitality, he told me that not
only could we use the facility at no charge, but also that his church would
provide all our meals as a missions project!

We decided that we would invite 300 leaders to this event, and we
called it a "Gideon's Army." We scheduled it for October 1993, and in order to make sure we invited the right people, we held regional SWN meetings in Northern Europe, Oceania, and Southeast Asia earlier in the year.
One of the major differences between the AD2000 events and the former
Lausanne events had to do with financing. The Billy Graham Evangelistic
Association had paid the participants' travel expenses for the Lausanne
meetings, but AD2000 wisely insisted that their meetings be self-financed

with the leaders raising their own travel funds. In my mind, this was an important missiological advance, helping to break the syndrome of Third World financial dependency on the West that some of the pioneer missionaries unwittingly had established.

The 300 leaders showed up from every part of the globe, including, by the way, five from the Middle East. It was one of the most magnificent meetings I had ever led. Not only did we all quickly get on the same page as to how strategic-level spiritual warfare could pave the way for fulfilling the Great Commission on every continent, but the delegates also solidly networked with each other and cemented numerous personal relationships that would help their ministries enormously in the years to come. Many still point to the 1993 Gideon's Army meeting as a high point in their lives. The SWN had become truly international!

Before I go on, I need to tell one fascinating story. While the Kwang Lim Prayer Mountain was elegant, it was furnished for a Korean constituency. We hadn't anticipated this ahead of time, but when we arrived to spend the week, we found that the dormitories had no beds! Koreans are used to sleeping on the floor! However, most of our 300 were international dignitaries used to 4- or 5-star hotels! When Sundo Kim saw that I was beginning to panic, he told me to calm down. He immediately placed a telephone call to an army general who was one of his elders. Sure enough, before the day was over, army trucks began to roll in and, by night, everyone had a bed! This was an unforgettable happening, and my admiration for Kim's leadership abilities went off the charts!

National Conference on Prayer and Spiritual Warfare

Four months after Gideon's Army, we had scheduled our first public event in the United States, featuring what we had been learning about spiritual warfare on all three levels. In order to cover the up-front costs, John Maxwell, pastor of the Skyline Wesleyan megachurch in San Diego, agreed to help. His church had given me one of the best examples of vigorous church growth in the nation, and we had become good friends.

John did his Doctor of Ministry studies under me at Fuller. I began to use him in some of our Fuller Institute conferences to give him some national exposure. He joined my Global Harvest Ministries board, and for a time he served Doris and me as our fuctional pastor. As I have previously mentioned, he had put together the prototype of a pastor's prayer team, which helped me greatly to understand personal intercession. In fact, John's first book on leadership, *The Leader Within You,* was his doctoral dissertation. Since then, Maxwell has become arguably the nation's number-one trainer in leadership with his numerous subsequent books appearing as *New York Times* bestsellers and circulating more than 10 million copies!

We contracted for the use of the Melodyland Christian Center's facilities in Anaheim for the conference. Just to mention a few from our extensive list of speakers, we had Ed Silvoso, Cindy Jacobs, Doris Wagner, Dutch Sheets, John Dawson, Dick Eastman, George Otis, Jr., Alistair Petrie, Chuck Kraft, Joy Dawson, Frank Hammond, and many more. A couple thousand people showed up, which was more than we had planned for. We all did our best but, to be honest, the conference was disappointing, not to say a disaster! I'll spare the details, but few look back to the event as something special in their lives like we did Gideon's Army in Korea. A notable exception would be our youngest daughter, Becky, who first met her future husband, Jack, there at Melodyland!

Praying Through the Window

In 1991, Luis Bush awakened in the middle of the night while he was in Bangladesh and wrote me a letter. He said, "Peter, if we are to see a spiritual breakthrough and an advance of the gospel so that the church is established in the 10/40 Window by A.D. 2000, it is going to take an enormous prayer and fasting initiative. We need a mighty army of strategic-level prayer warriors saying: *Lord, give me the 10/40 Window or I'll die!* We need at least one million who are prepared to pray until breakthrough occurs." *One million?* I wondered if Luis was serious!

Not long after that a small group gathered with Doris in Colorado Springs to pray and seek God's direction. They boldly asked the question: "Might it be possible to do as Luis Bush suggests and mobilize one million Christians to pray for the nations and the unreached peoples of the 10/40 Window?" Their response: "Why not? Let's go for it!" They thought at the time they were exercising great faith. However, before it was over, they would look back and say, in undisguised delight, "Oh, we of little faith!"

The United Prayer Track went into action and we projected a series of "Praying Through the Window" initiatives in the month of October, every two years for the rest of the decade, starting in 1993. For *Praying Through the Window I,* we focused prayers on the 62 nations of the 10/40 Window. One million? Before we were through we had no fewer than 21 million believers around the world committed to praying for the same two nations on each of the 31 days of October 1993! We had published a prayer calendar and circulated it in multiple languages.

For *Praying Through the Window II,* we selected the "100 Gateway Cities" of the 10/40 Window and published not only a daily prayer calendar but also a book with a description of each one of the cities. We were able to account for 36 million believers praying in one accord through October 1995!

Praying Through the Window III was for the unreached peoples. The AD2000 Unreached Peoples Track had identified 1,739 unreached people groups of significant size in the 10/40 Window. The Prayer Track grouped them into 146 clusters for the prayer calendar and for another book that we then published. By now, counting was becoming more difficult, but our best estimate was that well over 50 million believers joined together in synchronized prayer through the month of October 1997.

Mixed with all of this were numerous innovative prayer initiatives throughout the world, such as Marches for Jesus, prayer journeys, prayer expeditions, spiritual mapping consultations, mobilizing children for prayer, praying through Ramadan, cardinal points prayer, prayerwalking and so many others that I remember announcing in an international AD2000 gathering in Korea, GCOWE '95, that the prayer movement was "out of control!" I then summarized a good bit of what we had learned in my book *Praying with Power,* which, by the way, is back in print.

Celebration Ephesus

Although it wasn't originally planned that way, "Celebration Ephesus" in 1999, the climactic event for the United Prayer Track, also became, by default, the last large international event of the whole AD2000 Movement. Luis Bush and Thomas Wang had envisioned the final celebration of the decade, which arguably had advanced the spread of the gospel worldwide more than any previous initiative, to take place in Jerusalem in the year 2000. I must say that I had my doubts when I first heard it.

Doris and I had gone to Jerusalem in 1996 for an event with Yonggi Cho, which included a March for Jesus. While we were there, we could not get over the pervasive and stifling grip that the spirit of religion had been able to maintain over the whole city. Could that demonic force be overcome?

Because AD2000 embraced Christian leaders from virtually every nation in the world, including Arab nations, which were declared enemies of Israel, I could hardly imagine the Israeli government, for whom freedom of religion has never been a high value, issuing visas to all who needed to attend. Despite four years of preparation, generous financing and glowing promises from the Israeli government, circumstances unfortunately turned around and the meeting had to be cancelled. Thomas Wang later lamented that it was "the saddest moment in the Movement's history."

Fortunately, Celebration Ephesus, held a year previously, turned out to be one of the greatest moments of the decade, even though it was sponsored by only one of the tracks, namely, the United Prayer Track. One of our major initiatives, in cooperation with YWAM, had been the "Reconciliation Walk," a massive demonstration of identificational repentance on the part of Christians for atrocities committed by our ancestors at the time of the Crusades against innocent Muslims and Jews. For two years committed prayer warriors walked every step of the known routes of the Crusades in a mode of intercession and identificational repentance. I helped send the group off from Cologne, Germany, the starting point of the Crusades, and Doris and I joined them a year later in Istanbul, Turkey.

While in Turkey, we also toured the restored ruins of the ancient city of Ephesus, including the stadium in which the followers of Diana of the Ephesians had rioted against the apostle Paul. As a small prophetic act, I actually read the Reconciliation Walk statement of repentance to our Muslim Turkish guide, and he was visibly moved by the gesture. After we had done that, God gave me, during a time of meditation, one of the few literal visions I have ever had. He showed me the stadium, which had been very nicely restored, full of believers with banners praising Jesus Christ. Because the idol worshipers in Paul's time had shouted, "Great is Diana of the Ephesians" for *two* hours, God showed me a picture of Christians lifting up praises to Jesus in the same place for *four* hours!

The Centerpiece and the Finale

When we returned home, we got to work. *Praying Through the Window IV* had been scheduled for October 1999. By then, however, the prayer movement had grown so rapidly with different initiatives starting spontaneously all over the place that coordinating it like we used to do was no longer possible. We decided to make what we were now calling "Celebration Ephesus" the centerpiece for the United Prayer Track in October 1999, and we also realized that with it the activities of the Prayer Track per se would come to an end.

We sent word out to the people in our network that we had been building for years, and 5,000 of them from 62 different nations of the world found their way to Ephesus at their own expense. The weather was beautiful. Ross Parsley and the huge worship team and choir from New Life Church in Colorado Springs anchored the meeting for us. There were no sermons or exhortations, but just prayers and prophetic declarations from dozens of the top leaders of the many, many nations represented in the prayer movement. It was a literal fulfillment of the vision God had given me, namely, nonstop anointed worship for four hours in the very place featured in Acts 19. Many have since commented that it was the most exalted worship experience of their whole lifetime.

The finale was spine tingling. During Gideon's Army in 1993, Pastor Sundo Kim had brought his Kwang Lim Methodist Choir to the Prayer Mountain for a concert one of the evenings we were there. The group loved it, so I approached Kim about the possibility of taking his choir to Turkey in order to conclude Celebration Ephesus with their rendition of the "Hallelujah Chorus" from Handel's *Messiah*. He was delighted! The choir of 100 voices, as well as an orchestra with the exact 16 instruments for which Handel composed his piece, flew from Korea at their own expense along with a $20,000 cash gift for the victims of the recent earthquake in Turkey. Before they finished their number, done with the highest degree of professionalism, there was hardly a dry eye in the Ephesus stadium!

We finished Celebration Ephesus and the decade-long work of the AD2000 United Prayer Track with our minds and hearts resounding with:

The Lord Almighty reigneth!
Hallelujah! Hallelujah! Hallelujah! Hallelujah!
Ha- - - - le- - - -lu- - - -jah!!!

Notes

1. Ed Silvoso, *Transformation* (Ventura, CA: Regal, 2007), p. 162.
2. LCWE Intercession Working Group, "Statement on Spiritual Warfare: A Working Group Report," *World Evangelization*, December 1993, pp. 18-19.
3. Jack Deere, *Surprised by the Power of the Spirit* (Grand Rapids, MI: Zondervan Publishing House, 1993), p. 212 (emphasis his).

9

The Pierce Era
(1999–)

Introduction

When I arrived back home in Colorado Springs after Celebration Ephesus, I was exhausted. I don't mean that I was just a little tired, but way beyond that. Managing the AD2000 United Prayer Track had extracted eight strenuous years from my life. I was teaching more than a full-time load in Fuller Seminary and doing church growth conferences across the United States. During those eight years, I wrote the six-volume *Prayer Warrior Series* plus no fewer than 13 other books, to say nothing about relocating our home and Global Harvest Ministries from California to Colorado and building the World Prayer Center. I was 69 years old!

With all that, I felt a serious need to sit back, take my foot off the accelerator and coast along for a good while. I needed some quality R & R. Needed it? No, I felt I *deserved* it!

However, such was not to be.

No sooner had I unpacked my bags than prophet Chuck Pierce, supposedly my friend, approached me with a serious look on his face. He said, "Peter, are you still the apostle of the global prayer movement?" I immediately recognized it as a leading question, so I replied, "Of course," and waited for the other shoe to drop. It did! As it was dropping, I had to admit to myself that even during Celebration Ephesus, numbers of international prayer leaders who were close to me and whom I respected very much had come up and asked me, "What's next?" I cheerfully told them all that I had no answer for their question, and furthermore, I didn't know if or when I ever would have an answer.

But Chuck Pierce put a quick end to my lethargy. He looked me in the eye and said, "Peter, as the apostle of the global prayer movement, you are the one responsible for casting the vision for all of us. If you do not seek the Lord for the next vision right now, we are in danger of losing the incredible momentum that God has been granting us for a whole decade!" So much for my well-deserved R & R!

The 40/70 Window

I, of course, knew what I had to do. I began to pray and simply said, "Lord, where do You want us to go in the future?" I wish I could report that I had done a 40-day, or even a 3-day, fast! I didn't even play worship music and bask for a time in the presence of God. I steered away from embellishing my prayer with a touch of passionate eloquence. In fact, I prayed the prayer in the shower the morning after Chuck had spoken to me.

After breakfast, when I had gone to my desk in my home office, the revelation began to come thick and fast. I took out a yellow pad and began writing what I felt the Lord was giving me. I started with the fortieth parallel, and instead of counting 30 degrees *south* to the tenth, I counted 30 degrees *north* to the seventieth. This time we would no longer be praying through the 10/40 Window, but rather we would pray through the 40/70 Window. At around 10:30, I called Doris in her office in the World Prayer Center and told her to order some Taco Bell food and call the whole staff together for lunch in the conference room.

After we had eaten, I announced to the staff that God had just given us our next assignment. On one wall of the conference room we had a large map of the world with the 10/40 Window outlined in red yarn, which was held in place with push pins. I went over to the map, removed the two push pins on the tenth parallel, moved them north, and replaced them on the seventieth parallel. "There is our new prayer target!" I announced.

You would think I had lit the fuse on a fireworks display! The high voltage affirmation all around the table that this was truly what the Spirit was now saying to the churches was shocking. After a while, I noticed that Chuck Pierce hadn't been saying much. When things quieted down, I asked him what he was thinking. With a wry smile on his face, he nodded and said, "I've known for some time that we would be heading in that direction! Every demon in hell has just gone crazy!" As soon as he spoke, I feigned irritation and said, "Well, if you already knew, why didn't you tell me?" He nonchalantly replied, "If I had told you, it would have been *my* vision. You're the apostle. It needed to be *your* vision!" As usual, he was right.

The Pierce Era

I am well aware that I have just introduced a number of new names and thoughts that need considerable explanation, including Chuck Pierce, a Wagner home in Colorado Springs, the World Prayer Center, the 40/70 Window and apostles. I will weave the rest in as we go along, but first I want to pick up the Chuck Pierce thread and tell why this chapter is named "The Pierce Era."

How did Chuck Pierce come into the picture?

Our youngest daughter, Becky, who, as you know, was born in Bolivia, had been going through a very difficult transition in her life around 1990. Much to our amazement, Cindy Jacobs came to the rescue and invited Becky to move from her home near us in Pasadena, California, to Weatherford, Texas, where Cindy and Mike lived. Becky would help Cindy set up her first office for Generals of Intercession.

While Becky was still in junior high, she began working part-time in our Fuller Evangelistic Association office, and this continued through high school. By the time she graduated, she had developed skills in almost every aspect of office procedure. She had no inclination to go to college, so she continued on our staff full-time. Her education by apprenticeship had prepared her for what awaited in Texas.

Up to then, Cindy had managed Generals of Intercession from a makeshift desk in her living room. Mike had just left his employment at American Airlines to join with Cindy more actively in the ministry. Becky's work was cut out for her because Cindy had never been amenable to the details of office administration and things around that makeshift desk had not been too well organized. Soon, however, they came into shape and the office was moved to leased facilities outside of the home. The Generals' office soon began to function quite smoothly.

After this had been going on for a while, Doris and I began to hear from Becky about this person, who had connected with Cindy's ministry, named Chuck Pierce. Like many others, Chuck happened to be attending one of Cindy's conferences in Weatherford when Cindy called him out of the crowd for a prophetic word. She said, "You have a call similar to mine. You are called to bring healing to nations." When Chuck later asked her how she did this, he was as amazed at her response as I was at that lunch I told about in Washington, D.C., where Doris and I first met her.

As their friendship grew, Cindy visited Chuck along with his pastor, Robert Heidler, at Glory of Zion church in nearby Denton. During that meeting, God spoke directly to Cindy and said, "I want you to hire this young man (Chuck) and introduce him to Peter Wagner and Dutch Sheets!" Cindy obeyed, and it is comforting to know that our relationship with Chuck began with a prophetic word from God. That was in 1990, and within a year after that, Chuck began working with Generals of Intercession.

Right-Brained and Left-Brained

Pierce, a Baptist, had spent years in the business world, working in the oil industry. He had gone from being over the missions committee of his church in Houston, to serving as executive director of a local mission that helped restore young boys' lives, to being prayer director and mission executive for an organization that worked in the former Soviet Union and closed Eastern Bloc countries. God had gifted him as an intercessor and a prophet, but he was different from the stereotypical prophetic intercessor. Instead of being only right-brained, as most of them are, Pierce was equally left-brained. Besides doing some traveling ministry with Generals of Intercession, Chuck visited the office every week or two. Becky soon looked forward to Chuck's visits.

The fact is, Cindy Jacobs is wired for high voltage. Being both prophetic and creative, she never seems to be content with the status quo. New ideas and new projects are drawn to her like moths to a flame. Even though Becky tried to keep order in the office, for the most part, she was only partially successful. Then when things would seem uncontrollably chaotic, in would come Chuck Pierce, like a masked man on a white horse, for a day. Before he left, Becky would tell us, everything would be completely in order. She later found that Chuck had done graduate work in systems management!

So Doris and I were well briefed before we met Chuck Pierce in person. You may recall that around that same time, Doris and Cindy were making their frequent trips to Argentina with Ed Silvoso for *Plan Resistencia*. I had started inviting Cindy to lecture on spiritual warfare to my Fuller Seminary students from time to time, and we were busy organizing the Spiritual Warfare Network, as I explained in chapter 7. On a visit to California, in September 1991, Cindy was able to bring Chuck over to our house in Altadena, and we met him for the first time in our dining room. We bonded immediately, and our working relationship has grown and matured through the years until we have now informally adopted Chuck Pierce as our son and heir to Global Harvest Ministries. But I am getting ahead of the story!

New Tributaries

Speaking of the story, many new tributaries seem to spring up and begin to flow into the stream of my life. In the past, I somehow thought that the newest tributary was the most crucial and strategic one for the kingdom of God so far, and that it might well be the last. Over time, however, I discovered that evidently no stream was meant to be the last. From the moment I undertake a new assignment, I have learned to be on the watch for signs of the next. I sometimes look with no little envy at friends who graduated with me from seminary and who have spent an entire career concentrating on and perfecting one, and only one, area of ministry. One part of me wishes that I had the attention span and relatively uncomplicated life that they have had, but another part of me craves the adrenaline-stimulating challenge of a new assignment.

As you would have noticed, the style I am following, especially in the latter parts of this book, is not so much a chronological year-by-year narrative as it is a topical approach. I have taken things like our missionary career or the Church Growth Movement or the United Prayer Track to the end, although other important things had been going on simultaneously. This pattern will be even more evident in "The Pierce Era" chapter because I think it will be best to immerse ourselves in one tributary at a time. For that purpose, I am dividing the chapter into several parts. Keep in mind that the tributaries are all interrelated because they flow into the same stream, but each one has its distinct contribution to the big picture. The first one I want to describe has to do with the biblical government of the church.

Part 1: Establishing the Government of the Church

As you may recall, up through the 1960s, I was a card-carrying cessationist. Then, when I became aware of the disproportionate impact that the Pentecostal movement was having on Latin America, I gradually opened up to appreciating what the Holy Spirit had been doing through Pentecostals, but without desiring to become one. Through it all, even since the mid-1950s, I taught frequently on spiritual gifts, and I would always include the long list of biblical gifts in my teaching. Two of them on the list, of course, were the gifts of apostle and prophet. Even though I might have been regarded as inconsistent by my strict cessationist friends, surprisingly enough, I cannot recall ever suggesting that apostles and prophets were necessarily restricted to the early church, and consequently were not expected to be active in today's church.

For example, in my book *Your Spiritual Gifts Can Help Your Church Grow*, which first appeared back in 1979, I gave this definition of "apostle": "The gift of apostle is the special ability that God gives to certain members of the Body of Christ to assume and exercise general leadership over a number of churches with an extraordinary authority in spiritual matters that is spontaneously recognized and appreciated by those churches."[1] Even though I would fine-tune it a bit later, it wasn't a bad definition. So when the time came, I found myself open to the possibility of contemporary apostles, and contemporary prophets as well.

I began seriously to consider the apostolic movement in 1993. How did this happen?

Church Growth Methodology

You may remember that applying the four questions of church growth methodology helped me greatly in learning to appreciate and admire the Pentecostals in Latin America back in the late 1970s. This led to my paradigm shift out of cessationism. Once again, applying the same four questions produced the breakthrough in my mind concerning our contemporary apostolic movement.

By way of reminder, here are the questions once again:

1. Why does the blessing of God rest where it does?
2. Churches are not all equal. Why is it that at certain times, some churches are more blessed than others?
3. Can any pattern of divine blessing be discerned?
4. Do those churches that seem to be unusually blessed have any common characteristics?

As of 1993, it was becoming evident that on a worldwide scale the churches of the Global South (formerly called the "Third World") were experiencing more blessing than those of the Global North (formerly called the "Western World"). All missiologists were aware of three of the most outstanding examples: (1) the African Independent Churches; (2) the Chinese house churches; and (3) the Latin American grassroots churches. Only a few, however, would have recognized a fourth, namely, the American independent charismatic churches. I happened to be one of them because in the mid-1980s, I accepted the assignment to research and write an in-depth article on church growth for the definitive *Dictionary of Pentecostal and Charismatic Movements.* That research uncovered the fact that, at that time, the independent charismatic churches had become the fastest-growing group of churches in our nation.[2]

The Most Radical Change Since the Reformation

While studying these four movements, I came to realize that, indeed, a pattern of divine blessing today is discernable (question #3). In fact it became evident that we were looking at *the most radical change in the way of doing church since the Protestant Reformation!* If that is the case, question #4 needed to be answered. What are their common characteristics? Eventually, I was able to list nine radical changes, which are found in my book *The New Apostolic Churches.* But of all nine, the most radical change was apostolic leadership. This revelation came so clearly and precisely that I can still remember where I was sitting when it did come, namely, in a Fuller missions faculty discussion in the school's conference room.

From that day on, I became increasingly convinced of the immediate significance of Ephesians 2:20: "[The church has] been built on the foundation of the apostles and prophets, Jesus Christ Himself being the chief cornerstone." I have also paid much more careful attention to Ephesians 4:11: "And He Himself gave some to be apostles, some prophets, some evangelists, and some pastors and teachers." Apostles and prophets did not finish their task after the first century or two of the Christian movement; rather their ministry has never ceased throughout the whole history of the church. Not all churches today recognize this true biblical government of the church, but those that do constitute the new wineskin for churches of the foreseeable future.

"Authority" and "Individuals"

The core difference in these new wineskin churches is clearly *the amount of spiritual authority delegated by the Holy Spirit to individuals.* The operative words in this statement are "authority" and "individuals." Previously, church authority resided only in groups such as church councils or presbyteries or general assemblies or boards of elders or synods or other similar democratically oriented entities, but not in individuals. We are now seeing a transition from bureaucratic authority to personal authority, from legal structure to relational structure, from control to coordination, and from rational leadership to charismatic leadership (to use Max Weber's terms). This plays out on two levels, namely, the local church level and the translocal level.

On the local church level, the pastor is the *leader* of the church rather than an *employee* of the church. The church elders serve and support the pastor rather than supervising him or her. Pastors hire and fire staff, and they control the budget. Tenure is expected to be for life, not just for a number of years as in most traditional churches. The final authority in the church is the senior pastor.

Translocally, the final authority resides in the apostle. The apostle establishes an apostolic network of a number of churches, which is glued together relationally, not legally. Pastors and their churches remain in their apostolic network as long as the apostle adds value to them, and vice versa. This is a creative alternative to denominations.

I detail how these radical changes are occurring in multiple aspects of church life in my textbook *Churchquake!* published in 1999.

Where Do I Fit?

It is one thing to recognize that apostles are actually functioning in our churches today, but it is another thing to come to terms with how someone like me fits in. When these ideas began to congeal in my mind in 1993, my basic self-image was that of a teacher and a scholar. As I write this, however, my self-image has evolved. First I began to suspect that I might, indeed, have a gift and calling of an apostle. When I had come to terms with this, I referred to myself as a teacher-apostle. Now it has morphed to apostle-teacher. I am still a teacher, but my primary assignment from God is to serve as an apostle.

How did this change come about?

As I explained in chapter 8, by 1993, I had completed my transition out of cessationism by starting to believe in prophecy, the phenomenon that God reveals information directly to individuals. Some of this information is specifically for certain people, which would be labeled "personal prophecy." In 1989, Doris and I decided to begin a prophetic journal in which we would transcribe and preserve some of the personal prophecies we began receiving from time to time. By this writing, we have a total of 159 pages of single-spaced material. Looking back through the journal, it is interesting to see how some prophets had been hearing from God about my role as an apostle.

Three Prophetic Words

The first word was from Cindy Jacobs, an I-2 intercessor, during a conference she was holding in 1995, while she was still living in Colorado Springs: *The Lord would say today, "My son, Peter, today I put the anointing of apostle of prayer upon you. I put the mantle upon you of an Abraham, a patriarch, and I'm calling you forth into the land of promise."*

A couple of months later, I received a letter from one of our I-3 intercessors who lived in Dallas, Margaret Moberly, who was not in the habit of writing us personally at all: *An apostolic door has been sovereignly opened for you by the Lord Himself. Neither man nor demon will be able to shut it!*

I knew enough to take these words seriously, but as time moved on, I gradually dismissed them from my mind. I, apparently, wasn't ready to be "Apostle Peter"!

A couple of years went by, and in 1998, we were holding one of our GHM conferences, "Building Foundations for Revival," in Dallas, using the facility at Covenant Church. When I run conferences, I invariably keep them under strict control time-wise, but this one somehow got out of order, especially with unplanned prophecies springing up and even messages in tongues, which I had prohibited up to then. I was sitting in the front row, struggling to plan how I could get things back under control, when somehow or other I found myself kneeling on the platform with Jim Stevens of Christian International getting ready to prophesy over me in public. How I got there I still don't know! I glanced up and there was Charles Doolittle, one of our recognized intercessors, standing over me. Charles was a six-foot-four muscular African-American police officer on the Glendale, California, police force, with an aggressive look on his face and holding a huge three-foot sword over my head! I quickly decided that I'd better behave myself and listen carefully! Here is what Jim Stevens said:

> Even from this day forward, even from this national conference, there shall be a release on your spirit. Whether you want to say "apostle" or not is of no effect, says God. The title shall rest, the anointing shall rest, and men will give it to you. It is not something you have sought for your own; men will place it upon your back and upon your spirit and they will draw the apostolic from you!

I have since considered that time to be my prophetic ordination as an apostle. From then on I knew that God had called me to be an apostle, but I still couldn't bring myself to talk about it outwardly because I didn't know what kind of apostle I was. By then I had met and interacted with many recognized apostles, and I knew that I wasn't like any of them. They were all leaders of apostolic networks and they had numbers of churches and ministries, which they oversaw. I did not have a network, nor did I have a desire for one.

It was then that a friend from England suggested to me that there might be a difference between "vertical" apostolic networks and "horizontal" apostolic networks. Vertical networks would be the kind I have just described; the kind, for example, that the apostle Paul led. Horizontal networks, on the other hand, would involve bringing together leaders from different streams for certain purposes. The apostle James would have done this in the Council of Jerusalem. Eureka! That is exactly what I do! Organizing the international prayer movement would be a good example. That is probably why the first prophetic word I received from Cindy Jacobs mentioned "apostle of *prayer*."

The New Apostolic Roundtable

From then on, I outwardly began to recognize that I was, indeed, an apostle, and I actually tried functioning as one. Among other things, in 1999, I organized and led a group of around 20 vertical apostles, calling it the New Apostolic Roundtable (NAR). The fact of the matter is that most vertical apostles minister full-time in their own spheres of authority and they rarely have opportunities for meaningful interaction with their peers. They loved getting together with each other in NAR! We would meet annually for two days, catching up with each other and discussing issues that were important to us.

Chuck Pierce, of course, was a member of NAR, and, as we had been doing in the world prayer movement, we functioned as apostle and prophet and attempted to model to others how a team like this could function. In one of the meetings, we were discussing the issues of how apostles were officially recognized as such by the Body of Christ. This brought up the difference between the *gift* and the *office* of apostle. What is the difference? The gift of apostle is given by the grace of God to those whom He chooses (see 1 Cor. 12:11,28). Such is not the case with the office. The office is not given by grace; it is awarded by works. The works are the fruit of the gift, exhibited over a period of time in the life and ministry of the apostle. God does not give the office, but rather the Body of Christ, through its appropriate representatives, commissions the apostle on the basis of the fruit that has been observed. The church gives the office.

Before we finished discussing this, Bill Hamon looked at me and said, "Peter, have you ever been commissioned an apostle?" I had never given it much thought, and I answered, "I don't think so. Who could even do it?" Without a moment's hesitation, he stood up and said, "We can do it right now! C'mon!" The next thing I knew, the whole group of apostles (representing the Body of Christ) had surrounded me with prayers and prophecies and together they anointed me with oil and commissioned me an apostle. From that time on, I officially had the office.

Please notice one thing in passing: Some detractors of the apostolic movement scornfully refer to "those self-appointed apostles." Apostles do not appoint themselves. God gives them the gift, and the church gives them the office. You can see from what I have said that this was not something I personally desired or strived for. It took me three years from the time I first knew I was an apostle until I would agree to accept the title. In fact, I once did a survey of more than 100 recognized apostles and I found that the time it had taken them to accept the title ranged from 1 year to 10 years, and the average was 3 years, as happened to be my case. There is no such thing as a *true* "self-appointed apostle"! I italicized *"true"* because certainly there are some *false* apostles who have appointed themselves. However, in this book I am only referring to true apostles.

What Is an Apostle?

The literature on apostolic ministry had been quite sparse in those days, and in the books I had found I could not locate a clear definition of what an apostle was, at least a definition that satisfied me. It took me quite a while to fashion one of my own, but the conclusion I came to has been fairly well accepted by leaders in the movement.

"An apostle is a Christian leader gifted, taught, commissioned and sent by God with the authority to establish the foundational government of the Church within an assigned sphere of ministry by hearing what the Spirit is saying to the churches and by setting things in order accordingly for the expansion of the kingdom of God."[3]

With this as a beginning, over the years I went on to develop a four-page position paper on "What Is an Apostle?" I also wrote five books on different aspects of apostolic ministry, some of which soon became obsolete, so I combined my thoughts in a sixth book, *Apostles Today,* which is hopefully my last book on apostles.

I am supposed to function as a horizontal apostle, which means that I bring Christian leaders together for different Kingdom-oriented purposes. I don't have any personal qualities or abilities to do such things on

Chuck D. Pierce (left), Founder of Glory of Zion International and Global Spheres, Inc.

In one of his rare seemingly relaxed moments, Chuck Pierce, in our home in Colorado Springs, is likely hearing from the Lord as to what next steps need to be taken for Global Harvest Ministries to remain in the stream of God. His title is "GHM Watchman."

my own, but I do see the Holy Spirit activating my gift in remarkable ways. I think, for example, of Celebration Ephesus, which I told about in the last chapter. Imagine 5,000 leaders from 62 nations accepting my invitation to come together for one day in the restored ancient stadium of Ephesus, all at their own expense. I recall that Billy Graham had paid something like $25 million to convene a similar event, but this one cost me nothing except our own travel expenses. In fact, we left behind $70,000 for Turkey's earthquake relief! This has to be the Holy Spirit!

A Name for the Movement

As soon as I began understanding this new wineskin movement of the church, I realized that it was going to need a name. After a number of unsuccessful attempts, I thought I had struck gold, namely, "The Post-denominational Church." For more than 400 years, the most functional structure for the Protestant church had been denominations. We now had a new structure radically different from denominations, so "postdenomi-national" sounded ideal. In fact, I began using it and writing articles on it. But not for long! All of a sudden I began getting letters from some good friends who were denominational executives. They were furious (to put it mildly!) because my newly coined term "postdenominational" clearly im-plied that the denominations they were leading had now become irrele-vant and relics of the past. The most forceful was Jack Hayford of the International Church of the Foursquare Gospel who, at a luncheon with fellow Christian leaders, persuasively convinced me that what I was doing should not be labeled "postdenominational."

After I left that luncheon, it quickly became clear to me that it would not be wise to lose friends over a name. So I wrote Jack and the other de-nominational executives a letter telling them I now realized they were right and that I would cease and desist.

The only catch in the change was that at the time I had already an-nounced a National Symposium on the Postdenominational Church to be held at Fuller Seminary in May 1996, so we had to live with the name a bit longer.

The gathering was amazing. Nothing like it had ever been convened previously. Around 500 leaders attended, and I was able to get almost 50 of them onto the platform to address the gathering. Bill Hamon says the meet-ing "was a historical occasion in God's annals of Church history. It was prophetically orchestrated by the Holy Spirit to fulfill God's progressive purpose of bringing His Church to its ultimate destiny."⁴ I realized again that it was only the anointing of God through my gift as a horizontal apostle that enabled me to call such a meeting.

But I still needed a better name.

The New Apostolic Reformation

After much struggle, the name I settled on for the movement I had been attempting to recognize is the New Apostolic Reformation (NAR).

I used the word "reformation" because, as I have said, these new wineskins appear to be producing at least as radical a change as those of the Protestant Reformation 500 years ago. The word "apostolic" connotes a strong focus on outreach, plus a recognition of present-day apostolic ministries. Furthermore, the affirmation of the contemporary gift and office of apostle undoubtedly constitutes the most radical of all the changes from the old wineskin to the new.

I added the word "new" because I found that many traditional denominations had incorporated "apostolic" into their official names but, nevertheless, they are now old wineskins. The name "New Apostolic Reformation" attempts to distinguish the new wineskin churches from them.

What, precisely, is the New Apostolic Reformation?

The New Apostolic Reformation is an extraordinary work of God that is changing the shape of Protestant Christianity around the world. For some 500 years, Christian churches have largely functioned within traditional denominational structures of one kind or another. Particularly beginning in the 1990s, but having roots going back for more than a century, new forms and operational procedures have been emerging in areas such as local church government, interchurch relationships, financing, evangelism, missions, prayer, worship, leadership selection and training, the role of supernatural power, prophecy and other important aspects of church life. Some of these changes are being seen within denominations themselves, but for the most part, they are taking the form of loosely structured apostolic networks. In virtually every region of the world, as Philip Jenkins has documented, these new apostolic churches constitute the fastest-growing and most influential segment of Christianity.⁵

The only final verification that any new terminology is useful is that other people begin using the terms. This, I am happy to report, is actually happening. You will find "NAR" in quite extensive use on the Internet, especially by critics of the movement. In fact, during the 2008 election, some liberals vilified Sarah Palin as being affiliated with the NAR! Although I cannot verify any direct connection, I do hope that such allegations did not contribute to her failure to be elected vice president!

Apostolic Ministries

Once I recognized that I had the spiritual gift of apostle, and particularly after my commissioning by the New Apostolic Roundtable, I found myself using more and more of my time in apostolic ministries. From time to time, for example, certain other apostles would approach me with requests that I agree to be their apostolic "covering." It took a while to work this through in prayer because I had no desire to become a vertical apostle. Over time, however, the Lord indicated that He wanted me to provide alignment (we have now found "alignment" to be a much more satisfactory term than "covering") to some fellow apostles. As I analyzed it, I concluded that the New Apostolic Roundtable was simply a fellowship group with no mechanism for formal alignment.

In order to move forward, I then disbanded the New Apostolic Roundtable and organized Eagles Vision Apostolic Team (EVAT) in 2000. While some members moved from one to the other, some didn't. I agreed to provide primary apostolic alignment to those who decided to join EVAT, but I specified that it was an alignment with individuals only, not with the churches or networks or ministries that they represented. This is how I avoided establishing a pure vertical network. It obviously wasn't exactly a horizontal network either. I have sometimes thought about calling it a "diagonal network"!

In order to seal the covenant relationship, EVAT members agreed to contribute a monthly sum toward my salary and benefits. The Global Harvest Ministries board of directors fixes the amount of my salary, and the EVAT contributions have generally covered what was required. We keep in touch through an annual meeting, as well as through seeing each other frequently during the year. I set the membership limit at 25, and this is the closest apostolic group to whom Doris and I relate. The mutual admiration and support contribute greatly to the effectiveness of our ministries.

International Coalition of Apostles

While EVAT provides my deepest apostolic relationships, the International Coalition of Apostles (ICA) provides the broadest. I have built ICA on the model of a professional society of peer-level, mutually recognized apostles. Up to 400 apostles, 25 percent of whom live outside of the United States, have agreed to pay dues, attend an annual meeting and adhere to the professional standards of Christian apostles.

ICA came about as the result of a spontaneous meeting of several apostles in Singapore in 1999. I do not have a record of all who were there, but I am sure of Ed Silvoso, Lawrence Khong and John Kelly. They all agreed that there should be some organization that brought apostles together, and John Kelly was the one who picked up the ball and established the first ICA office in Ft. Worth, Texas. While Kelly, a vertical apostle, was the founder of ICA, he soon recognized that my gift of horizontal apostle might be more effective in running the organization than his, so he invited me to become ICA's presiding apostle. We then moved the office to Colorado Springs under Global Harvest Ministries.

Let me pause and point out how different ICA is from apostolic ministries of the past generation, many of which were characterized by a lust for power and control. When I say this, I have no intention of degrading the pioneers of the apostolic movement who arose post-World War II, such as the leaders of the Latter Rain Movement. They were pioneers. They were risk-takers. Their positive contributions to God's kingdom far overshadowed any mistakes they might have made!

However, the new generation is different, as exhibited by John Kelly. With the mandate he received for ICA, he could easily have pushed on through and built his own kingdom. But Kelly's greater desire was for the kingdom of God. He then approached me, and along with me, Chuck Pierce, and through the years the three of us, with our distinct spiritual gifts, have guided ICA into the most influential grouping of apostles currently known.

Horizontal Networks

Although I will not attempt to explain them in great detail, I want to list together the horizontal apostolic networks that God has assigned me to establish other than the New Apostolic Roundtable, EVAT and ICA:

- **The Apostolic Council for Educational Accountability (ACEA).**
  This was organized in 1998 in order to connect the educational leaders of the different apostolic networks. I will tell the story in part 4 of this chapter, "Equipping the Saints."

- **The Apostolic Council of Prophetic Elders (ACPE).** Up until now I haven't said enough about prophets as an essential part of the government of the church. Because I am an apostle, I have naturally stressed the work of apostles, but you will remember that I have frequently mentioned prophets such as Chuck Pierce and Cindy Jacobs and Bill Hamon. Look at 1 Corinthians 12:28 to see what an essential role prophets have: "And God has appointed these in the church: first apostles, *second prophets*, third teachers, after that miracles, then gifts of healings [and other spiritual gifts]." I would not want to move one step as an apostle without being properly aligned with prophets. Consider that "Surely the Lord GOD does nothing, unless He reveals His secret to His servants the prophets" (Amos 3:7). Chuck Pierce and I have teamed for more than a decade in attempting to model an effective biblical relationship between apostle and prophet.

  ACPE began when a group of prophets under Cindy Jacobs decided that they needed to group together on an ongoing basis to build relationships and establish mutual accountability. Cindy then invited me to provide apostolic leadership to the group even though I was not a prophet. I agreed that it fit into my role as a horizontal apostle, and in 1999, I began to convene ACPE on at least an annual basis. Around 20 to 25 prophets have been active in ACPE through the years.

- **The International Society of Deliverance Ministers (ISDM).** Doris first began her deliverance ministry in the mid-1980s, and she soon became one of the best known in the field through her teaching ministry and her two books, *How to Cast Out Demons* and *How to Minister Freedom*. As we began meeting other deliverance ministers all over the country, we noticed they had few connections with peers and some felt alone and even shunned by other believers. Consequently, we started a small roundtable in 2000 and then we co-founded a professional society in 2003 called ISDM. Now ISDM has up to 200 dues-paying members who feel affirmed and encouraged in their deliverance ministries. Our goal is to raise the water level of integrity of deliverance ministries throughout the nation.

- **The Hamilton Group** and **Apostolic Council for Kingdom Wealth.** I will explain more about these two apostolic networks in part 5 of this chapter, "Dominion, Wealth and Transformation."

Apostolic Summits

While growing in understanding apostolic church government, as I have related, most of my involvement was within the United States. I did connect some, and I learned a great deal from, apostles in Great Britain, which at that time was 5 to 10 years ahead of us in developing apostolic ministry. I had some help from a few other apostles, such as Lawrence Khong in Singapore and some apostles in Brazil, but not many. Consequently, because I am a missionary at heart, I developed a passion for helping to spread apostolic ministries around the world.

My first step was to research and attempt to identify the top 40 apostles in the world, representing all continents. On the supposition that one characteristic of apostles is that they have access to considerable finances, I invited them to what I called a World Apostolic Summit in Singapore in 2000. They would come at their own expense, and we would book a five-star hotel for our meetings. Almost all of them came, most of them not knowing the others beforehand. It was an amazing meeting, with great freedom for discussion since we were all peers. The Summit turned out to be a one-of-a-kind meeting instead of an ongoing apostolic organization. I could not find any social glue that would bind these apostles from different parts of the world together for the long haul.

It then became clear that a better approach might be to bring together apostles of the same or similar cultures or geographical areas and see if they would be inclined to form horizontal apostolic networks of their own like ICA. So, along with Chuck Pierce and John Kelly, I convened a series of apostolic summits over the next few years:

- **Native American Apostolic Summit** in 2002 under Jean Steffenson in Colorado Springs.
- **European Apostolic Summit** in 2002 under Jan Aage Torp in Oslo, Norway.
- **Nigerian Apostolic Summit** in 2002 under Enoch Adeboye in Lagos, Nigeria.
- **Southern Europe Apostolic Summit** in 2003 under Bruno Interlandi in Naples, Italy.

- **Former USSR Nations Apostolic Summit** in 2004 under Sunday Adelaja in Kiev, Ukraine.
- **East Africa Apostolic Summit** in 2004 under Jackson Senyonga in Kampala, Uganda.
- **China Apostolic Summit** in 2006 under David Wang and Ernest Chan in Hong Kong.

As I reported in the case of the World Apostolic Summit of 2000, these meetings were wonderful occasions, and I'm sure they helped open the minds of all who attended toward the new apostolic wineskins for the church. However, my hopes that they would spark apostolic alliances like ICA within their respective cultures went largely unrealized. There were a few short-lived attempts, but nothing permanent that I know of. As I look back, I can now see that the apostles who gathered in each event were almost all vertical apostles. Their assignment was to care for and expand their own apostolic networks, and that is more than a full-time job for most vertical apostles. Organizing and managing a horizontal network such as ICA was outside the spheres to which God had assigned them. Few, if any, of the apostles we met had the gifts and calling of a horizontal apostle.

It should go without saying that I was quite disappointed that my vision for these summits sparking active apostolic alliances around the world went largely unfulfilled.

The Second Apostolic Age

In conclusion, I am thankful to God and gratified that He has allowed me to be a front-row spectator, and even a participant observer, of the historic beginnings of the Second Apostolic Age. The First Apostolic Age took place in the first couple of centuries after Christ. Then, for some 1,800 years the biblical gift and office of apostle was virtually neglected by the wider Body of Christ. By this I do not mean to imply that apostles did not exist. Who could deny that Luther or Wesley or Savanarola or Jonathan Edwards or Hudson Taylor were apostles? I do mean, however, that the church, until recently, was not prepared to interpret literally Ephesians 4:11 and affirm the gift, office and ministry of apostles in our days.

If I were asked to fix a date for the beginning of the Second Apostolic Age, I would say it was 2001. This is when a critical mass of the Body of Christ began to agree that the foundation of the church is, indeed, apostles and prophets and that they should be openly recognized as such in our churches today. One of the tangible signs of this was the activation of the ICA, which took the shape it has today in 2001. I explained its origins a few pages back, but it is interesting to note that for the first time, hundreds of apostles from different streams now had a vehicle through which they could recognize and affirm the gifts and offices of apostle that all of them had received. My great satisfaction is that when I go, I do not have to leave behind the thought that the Second Apostolic Age may come soon. It is already here!

Part 2: Colorado and The World Prayer Center

I have mixed feelings about writing this section. Let me explain some of the reasons why.

I want to tell the story of how we moved from Pasadena, California, to Colorado Springs, Colorado, in 1996, undoubtedly the most significant change that Doris and I made since moving from Bolivia to the United States in 1971. The good news is that the relocation opened up fascinating and extraordinary vistas of ministry for the kingdom of God that we would never have dreamed of without it. The bad news is that the human agent whom God used more than anyone else to nurture us through the change was Ted Haggard, then Pastor of New Life Church, but since exposed and asked to leave the church when his immoral sexual contacts and drug use were revealed. My first intuition was to leave Haggard out of these memoirs entirely, but as you will soon see, that would not have been possible. The following is my view of how those events unfolded.

Prophetic Forebodings

Toward the end of the last section, I explained how important it is for apostles to be properly related to prophets. Apostles, more than others, are those who are designated to hear what the Spirit is saying to the churches. Sometimes apostles hear this directly from God, and other times they hear it through the prophets with whom they are connected. In my case, I estimate that I hear more than 50 percent of what the Lord wants to say through me from prophets. For this reason, I consider my relationship with Chuck Pierce and other prophetic friends as absolutely essential for my apostolic ministry.

One of the best-known prophets in America is Bill Hamon, founder of Christian International. I remember that when I first started researching prophets at Fuller in the late 1980s, Hamon's name came up frequently. You may recall that I explained in chapter 8 how his book *Prophets and Personal Prophecy* helped more than any other to wrap my mind around the theological constructs of contemporary prophecy. Through this, Hamon became a distant hero for me and I never imagined I would ever get to meet such a distinguished personality. I did not think that "Bishop," as his friends call him, even knew that I existed. Yet one day when Doris and I were in Phoenix for meetings in 1992, our friend Hal Sacks told us that Bill and Evelyn Hamon were in town as well, and they would like to meet with us!

The Hamons were in a hotel suite, and when we entered we saw a tape recorder on the table. Did this mean that he was actually going to prophesy? It did, and the prophecy fills no less than three single-spaced pages in our *Prophetic Journal*! I'll quote from this prophecy again later, but for now, here is part of what he said: "Fear not, man and woman of God. Your financial affairs are in My hands, and I'm about to give you a better, different place of your permanent residence and of your permanent headquarters where you can reside, a more spacious, roomier place."

I need to explain what a disturbing word this was for us! Here I was, a 62-year-old tenured professor in Fuller Seminary, living in a nice, paid-for, Spanish-colonial home in the foothills of the San Gabriel Mountains in sunny Southern California. A graduate school professor, by the way, has got to be one of the easiest jobs in America. My idea was to stop teaching when I was 70, and then do whatever I felt like whenever I wanted to for the rest of my life. What could Bill Hamon's prophecy possibly mean? I dutifully entered it into our *Prophetic Journal* and went on with other things.

However, I could not rest. Before long, two of our I-2 intercessors, Cindy Jacobs and Jean Steffenson, totally apart from each other, prophesied to us that we would soon be moving to Colorado Springs! We honestly thought they had missed it, just as Paul missed it when he thought he should go to Bithynia, as recorded in Acts 16:7. We should have listened more closely! God was trying to tell us something!

The Invitation to Colorado Springs

In chapter 8, I told all about Luis Bush and how we joined forces with him in coordinating the United Prayer Track of the AD2000 Movement, which by design was scheduled to operate only until the year 2000. One thing I didn't mention was that Luis's headquarters were in Colorado Springs where he frequently called us track coordinators together for meetings. In one of those meetings, Doris and I met Ted Haggard, founding pastor of New Life Church, a missions-minded megachurch. We became friends, and whenever we were in Colorado Springs, we attended New Life.

During the AD2000 leaders' meeting in December 1993, Ted and his wife, Gayle, invited Doris and me to lunch. He shared with us a long-standing burden he had felt for establishing a World Prayer Center in Colorado Springs, and he challenged us to begin to pray about being a part of it. He argued that the effectiveness of Global Harvest Ministries and the United Prayer Track could be measurably enhanced by shifting our base to a World Prayer Center. We prayed, our intercessors prayed, and by December 1994, we agreed in principle to move ahead. We scheduled a meeting for February 23, 1995, to get together in Colorado Springs and make the final decision.

There were some important details to care for in the interim. First we increased the level of personal intercession on our behalf. Then I met with my dean of the Fuller School of World Mission and negotiated arrangements for me to continue to teach my full load (plus!) of seminary courses by commuting to Pasadena for week-long intensives throughout the year.

As planned, we held our meeting with Haggard in New Life Church on February 23, joined by George Otis, Jr., of The Sentinel Group, who at the time was committed to join us in the project. We put all of our thoughts, positive and negative, on the table, and then we came to financing. The architect had estimated a cost of between $3 million and $4 million for the building. So we made a telephone call to Paul Traxel in Germany, the man whom you will recall helped us to start Global Harvest Ministries in 1991. We cast the vision to Paul, and before we had finished the call, he had committed $1.5 million to start the project! Doris and I looked at each other and said, "There's no turning back!"

Crossing the Rockies

We planned on an 18-month period to get ready to move. Many details had to be cared for, including, of course, selling our house and finding a place to live in Colorado Springs. We retained a realtor from New Life Church, and Doris flew to Colorado Springs. She found a house on eight acres of Ponderosa pines in the Black Forest area that she liked. When she called, I changed my travel plans and quickly flew to be with her in

Colorado Springs. I liked the house as well, so we made an offer, but someone else had just bid more, and we lost it.

We were sad, but here is where intercessors come into the picture. We went house hunting again, and we did find one house that I liked, but Doris had serious reservations. You've got to understand that I am a buyer, not a shopper! My attention span, even for finding a house, is very short. On the other hand, Doris has the persistence to look and look until she knows it's right. So in order to help solve our family dispute, we agreed to call in our intercessors. It so happened that Cindy Jacobs, who was by then located in Colorado Springs, was holding a conference at which four of our I-2 intercessors happened to be present—Cindy herself, Chuck Pierce, Beth Alves and Jean Steffenson. So we were able to load all six of us into a van and visit the property that I liked. None of the intercessors liked it at all! In fact, some were spiritually repulsed! Doris won! It turned out, however, to be a good thing.

Why?

On our way back, Doris insisted that we all take a look at the property we had lost, which we did. The eight-acre lot next door had a "For Sale" sign, but Doris and I had asked about it previously and we were told that a physician had purchased it. Nevertheless, Cindy said in an authoritative, prophetic voice, "Doris, you take the phone and call that number!" Doris did, and the owner seemed open to talk about it!

My problem, however, was that I did not at all desire to supervise the complicated process of constructing a new home from the next time zone. But Beth Alves spoke up and suggested that perhaps Ralph Femrite, who had just retired as a colonel from the Air Force in Colorado Springs, would be willing to supervise it. Ralph's wife, Tommi, happened to be another one of our I-2 intercessors. I said, "If Ralph will do it and if we can make a deal, let's go for it!" That van ride turned out to be an extremely important event in our lives. Ralph was willing, and the upshot is that we have been living in our dream home since we moved to Colorado Springs in June 1996. Once again, thank God for intercessors!

Ready to Move

Not long after we began Global Harvest Ministries, one of my Fuller students, a Japanese-American, Kay Hiramine, came on board as a volunteer. Before he arrived at Fuller, Kay had been in the business world, and at one point he was the number-one salesman for Proctor & Gamble Food Division in the nation. Kay noticed that we had been doing all our conferences through The Charles E. Fuller Institute, but GHM itself was suffering financially. It didn't take him long to suggest that we shift to doing our conferences through GHM, which we did. We asked him to come on staff full time to head up our new GHM Ministries Division. He also developed our resource center, which we called The Arsenal. These were good moves because they greatly increased our revenue flow.

We had finalized our plans to move to Colorado Springs in June 1996, but two months before, in April, we received some shocking news. Paul Traxel informed us that he could not deliver on his promise to provide our initial $1.5 million for the World Prayer Center! Paul, as we knew, was in close partnership with his father and brother in all their enterprises. No important decision could be made without unanimous consent of the three. They had all been in favor of the $1.5 million gift until something happened in Germany. Remember that I explained how we became involved in strategic-level spiritual warfare and the Spiritual Warfare Network, back in chapter 7? I also brought up the severe opposition from some like the Fuller Seminary theology professors. Well, it turns out that a German theologian, Wolfgang Buehne, wrote a book in German arguing that Peter Wagner was a heretic because of his views on warfare. Paul's father received a copy of the book, took it at face value and proceeded to veto the agreement for the promised gift to Wagner, the heretic! Paul profusely apologized, but his hands were tied.

This, of course, postponed initiating the construction of the World Prayer Center, for which we had conducted a high-profile groundbreaking ceremony in December 1995, attended by more than 500 celebrities from the prayer movements of Asia, Africa, Europe and Latin America as well as North America. We had hoped the WPC would be ready for us to move into before we arrived in Colorado, but no such thing!

At the time of our WPC groundbreaking, we also held another powerful private groundbreaking and anointing ceremony for the eight acres in the Black Forest area where we were going to build our home. Our family, almost all of our I-1 and I-2 intercessors, and several others were with us. We worshiped the Lord, anointed the boundaries with oil, took communion, and opened the heavens over the property. All this contributed to our very comfortable and peaceful homestead, including waterfalls, an antique tractor collection, a 115-year-old log cabin we use as rustic guest quarters, a half mile of ATV trails through the woods, a 9-hole Frisbee golf course, horseshoe pits, flowers in the summer time and a llama named George.

For the first time since she was a kid, Doris is operating a Case SC tractor. This is the first vehicle she learned to drive back on the farm in St. Johnsville, New York. She drove tractors long before she drove cars. This is one of the most prized tractors in our collection.

I am driving off the truck another addition to my antique tractor collection. With seven antiques from 1929 to 1944 running, in addition to my working John Deere 4600, I consider my collection complete.

In partial compensation for the delay in construction, Paul Traxel agreed to cover the rent of temporary facilities in Colorado Springs for GHM offices until the World Prayer Center was completed, plus paying for the move of our office furniture, as well as moving us and our staff members from Pasadena to Colorado Springs, which he did. For the first year, Doris secured office space in a commercial building; then when the lease was terminated, David C. Cook Communications very generously leased us empty space in their facilities for the second year at $1 per year! We still thank God for David C. Cook coming to our rescue!

The World Prayer Center

When we arrived in Colorado Springs, the challenge of raising funds for the World Prayer Center became our passion. It drove us to our knees because we had never undertaken anything like it before. God began to open the door with some donors here in the United States, but, surprisingly, He began to give us promising contacts with businesspeople in Asia who largely carried the project. This was some of the fruit of the relationships we had been building through the United Prayer Track of the AD2000 Movement. After the construction began, the projected cost of the building rose to $5.5 million, and God was providing the needed money month by month, especially from Asia. This continued until the devastating Asian financial meltdown hit that part of the world in 1997. Our revenue stream suddenly dwindled to almost nothing. At that point, New Life Church took out a bond issue to complete the project. In round numbers, it turned out that GHM had raised $3.5 million, and New Life had added $2 million for the World Prayer Center building.

It was a great day of rejoicing when we physically moved our offices into the World Prayer Center on September 19, 1998. We held an exuberant praise service and a moving ceremony of Native American dedication put together by Jean Steffenson. The World Prayer Center was built on land occupied at one time by Southern Cheyenne. Our close friend, Jay Swallow, who is a Southern Cheyenne apostle, gathered some Indian friends, brought in some dirt and ceremoniously poured it into my hands, indicating that we now had permission to use the land for the glory of God.

Chuck Pierce Joins the Team

This is the time that Chuck Pierce permanently joined our team. As the magnitude of the operation of the World Prayer Center became clearer, I began to realize that it would require a hands-on leader with skill sets that I did not have. Chuck Pierce, with his background in the business world and his training in systems management, had those skills. He had served as prayer leader for the United Prayer Track and the Spiritual Warfare Network. Furthermore, by then he was relating more closely to Doris and me as a prophetic intercessor. We had to negotiate with Cindy Jacobs to allow him to switch from Generals of Intercession to our team, and that was not an easy decision for Cindy. Finally, however, we all concluded that it would be best for the kingdom of God. In June 1998, Chuck moved his family to Colorado Springs from Denton, Texas, for the time it would take to get us organized and moving forward. It ended up taking two years before he felt released to move back to Texas.

Chuck accepted the invitation to join the board of Global Harvest Ministries as a vice president, along with Doris, and I appointed him director of the World Prayer Center. After Chuck came, we formed a new nonprofit called Wagner Institute for Practical Ministry of which I was president and my vice president was Kay Hiramine. Doris and I had worked closely with Kay for six years. He helped us move our conferences to a new level: We established Wagner Publications to produce cutting-edge books on prayer, spiritual warfare, deliverance, and other topics; we organized the Apostolic Council for Educational Accountability, which I will explain more about later; we founded Wagner Leadership Institute; and our budget for everything, including Global Harvest, exceeded $5 million annually. We never could have reached that level without the entrepreneurial skills and commitment of Hiramine.

Chuck Pierce, on the other hand, was implementing our vision for the world as in *World* Prayer Center. He was working on strategic communications and missions. He focused, with us, on the 10/40 Window, then the 40/70 Window. He formed the Eagles of God team of strategic, prophetic intercessors who could quickly move into the nations of the world on short notice. He helped me anchor Celebration Ephesus, which I told about in chapter 8, and we functioned there as an apostle-prophet team. When Alice Smith moved aside as our long-term I-1 Intercessor, Chuck took her place and has been handling that responsibility ever since.

"A Time of Reorganization"

In November 1998, Chuck prophesied: "God says, 'I am beginning a time of reorganization of My people. I will realign within their minds, their ministries and their relationships. I must create My authority in the earth. I will promote some and create new spheres of authority for others. I will begin the year with this realignment, and it should be completed by mid-March.'" And in December, he added: "If you will pray, I will complete the realignment of My purposes by March 17."

As we went into 1999, I began to feel uneasy about leading two ministries, GHM and Wagner Institute. I noticed that Chuck was much more comfortable on the GHM side of the offices rather than the Wagner Institute side. It was on March 18 that I called a leadership meeting and we decided to phase out Wagner Institute as a separate ministry and place it under GHM. This was a very difficult decision. Just around this time, Kay Hiramine had been receiving prophetic words to the effect that his season with GHM was ending. He resigned three months later. It was very sad to lose Kay after six years of working closely together, but it turned out for the best.

Actually, Chuck knew that this was exactly what God wanted me to do. We had walked arm in arm through the months of transition, and from time to time, Chuck would nudge me with a prophetic word that would invariably be a word in season. When the consolidation was finally over and he told me that he had known all along what was going to happen, I said, with a tinge of rebuke, "Why didn't you tell me sooner? You could have saved us months of grief!" He calmly replied, "Peter, I couldn't tell you because you weren't ready. You would have messed the whole thing up!"

Beyond the World Prayer Center

Consolidating GHM wasn't the only "realignment of ministries and relationships," as Chuck's prophecy had mentioned. Although Haggard and I had enjoyed seven years of positive, symbiotic relationship, beginning in 1993, even during those seven years fissures between us had begun to develop.

The legal arrangements for the project were never really comfortable. What happens when you build a building on someone else's property? We tried forming a separate WPC, Inc. corporation, but that didn't work. As we discussed it, we eventually discovered that the root of our growing discomfort was that we had been operating on conflicting assumptions. The understanding that I had from the beginning was that GHM/World Prayer Center would be seen by the public we were serving as a ministry distinctly separate from New Life Church, even though it happened to be located on New Life property. As far as I recollect, that was Haggard's original

proposition to me, and on that basis we moved to Colorado. Haggard's recollection, however, was quite different. He claimed that from the outset he
wanted both GHM and WPC to be regarded as ministries of New Life
Church. This, as you can imagine, was a deeply disappointing turn of events.

I felt I had no choice but to accede to Haggard's wish and dissolve the
separate WPC corporation, turning the World Prayer Center building over
to New Life as their sole property. In return, New Life agreed to give GHM,
which remained a separate corporation, our office space and the use of
common areas rent-free as long as either Doris or I remained in ministry
and desired to stay. We were expected to pay only "triple net," which is the
cost of utilities, maintenance, cleaning, insurance and the like.

All this might have been workable were it not for two other developments. First, strangely enough, Haggard and I found ourselves drifting
apart. We seemed to be carving out different pathways regarding doctrine
and philosophy of ministry. Second, it appeared to me that Haggard had
developed a very strong aversion to prophecy and prophetic ministry,
which by then had become deeply embedded in Global Harvest Ministry's
DNA. Let me explain both.

Positioning for the Future

Although I wouldn't have anticipated this, Haggard began moving toward
the traditional evangelical stream that we had come from. Our background was the Fuller Seminary, National Association of Evangelicals,
Christianity Today, Billy Graham end of the evangelical spectrum. One reason we were attracted to Haggard at first was that he had come from the
Oral Roberts University, independent charismatic, *Charisma* magazine,
Smith Wigglesworth end of the spectrum. At first we successfully brought
the two together. Then it became clear that Haggard was becoming more
evangelical while I was becoming more charismatic. For example, I could
not understand why he assiduously desired strong relationships with the
National Association of Evangelicals, which did not fit at all with our apos-
tolic/prophetic stream of Christianity.

By 2004, Doris and I felt it was time to have a heart-to-heart talk with
Haggard, which we did. I had even diagrammed the process that our relationship had gone through since we met in 1993, showing how we had
steadily been drifting apart. I raised the question as to whether Doris and
I were properly positioned as members of New Life Church for God's new
assignments over the next 10 years. Haggard conceded that we probably

were not, and he said, "Where are you going?" I had brought with me an article from the current *Charisma* magazine on the 50-state tour that Chuck Pierce and Dutch Sheets were doing on behalf of the U.S. Spiritual Warfare Network. I pointed out that Chuck and Dutch were apostolically aligned with me, and that I probably really belonged in Dutch's church, then called Springs Harvest Fellowship, and now Freedom. Haggard agreed and prayed a blessing over us. Afterward, Doris and I both felt that Haggard was in all probability happier about our leaving than we were about going!

Unfortunately, our relationship with Haggard went downhill rapidly from that point on. An unpleasant situation developed when a couple of months later we discovered that he had used certain Wagner family members to illustrate what he called "The Markers of Self-Love" in a Sunday sermon. This required another face-to-face meeting, which, unlike the first, felt decidedly adversarial in nature. The following is my view of the meeting: At one point, Haggard expressed his disagreement with the direction we were headed, as shown on our previous diagram, warning us that if we persisted in promoting the apostolic/prophetic government of the church, we would lose our national influence. As I recall, he said that the market indicators he was observing showed that I had been heading in the wrong direction and that I was in danger of not finishing well. He seemed to me to be so agitated that he implied that I was an old man and I should try to finish well by retiring and going off the scene as Oral Roberts has done. Doris and I were speechless when we heard him say, as we remember it, that he had never invited us to Colorado Springs!

Secrecy Exposed

As Haggard moved more and more toward NAE and traditional evangelicalism, he gradually distanced himself from some of the more expressive forms of the charismatic movement, such as prophecy. He was cordial to Chuck Pierce, but never close and supportive. In fact, during the two years that Chuck lived in Colorado Springs (1998 to 2000), he became a tithe-paying member of New Life, but he was never invited to speak to the congregation.

Haggard's secret sexual contacts with two men and occasions of drug use were exposed beginning in November 2006. For eight years before that, Cindy Jacobs had been gently warning me of his immoral behavior about which God had been speaking to her. Furthermore, Jill O'Brien, another of our closest circle of prophetic intercessors, had been hearing the same thing. In fact, Jill had developed some expertise on the matter because she had been married to a man who practiced homosexual behavior for five years. She said, "Peter, I can smell it a mile off!" On one occasion, Jill even sat me down and gave me a one-on-one very forceful admonition that his immoral behavior was going to be uncovered and that I wasn't taking it seriously enough!

I, however, didn't really know what to do with all this. I believed Cindy and Jill, but I had no evidence that I could present. It was Cindy who finally took the bull by the horns, so to speak. At a certain social occasion in our home, Cindy took Chuck Pierce along with Ted and Gayle Haggard into another room and talked to them about what she and many others with whom she had been in touch had been hearing from the Lord concerning his immorality. Haggard denied it with his characteristic charm and concluded the conversation as rapidly as he could. From then on he distanced himself from Cindy, even suggesting to some, including Doris and me, that she was a false prophet.

One reason why Haggard was distancing himself from the New Apostolic Reformation was that some of the leaders in the National Association of Evangelicals had already come out against it. When the time came that he being considered for the office of president of NAE, this question naturally came up. Ted then went on record as saying, "I do not embrace the modern prophetic movement represented by Dr. C. Peter Wagner and others, nor have I ever!"[6] His public opposition to what we were doing had now escalated to the point that Chuck Pierce, Cindy Jacobs and Dutch Sheets refused to step foot on New Life Church property, including coming into our GHM offices in the World Prayer Center.

Now what? Because Chuck was vice president of GHM, we had to hold our annual 2005 board meeting in borrowed facilities off campus rather than meeting in our own conference room as we usually did. We were becoming convinced that the World Prayer Center was not a friendly place for us to be. In fact, in an unguarded moment, a New Life Church janitor told one of our staff that New Life leadership was circulating the word that GHM had "overstayed its welcome" in the World Prayer Center!

A New GHM Facility

A major reason why I have been able to do enough to fill a book like this is that Doris has served, since we were missionaries in Bolivia, as my administrative anchor. Take finances, for example. With the exception of a period of time around the turn of the century, when we had some surplus, GHM has survived year in and year out on the brink of going from the black to the red. Ordinarily we have lived from payroll to payroll, nothing more. As president, I do worry about this and pray for God's supply. However, and maybe I shouldn't admit this, I estimate that I may do about 5 percent of the worrying and praying. Doris has consistently picked up the other 95 percent of the financial burden. And somehow or other, payroll after payroll, we seem to pull through by the grace of God.

A corollary of her role would be that the task of finding a new location for GHM would largely fall to Doris. As sociologists tell us, significant changes like this usually are moved by a combination of "push" and "pull" factors. For example, our move from California to Colorado was motivated mostly by pull factors. In this case, however, push factors dominated. We needed to leave the spiritual oppression of the New Life Church campus and take whatever might come along as our destination. We looked at the possibility of building out some empty space in Dick Eastman's Jericho Center. We considered sharing space with Springs Harvest Fellowship in a new facility they were looking at. But neither of those ideas worked out. Doris was almost ready to sign a lease on another available office building, even though we knew that in it we would be cramped to our limits. But before she did, God intervened.

Here's how it happened.

While I was teaching in Wagner Leadership Institute in Red Deer, Alberta, a friend approached Doris and suggested that she look at the facility recently vacated by DAWN Ministries. This was an interesting connection, because Jim Montgomery, the founder of DAWN, was a member of our 120 Fellowship Sunday School class in Pasadena, and we had been very close for years. However, Jim had been ousted by a hostile board takeover, DAWN was relocating to Orlando and their facility was for sale.

Doris inspected the two buildings, which had a total of 20,000 square feet. She immediately saw that the space was more than adequate for all of our GHM needs, plus classroom space for Wagner Leadership Institute. Doris happened to know the DAWN representative personally, and she soon learned that the ministry needed the revenue from the sale of the building very badly. She correctly assumed it was a buyer's market. The facility was appraised at $1.95 million, and the asking price was $1.9 million. When Doris hesitated at the price, her friend said, "Make me an offer!" Doris countered with what she thought was a ridiculous price, and she said, "$1.5 million." He immediately replied, "Sold!"

"It Was on Sale!"

I was having lunch with Mel Mullen in Red Deer when my cell phone rang. When I saw it was Doris I put it on speaker phone so Mel and his wife, Heather, could greet her and get in on the conversation. When the greetings were over, she said, "I just bought our new facility!" I was aghast! I said, "Why in the world would you do such a thing without even asking me?" She calmly replied, "Because it was on sale!" Now, I had heard those words about buying things at the grocery store or buying a new dress, but never about buying real estate!

After telling me that it was the DAWN property, she said that they had calculated we would need $300,000 as a down payment in order to get a $1.2 million loan. My faith was not very high for $300,000 until Mel Mullen said, "This is easy. Just get 30 of your friends to donate $10,000 each, and I will be the first one!" So we pressed on forward under the blessing of God, not only for the $300,000, but also for an additional $150,000 to begin renovating the buildings.

It was not that easy moving from a modern, state-of-the-art facility to a fixer-upper. We had two buildings, the main one a former medical rehab building from the 1970s, which was a challenge both physically and spiritually. We had to replace the bathroom fixtures, all the windows, remove walls, redo ceilings, update the electrical system, build fire escapes, recarpet the whole building, repaint the interior and replace the heating and air conditioning. Then our intercessors went to work and did some intense spiritual housecleaning, going back to Native American activities, then addressing contamination related to the time when it was a medical rehabilitation center and, finally, dealing with spirits that had gained access through the hostile takeover of the ministry that preceded us. It was a fierce battle, but God was good, and now we have enjoyed working under an open spiritual environment once again.

We were ready to push on once again into God's new seasons for us!

Part 3: Prayer for the Harvest

As you will recall, Global Harvest Ministries was birthed as a prayer ministry. I explained in chapter 8 how Luis Bush invited me to coordinate the AD2000 United Prayer Track, how Doris resigned from Fuller in order to administer the global prayer movement, and how we soon founded GHM as our central office in Pasadena. Subsequently, we moved to Colorado

Springs and helped build the World Prayer Center. This majestic building, surrounded by more than 50 flags of the world, became the international nerve center of worldwide prayer, first for the 10/40 Window and then for the 40/70 Window.

Reporting the Results of Prayer

So many prayer reports kept pouring into our GHM offices that it was almost impossible to keep up with them all. Even so, we had decided to attempt something that no previous prayer movement, to our knowledge, had done. First, as I detailed in chapter 8, we mobilized probably the largest prayer army ever known, namely, up to 50 million believers through every continent praying for the same people group in the 10/40 Window on the same day throughout the month of October in 1993, 1995 and 1997. But second, we promised them that we would give them a report of what happened in each of the years. Nothing encourages intercessors more than hearing that their prayers were indeed answered.

Our point person for this was Beverly Pegues, who led the Christian Information Network, located near to us in the World Prayer Center. Beverly combines the spiritual gifts of an experienced intercessor with quality administrative and management skills—a rather unusual blend of exactly what was needed for the prayer movement. After 21 million believers prayed for the 62 nations of the 10/40 Window through the month of October 1993, she spent countless hours in processing the reports, and then produced a remarkable book, *WindowWatchman*, which contained three-page chapters updating the prayer movements in each one of the 62 nations of the 10/40 Window! Following the thrust of October 1995, she wrote *WindowWatchman II*, a 432-page update on answers to prayer in the same 62 nations. Following our 1997 initiative, Luis Bush joined Beverly in writing *The Move of the Holy Spirit in the 10/40 Window*, arguably the most detailed and uplifting report of a sustained prayer movement ever published.

Let me give you a couple of examples of powerful prayer. Dick Eastman's Every Home for Christ is one of the largest and most effective evangelistic/church planting agencies existing. Here is their report:

- 1989-1992: average of 410,000 conversions in the 10/40 Window per year. *Then Praying Through the Window began!*
- 1993: 1,260,000 conversions
- 1994: 1,485,000 conversions

This reflects a 300-percent increase in conversions in one year! Even the most skeptical would have to think twice before they denied a cause-and-effect relationship between massive prayer and the salvation of souls!

Even though I mentioned this second example previously, it bears repeating because it is one of the most remarkable missiological reports on record. At the beginning of the decade of the 1990s, there were 1,739 unreached people groups of significant size in the 10/40 Window. By the end of the decade, only 500 of them did not yet have a church-planting movement, and many of those remaining 500 had already been targeted by various church-planting agencies!

More recently, Patrick Johnstone, one of our foremost missions researchers and author of the renowned *Operation World* in its several editions, released another amazing set of statistics regarding what has happened in the 10/40 Window since we began praying for it in 1991.[7] Here they are:

- In 1990, 2.5 percent of the population of the 10/40 Window were Christ followers, but in 2005 it had gone up to 4.5 percent.
- In 1990, there were 87.5 million Christ followers in the 10/40 Window, but in 2005 there were 205 million. This is an increase of no fewer than 117.5 million believers!
- Over that time, the average annual growth rate of Christ followers was 5.4 percent per year, while the population growth rate was 1.5 percent per year. This indicates that the great majority of growth was conversion growth, not biological growth.

This is what we were praying for!

Disappointment

One of the most valuable things I learned early in life, I think mostly through earning three varsity letters a year in high school athletics, was not only how to lose, but how to lose well. We may get knocked down, but we do not stay down. We learn from our defeats. John Maxwell labels the experience "failing forward"! I mention this because I have so many friends whose spirituality does not allow for them to ever admit defeat. When I suggest that "I lost this one," they invariably try to correct me as if it might be an insult to God to confess that I had failed!

During the Praying Through the Window initiative, I did suffer a disappointing defeat in Japan. As I have said, I became associated with David

Yonggi Cho of Korea, and I joined his Church Growth International board in the mid-1980s. Among other things, I enthusiastically adopted the goal that he had set for the evangelization of Japan. Toward the beginning of the 1990s, Cho began visiting Japan once a month, he learned the Japanese language and he projected a goal of 10 million born-again Japanese by the year 2000. This was a substantial risk, since, of all the nations of the world, Japan has been one of the most notoriously resistant to the gospel. Of a population of 125 million, Japan had fewer than 1 million believers, even though the gospel had been freely preached for a century, and especially since World War II.

What did that have to do with me? I made the evangelization of Japan one of my highest priorities for the 1990s. I literally believed in Cho's 10 million. I wrote about it, I spoke about it in public meetings and I visited Japan many times to help open the doors. One of those visits embraced an unforgettable spiritual experience on my part and on that of the Japanese Christian leaders I was ministering to.

A Prophetic Prayer

I was planning to minister in Japan with Yonggi Cho in August 1990. Just a couple of days before I was to leave, it so happened that Cindy Jacobs and I were among the speakers in a large conference in Indianapolis where I shared my passion for 10 million Japanese believers by 2000. Unexpectedly, the leader of the meeting called Cindy to come forward and pray for my coming visit to Japan. Cindy's prophetic prayer said in part:

> Lord, I thank You that You are sending Peter Wagner to Japan. Father, it was the American people who caused great devastation when they dropped the bombs on Hiroshima and Nagasaki. Lord, I thank You that You are sending back an American to undo the atrocity of Hiroshima and Nagasaki. Father, Peter will be used like a nuclear bomb in the Spirit to break apart the darkness that Satan has worked against the nation of Japan and the Japanese people. . . .

I didn't know how profound this prophetic prayer was until I stopped off at my home in Pasadena for one day to repack my bags for Tokyo. While I was praying for Japan the morning of the day I was to leave, for the only time I can remember, I began to weep profusely for a nation! When I finally calmed down, the phone rang and it was Doris, who had stayed in Indianapolis on the prayer team. She said that her team had been praying for Japan and they sensed that the Lord wanted me to repent for the sins of dropping the atomic bombs in World War II. Such a thought had never previously entered my mind, but, with the background of Cindy's prophecy, I had no choice. I took it as a divine assignment.

Immediately, I opened my Bible to Nehemiah, where he confessed to God that his father's house had sinned (see Neh. 1:6). Dropping the atomic bomb was a sin of my fathers, not my sin, because I was only 15 when the war ended. But then Nehemiah went on to say, "and I have sinned." I didn't fight the war, but God reminded me that I had deeply hated the Japanese people! Yes, I had sinned! Furthermore, He showed me that there were 15-year-old boys in Hiroshima who didn't fight either, but they were now dead or disabled. I started weeping again with twice the intensity!

The Congregation Melted

When I arrived in Tokyo, and it was my turn to speak, I had previously found two representatives from Hiroshima who had suffered, and two from Nagasaki, and I brought them on stage. I taught on remitting the sins of the past through identificational repentance, and then with more tears, I repented to those who were on the stage with me. By the time I finished, the whole auditorium, seating 1,000 influential church leaders, was filled with the noise of weeping, and handkerchiefs showed up from wall to wall. Yonggi Cho himself came up on the platform and confessed his hateful feelings toward Japanese as a Korean. Pastor Hiroshi Yoshiyama later wrote, "The congregation melted in tears and repentance. We have never had a conference like this before." In fact, a whole book about the event was published in Japanese. I have a copy, but I cannot read it!

This was not the only such event in Japan, through the 1990s. Once, in a moment of excitement, I prophesied that pachinko parlors (gambling establishments) all over Japan would be turning into churches. Numerous prayer journey teams from several other countries traveled to Japan and prayed at key power points. They did warfare against some of the highest profile principalities and powers over the land. Cho continued to minister to large crowds every month, and I joined him from time to time. I was convinced that we had used the weapons of spiritual warfare properly on behalf of that nation and that we would literally see the 10 million before 2000.

However, it was not to be. Through the 1990s, the rate of church growth in Japan remained unchanged, and the year 2000 saw fewer than 1 million

Doris and I are opening the door to one of our two new buildings in Colorado Springs, Colorado, to house Global Harvest Ministries and Wagner Leadership Institute. This is the building that Doris bought while I was in Canada because "it was on sale!"

Soon after we moved to Colorado Springs, we acquired some llamas. After a brutal bear attack, George, the llama I am feeding, turned out to be the only survivor. I still feed him every morning.

believers in the country—the same number as in 1990, and far short of the
10 million goal! Later, Cho admitted publicly in his newsletter that he had
set the goal of 10 million believers in his flesh, not through God's revelation. Because I had associated with him so closely, I had to confess the
same thing for myself.

People may rationalize this in one way or another, but I cannot join
them. I set a goal, I did not reach the goal, even with sincere dependence
on God, and I admit that I lost! This, as you can imagine, was a major disappointment!

"Operation Ice Castle"
Ana Méndez, our Spiritual Warfare Network coordinator for Southern
Mexico, had been leading intercessors in fervent prayer for the 10/40 Window, to the extent of even establishing a physical 10/40 Window prayer
tower in Mexico City. Ana had been a priestess of voodoo before she was
saved. In fact, she was radically converted to Christ in an insane asylum
and instantly healed. They would not release her immediately, so she began ministering to her fellow patients and delivering them from the demons that were tormenting them "through," as she says, "the amazing
empowerment of Christ that gave me the faith and boldness to do it."[8] By
the time she was released, she had practically emptied the whole facility!

Ana, who now lives in Jacksonville, Florida, with her husband, Emer-
son Ferrell, was praying in her prayer tower when the Lord showed her that
one of the major strongholds of darkness over the whole 10/40 Window
was on Mt. Everest in the Himalaya Mountains. When she shared with our
office the possibility of doing a prayer journey there, Doris not only agreed,
but she said, "I'm going along!" Ana had a vision of the Himalayas as a
huge castle of ice, so we named the expedition "Operation Ice Castle." This
was our first direct assault on the Queen of Heaven. The original name of
Mt. Everest in Nepali is *Sagarmatha*, meaning "Mother of the Universe"!

So, in September 1997, a team of 24 strategic intercessors was deployed in Nepal. A group led by Doris, hobbling on a cane because of a deteriorating hip, prayed for three weeks in a rustic hotel, with no hot water
and very marginal food, at 13,000 feet. Others prayed in the Everest Base
Camp at 18,000 feet. Ana, along with a team that had taken Alpine training with her in Mexico and Peru, crossed bottomless crevasses and scaled
the mountain to 20,000 feet. There they performed a series of dramatic
prophetic acts at a site that they perceived to be the territorial power point

of the Queen of Heaven. This involved such strenuous physical, emotional and spiritual security risks that we kept the strategic expedition a secret until all were safely home.

The Surgery Hall of Fame

Doris's personal physician, Brian Olivier, once said, "This woman should be a candidate for the Surgery Hall of Fame." Of course there is no such organization, but if there were, she would probably qualify. At last count, she has had 28 surgeries!

One of the most outstanding events sponsored by the United Prayer Track was the Gideon's Army gathering in South Korea, in 1993. You may recall the story from the last chapter, especially the part where host Sundo Kim had to call an army general to provide beds for his Western guests in Kwang Lim Prayer Mountain. However, I did not mention our sadness that Doris was not able to be with us for such a memorable occasion. She and I had been planning and working toward Gideon's Army for three years! Leaving her home was one of my most emotionally painful moments.

However, it was better than the alternative, which was the possibility of losing her altogether. About two months before Gideon's Army, Doris taught her first ever public seminar on deliverance, which happened to be in Malaysia. The enemy did not like this one bit! Just minutes before she was to begin her first session, some insect bit her on her right shin. She scratched it a little and paid no more attention. Four days later, however, we arrived in Singapore for some ministry I was doing at Lawrence Khong's Faith Community Baptist Church, when suddenly the bite became severely infected. She was rushed to the hospital for emergency treatment of flesh-eating bacteria. We were later told that she had been just a couple of hours from death! Our intercessors had been alerted immediately, and we attribute her survival to God's power through prayer.

To give you some background, Lai King Pousson, a noted Singaporean intercessor, was one of our United Prayer Track coordinators for Southeast Asia. Doris had been planning on accompanying me to my teaching assignment in Faith Community Baptist Church, but that morning she felt a little sick. She thought she had food poisoning and decided to stay in the hotel. A couple of hours later, the Holy Spirit said clearly to Lai King, "Call Doris now!" So she called the hotel and discovered that Doris was suffering from a high fever and no longer had the strength even to get out of bed! Lai King immediately sent a physician friend to the hotel, who personally drove her to the hospital, and her life was saved. Two more hours and it would have been too late!

After four days in Singapore, the doctors agreed to let me try to transfer her to Huntington Memorial Hospital in Pasadena, where our daughter, Karen Potter, was an intensive care nurse. The 20-hour airplane trip was pure torture—by far the worst trip of our lives, even worse than our airplane crash in Guatemala! The medical team in Pasadena found that the infection had gone to the artificial knee that had been implanted two years previously. They operated, and the good news is that they did not have to remove the prosthesis. The bad news is that they diagnosed a severe "septic joint," and she ended up in the hospital for two months with twice daily, "last-ditch," intravenous antibiotic injections of maximum strength. Meanwhile, Gideon's Army came and went. But her knee was saved and she is still walking on it!

Her Engine Runs Good, but She Needs Body Work!
That wasn't the only close call. I was ministering in Japan in 1988, and I made my normal daily call home. The first thing I heard Doris say was, "I'm going to be all right!" I had no idea there was anything wrong!

What happened?

A few weeks earlier, Doris had her right foot and toes reconstructed because of Charcot disease. While I was in Asia, the surgeon had removed the pins and sent her home with a good prognosis. Alone in the house, she awakened at 4:30 A.M., struggling to breathe. She dialed 911 and was rushed to the hospital, once again Huntington Memorial where our daughter worked, with serious blood clots in the lungs. When she arrived, she only had a surface the size of a naval orange inside her lungs with which to breathe! She was told that she would not have had much more time.

I immediately said I would jump on a plane and rush home. But, typically, she told me that it would make little sense because, even though she would be in the hospital on blood thinners for 10 more days, the crisis had passed and "I'm going to be all right!" True to her missionary nature, my ministry in Japan was more important than my sitting next to her hospital bed!

The first crisis I told you about related to her knee replacement, and this one to her reconstructed right foot. The enemy somehow has chosen joints as points of physical attack for years. Back in Bolivia, she needed part of her right index finger amputated. Doris's arthritis started when she was in her 30s, and it has increased ever since. She has had three back surgeries, both knees replaced, both hips replaced, one shoulder replaced, her right thumb reconstructed, her left foot reconstructed (four surgeries), her right ankle and foot reconstructed (three surgeries), and her left knee cap removed.

She has learned to get around on her walker, her C.R.O.W. (Charcot Restraint Orthotic Walker) boot, and her electric scooter. When people ask me how she is, I frequently reply, "Her engine's running real good; she just needs body work!" Every time doctors have recommended surgery, she says, "Let's get on with it. I've got places to go and things to do!"

From "Queen's Palace" to "Queen's Domain"

The massive research project of spiritual mapping that we did in a unit of the World Prayer Center called the "Observatory" uncovered the reality that the principality of evil named, among other names, the Queen of Heaven could well be the highest-ranking agent of Satan to keep human beings in spiritual darkness. The goddess worship that she spawns is spread throughout the globe and has historic roots going back to the land of Mesopotamia that surrounded the Garden of Eden. Because Turkey has been one of her primary bases of operation, we labeled our initiative that culminated with Celebration Ephesus in 1999 "Operation Queen's Palace."

Some historians consider Diana of the Ephesians to be the most worshiped deity in the Roman Empire. Her temple in Ephesus was one of the seven wonders of the ancient world. We called it her "palace" because it syncretized ancient Cybele worship, the Moon Goddess, and allegiance to Mammon. The temple, in fact, housed the first attempt at a world bank. Ephesus, not surprisingly, was the site later chosen by the Church to convene the famous Council of Ephesus in 431 where Mary was officially declared the "Mother of God."

When I received the word from Chuck Pierce that I told you about in the beginning of this chapter, and I then cast the vision for shifting from the 10/40 Window to the 40/70 Window, the name of this new initiative became "Operation Queen's Domain." Why? Because, mainly in the form of the Counterfeit Mary, the Queen of Heaven had deeply penetrated and corrupted much of the traditional Christianity of the western section of the 40/70 Window.

Our strategy was to send at least one well-equipped prayer team to each of the 62 nations of the 40/70 Window over a period of six years. We attempted to train the intercessors and encourage them with large annual prayer gatherings, which took us to Hannover, Germany (2001), Sofia, Bulgaria (2002), Almaty, Kazakhstan (2003), Santiago de Compostela, Spain (2004), and Rome/Pozzuoli, Italy (2005).

One of the distinctive characteristics that would fan out through the 40/70 Window was performing prophetic acts. These demonstrations in the natural realm, initiated by the Holy Spirit, are intended to create conditions through which God acts supernaturally. Biblical examples would be Jeremiah burying his underwear (see Jer. 13) or Isaiah going around naked (see Isa. 20).

One of these prophetic acts was done by a team of strategic intercessors that Chuck Pierce had organized under the rubric "Eagles of God." As Chuck was planning strategy with a team to go into the Queen's Domain, one of his other personal intercessors wrote him that she had heard God say that the team was to bury a gold coin in each of the 10 cities they had earmarked for prayer. As Chuck shared it with his group, Doris mentioned that in our last conference someone had donated a bag of small gold coins and she hadn't sold them as yet. When she opened the bag and spilled them on the table, there were exactly 10 coins, one for each city! Not only that, but each coin was imprinted with an eagle, as in Eagles of God! Needless to say, it greatly fired up the intercessory team!

Mad Cow Disease

Doris and I are beefsteak eaters. When time permits on our domestic and international trips, we like to try out the finest prime steak houses. We found some excellent steak houses in Hannover, Germany, where we convened our first international meeting for our 40/70 Window prayer initiative in 2001. Incidentally, it turned out to be one of our most significant prayer gatherings. Some 2,500 intercessors came together from no fewer than 64 nations of the world in order to share our experiences, make new connections and renew our commitment to pray for a massive harvest of souls through this part of the world. The 40/70 Window divided itself roughly into two theaters, which we called Target Europe in the western area and Target Silk Road in the eastern area. From Hannover, 126 teams of enthusiastic intercessors fanned out for prayer journeys into 56 of the 61 nations of the 40/70 Window!

But back to steak houses. As we dined at some of the restaurants, I began to notice that the menus all indicated that they were serving

"Argentine beef" or "American beef." It suddenly dawned on me that the reason the German steak houses couldn't serve German beef was because of a devastating epidemic of mad cow disease that had been reported in the media! Because Doris and I are farmers, we became incensed that innocent German farmers could be victimized by this terrible plague.

I hadn't given much more thought to it, however, until I was enjoying one of our plenary sessions in which the presence of God had obviously fallen. Much to my surprise, a word from the Lord came to me quite clearly: "Take authority over mad cow disease!" Such a thing had never occurred to me, so I began to pray over it, and when I did, it came even more strongly. Because I was in charge of the meeting I needed to ask no one's permission, so I made my way forward. By the time I got on the platform I could sense a strong divine anointing. When I began to describe the scenario to the crowd, I broke down into an embarrassing fit of weeping and sobbing. By then I knew that God wanted me to take the apostolic authority He had given me and decree once and for all that mad cow disease would come to an end in Europe and the U.K., which I did. The whole assembly noisily agreed with me with sustained cheers and applause.

That was October 1, 2001. A month later, a friend of mine sent me a newspaper article from England saying that the epidemic had broken and that the last reported case of mad cow disease had been on September 30, 2001, the day before the apostolic decree!

Up until then I had been reasonably aware of the potential power of apostolic decrees. The one I had known best was the decree that apostle James made in the Council of Jerusalem, which opened the door of the kingdom of God to Gentiles as well as Jews. Since Hannover, I have been cautiously moving toward using apostolic decrees a bit more, although I have yet to experience again as dramatic an effect as the eradication of a plague like mad cow disease.

Prayer Saturation for the 40/70

Few prayer leaders have prayed and prophesied in more nations of the world than Chuck Pierce. His Eagles of God team, which I just mentioned, is an extraordinary, committed band of around 50 professional-level intercessors, ready to go any place in the world at their own expense and at a moment's notice. When Chuck hears from God as to nations and cities that are ripe for prayer, he typically pulls together anywhere from 6 to 20 Eagles to accompany him. They have two tasks: (1) to pave the way for

promising breakthroughs that will produce evangelistic fruit, and (2) to
see demonic barriers of the highest strategic significance demolished.
These are high-risk assignments and the teams are well trained and su-
perbly conditioned.

We called our international gathering in Hannover "Gideon's Army II,"
with Gideon's Army I being our meeting in the Kwang Lim Prayer Mountain
in Seoul, in 1993, which I told about in chapter 8. Subsequently, Gideon's
Army III was held in Almaty, Kazakhstan, in 2003. Apostle Kim Sam Seong
anchored this meeting in his dynamic Grace Mission Center, a thriving
church of 6,000 members. Whereas in Hannover we prayed mostly for Target Europe, in Almaty we focused on Target Silk Road, the two major divi-
sions of the 40/70 Window. No fewer than 1,900 leaders and intercessors
from 35 different nations, most of them in the Silk Road region, were present at the event. They were renewed and recharged for continuing their powerful ministry of prayer and spiritual warfare in the 40/70 Window.

Santiago de Compostela in northern Spain is arguably the number-one
destination for Roman Catholic pilgrimages, recently rivaling or possibly
surpassing both Rome and Jerusalem. It is the burial place of James the
brother of John. In a given year, 10 million pilgrims will walk hundreds of
miles to Santiago, not for healing, as they do at Lourdes or Fatima, but for
forgiveness of sins. In 2001, Apostle Paco Garcia took Doris and me to visit
Santiago and its famous cathedral, 1,000 years old! Unexpectedly, we found
that the principality ruling over that site of counterfeit forgiveness of sins
was none other than the Queen of Heaven whose statue this time took the
shape of a voluptuous woman seated on a replica of the tomb of apostle
James. While we were there, God clearly showed us that we needed to gather
prophetic intercessors in the huge plaza in front of the cathedral for one of
our major international gatherings in the 40/70 Window.

The event was conducted on a specially constructed platform in the
cathedral plaza. We called it "The Celebration of Praise," and it consisted
of two hours of continuous worship, punctuated by prayers from nine of
the top leaders from the 40/70 Window. Some 3,000 leaders and worshipers gathered from every corner of Spain, plus 30 other nations. It was
a glorious, unforgettable time, loosening the hold that the Queen of
Heaven, in some of her various adaptive forms, has maintained over much
of the 40/70 Window for millenia.

Our last stop, fittingly enough, was in Rome, as well as in nearby Pozzuoli, the place where the apostle Paul landed and walked to Rome. It is

said that more Christians were martyred in Pozzuoli than in Rome. Hundreds and hundreds flew into Italy to be with us in the finale of praying through the 40/70 Window. While we were praying in the rooms under the Pozzuoli stadium where the lions were caged and the Christians imprisoned, God visited us by pouring down gold dust over the group. I know that many others have reported this phenomenon as well, but this was the only time I have experienced it.

A sign of gold from heaven was great encouragement to me that God would use me down the road as one of His agents for the coming great transfer of wealth. I'll tell more about that later.

Part 4: Equipping the Saints

As you would have gathered by now, I am an inveterate teacher. While I was studying at Fuller in the early 1950s, I taught an adult Sunday School class every Sunday. In the Bolivian jungles, I ran a Bible institute. When I moved to the Andes Mountains, I taught in and later directed a theological seminary. Back in the United States, I taught for 30 years on the faculty of Fuller Seminary, and added an adult Bible class for 13 of those years. My extensive traveling ministry was mostly in response to invitations to teach.

For a while I foolishly imagined that my teaching career would come to an end when I finished my last class at Fuller in 2000. However, I must have temporarily lost track of Ephesians 4:11-12, which clearly says that God provided apostles, prophets, evangelists, pastors, and teachers specifically "for the equipping of the saints for the work of ministry." I never thought that my calling as an apostle and a teacher would end, so I should have known that I would never cease equipping the saints. I simply had to move into a new season.

The Prophets Step Up

True to form, God used prophets to speak into my life and point the direction for the future. The first was Bill Hamon, whom I have mentioned from time to time. This is from the prophecy he gave me in his Phoenix hotel room in 1992. I have already quoted part of it, and here is another part:

> "The work that I've called you to do over the next 10 years," saith God, "will be more productive and more effective than all the rest of your life put together. You are going to begin to touch new

leaders, and the leaders you touch are going to touch hundreds, and the hundreds are going to touch thousands, and the thousands are going to touch millions. I'm going to use you to cause a chain reaction," saith God. "I've not called you to speak to the multitudes; I've called you to speak to My key leaders."

While this word caused no immediate changes in my life and ministry, it did let me know for sure that my career would not be over when I left Fuller Seminary. For one thing, it was only the following year, 1993, that I began to research and teach on what I later called the New Apostolic Reformation. This became the framework for launching my post-Fuller career. As I moved forward, the next directive prophecy came from Cindy Jacobs.

Chuck Pierce's Birthday Party

On June 6, 1998, a group of friends gathered in our living room to celebrate Chuck Pierce's birthday. The candles had been blown out and some were cutting and distributing the birthday cake when all of a sudden Cindy Jacobs got this look on her face with which I had become quite familiar. She stared into space and said, "The spirit of prophecy is so strong!" Confusion reigned as we searched for a tape recorder. When we found one, she began prophesying and, surprisingly enough, the prophecy was not for Chuck on his birthday, but it was for me! Here are some excerpts:

> For the Lord would say, "I am going to build a seminary here in Colorado Springs. I am going to gather leaders from around the world." And the Lord says, "My son, the curriculum that I am going to put together in this school is like nothing that has been seen before. It is going to happen quickly. The Wagner Institute is so big that you cannot imagine how big it is. For it is greater than anything you could ever dream of."

That last line was very accurate. The idea had never entered my mind to start a school. Just the opposite! For me, running a school would not seem like a dream—it would be more of a nightmare! So I had the prophecy transcribed and I entered it into my *Prophetic Journal*. I dutifully prayed about it, but, since I received no further revelation from the Lord, I went on with other activities.

Resigning from Fuller

Things suddenly changed a month later on July 17. We were in the same living room, but this time with a small group of apostles. Rice Broocks was there, along with David Cannistraci, Lawrence Khong, Joe Martin, Dexter Low, Kay Hiramine, Cindy and Mike Jacobs, and others. We were eating pizza and just hanging out. At one point, I casually mentioned that down the road, after I left Fuller when I turned 70, I hoped to be able to teach in some of their apostolic schools. That prompted Dexter Low from Malaysia to say, "Peter, how old are you?" I told him I was 68. He continued, "Don't you realize that you're an old man? Don't you realize that you don't have many years of ministry left? Do you mean you're planning on giving the two best years of your life to Fuller and then give the leftovers to us?"

I was startled! Everyone else was silent, looking at me. So I said, "That sounds like you're asking me to resign from Fuller Seminary!"

Rice Broocks turned to Doris and said, "Doris, what do you think?"

Doris said, "I told him he should resign from Fuller three years ago!"

That was enough for me. I said, "Okay, I'll write my letter of resignation tomorrow!" And I did! I resigned my full-time position, agreeing to continue for a while on a part-time basis. When I wrote the letter, was it hard? I couldn't help but think of the wonderful years at Fuller, which I have told about in past chapters—my student days in the '50s, studying under McGavran in the '60s, joining the faculty in the '70s, and all that has happened since then. Doris still says, "That's when you were in your prime!"

The next morning, while I was in the shower, the revelation concerning Cindy's prophecy and the future Wagner Leadership Institute began to pour forth. It lasted for several days, and before I knew it I had in place all the necessary ingredients for a new school.

Actually, I should have read my *Prophetic Journal* more carefully. If I had, I might have remembered a prophecy from Emmanuele Cannistraci two years previously. In 1996, he said, "I'm going to give you strength; I'm going to give you an extended life, O man of God. You are needed. *When you break from your present position as professor and instructor*, you are going to be a pastor to pastors, an apostolic leader to a whole new breed of men and women. The latter house is going to be greater than the former."

Obviously, this explains why I received no revelation on Cindy's prophecy concerning WLI until the day after I officially resigned from Fuller!

A New Paradigm for Equipping

When I first began casting the vision for Wagner Leadership Institute (WLI), I felt like I was beginning a new career at 68 years of age! One reason is that I sensed a refreshing freedom to develop a philosophy of equipping the saints that had been percolating in my spirit for years. I trace it back to meeting Ralph Winter while I was studying church growth at the Fuller School of Mission back in 1968-1969. That is when Ralph was using his former nation of ministry, Guatemala, as a field for developing what he called "theological education by extension." I described this in quite a bit of detail in chapter 5, so I will not repeat it. Suffice it to say that the major feature of this radical new paradigm was focusing what he called "theological education" (by the way, I don't care for this term!) on "in-service," rather than "pre-service," students.

Up until then, the almost uniform assumption of all of us who were in educational ministry was that we train young people as well as we can in order for them to enter professional ministry after they graduate. That is "pre-service" training. This was working fairly well in the United States, but Winter had noticed that in the Third World (for example, Latin America), the great majority of those who were actually pastoring the churches across the continent were adults, with families, who had never had the opportunity to graduate from any ministerial school whatsoever. How, then, could we equip these mature pastors? Only by developing an educational system focused on "in-service" students like them. This was truly thinking outside the box in those days.

For different reasons, Donald McGavran had originally designed the Fuller School of World Mission on the "in-service" philosophy. The only students he would admit were those who had accumulated significant cross-cultural missionary experience, validated by fluency in a second language. I loved this way of designing a school.

Furthermore, as I also described earlier, I became involved in developing a Doctor of Ministry program for the Fuller School of Theology. Their Master of Divinity program was built on the "pre-service" model, but the D.Min. program was "in-service" for those who had earned their master's degrees and who had gone on to become experienced pastors or other leaders. I liked teaching in the SWM and D.Min. programs much more than teaching M.Div. undergraduates.

The Major Differences

With this as a background, I was ready to start WLI as an "in-service" educational institution. I realized from the start that in many ways it would be

180 degrees different from standard, traditional programs for training ministers. Here are some of the major differences:

- **No academic requirements.** Accredited theological seminaries, because they require a college degree for entrance, have eliminated 75 percent of America's population from their student body. Only 25 percent of American adults are college graduates. WLI, on the other hand, wants to be available to train *all* of God's saints for the work of the ministry.

- **Impartation along with information.** In WLI, I instruct my faculty not to focus primarily on transferring a body of knowledge from their heads to the students' heads, as much as imparting to them tools and anointing for fruitful ministry. As the students will tell you, they invariably suffer from information overload, but the information is secondary while the impartation is primary.

- **No exams or grades.** Because of the focus on impartation, I find it impractical to give exams or letter grades for the courses. The powerful impartation for ministry that the students receive validates the quality of their education, so exams and grades are not necessary. To close each course, the student must write a brief self-evaluation paper, telling how the course impacted their own life and ministry.

- **No resident students or resident faculty.** Because we at WLI are training in-service rather than pre-service ministers, it is impossible for most students to enter a residence program. The students have families, jobs, community involvements and ministries wherever they live. Most cannot give three years to full-time study. In addition, by using visiting faculty, it is possible to draw on the best in each field on a time-available basis.

- **Variable delivery systems.** There is no prescribed format for WLI courses as long as students have around 12 contact hours with the instructor. Some WLI schools use two days back to back; some use Thursday night, Friday night and Saturday; some teach

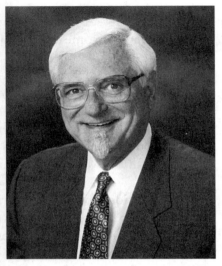

Doris and I enjoy living in the Black Forest Park region of Colorado Springs, where we have eight acres covered mostly with Ponderosa pines. I have cut out more than half a mile of four-wheeler trails and installed a nine-hole Frisbee golf course.

At this point, around the turn of the twenty-first century, I am finishing my teaching career at Fuller Theological Seminary and switching my attention to Wagner Leadership Institute. I am excited about this new paradigm for equipping the saints for the work of ministry!

Jay Swallow (left), a Southern Cheyenne, is one our our chief apostolic bridges to Native American nations in our country. We are praying for God's release of kingdom wealth at the grave of Alexander Hamilton, my four-time great grandfather, in the yard of Trinity Episcopal Church in New York City.

one night a week for several weeks; some teach every night for a week; some use conferences as their format. We have live web-casts in all our WLI Central classes, and numerous courses are available online.

- **Curriculum.** Courses are tailor-made to the needs of the students. Rather than required courses, WLI has six core areas that reflect the DNA of the institution, namely, Apostolic Ministries, Prophetic Ministries, Intercession, Deliverance, Signs and Wonders, and Spiritual Warfare. Students can fulfill this requirement in a variety of ways.

WLI Phase Two

WLI was a new wineskin that began very strongly under the leadership of our son-in-law, Jack Sytsema, married to our youngest daughter, Becky. However, Jack had to resign as WLI dean in 2004, when he and Becky felt they should move from Colorado to Florida in order to receive proper care for their two sons who have autism. Unfortunately, the replacements for Jack did not meet our expectations, and 2005 was a serious down year for WLI. By then I had become involved in other projects, and I could not go back to running WLI hands on. I was very discouraged, and I must admit I even considered the possibility of phasing out WLI.

At this point, however, Craig Davis stepped up to the plate. Craig, who lived in Florida, had enrolled in WLI. After he took a few courses, he liked it so much that he moved his family to Colorado Springs. He began to volunteer to help Doris in the GHM office, and it soon became evident that he possessed unusual skills at innovation, organization and management. Craig, by then an alumnus of WLI, started casting a new vision for the school, which I immediately saw as a potential Phase 2. I reorganized the staff and named Craig as WLI provost in 2006, serving under me as chancellor.

It didn't take Craig very long to revamp WLI Central in Colorado Springs and to begin to establish new regional WLIs across the nation. Back in 2004, Chuck Pierce had prophesied that we would have 12 WLIs in different parts of America. Through the years, I had made 10 to 15 attempts to start some, but I was never able to succeed because, as I later figured out, I mistakenly had in mind establishing cookie-cutter branches of our central school. Craig's approach, to the contrary, was to encourage potential regional chancellors to develop separate schools of their own, not branches of Colorado Springs, tailoring each one to the needs of the region. His plan worked well. Before long we had more than 20 WLIs in the United States and 12 international WLIs. Phase 2 was well under way. Unfortunately, an unanticipated death in the family forced Craig to move back to Florida, but by then he had built momentum and had trained Karen Kottaridis, whom I then appointed as dean. WLI has done well ever since.

"Now I Can Study!"

One of our strongest international schools has been Indonesia. I have taught there many times, and I have presided over a number of graduations, the last one presenting diplomas to almost 200 students. They build their graduation ceremonies around an elegant banquet in huge hotel ballrooms.

One of the most memorable testimonies came from Timothy Arifin, one of the best-known leaders in Indonesia, with a remarkable megachurch of 5,000 on the demon-infested island of Bali. Before he received his doctorate, he told the audience that a few years ago, God awoke him from sleep with one clear word, "Study!" As an obedient servant, he checked out all the Bible schools and seminaries in Indonesia, but none of them could serve him. He simply couldn't leave his church and enroll in a traditional school. Then one day he came across a WLI catalog, and he exclaimed, "Now I can obey the Lord! Now I can study!"

When Arifin first enrolled in WLI, his goal was to plant and provide apostolic leadership to 100 churches. I thought that was an awesome goal! Before he graduated three years later, however, he had already planted his 100 churches. At graduation he announced that studying in WLI had increased his faith so much that his new goal is 50 cities and 1,000 churches in his apostolic network! And he's well on his way to achieve his goal!

As I handed Timothy his diploma, I could only think in my mind, *Now that's what WLI is supposed to be all about!*

Accountability Rather Than Accreditation

Wagner Leadership Institute was only one of hundreds of new schools that had been springing up in recent years to equip the saints in the New Apostolic Reformation. Virtually every vertical apostolic network would routinely establish its own school to train leaders and others. Even before I started WLI, it became clear to me that the Body of Christ was spawning a new breed of educators. These educators, like me, had all been moving from a paradigm of theological education, centered in traditional seminaries and Bible schools, to a variety of new wineskins for training ministers. It wasn't long before my intuitions as a horizontal apostle began to kick in enough to make me realize that very few, if any, of these apostolic educators had ever been in contact with their peers from other networks or ministries.

In 1998, I felt the prompting of the Holy Spirit to attempt to get these educators together for the first time, so I wrote a letter to all of the apostles with whom I had been building relationships. I cast my vision for a meeting of educators and told them that this time I did not want the apostles to show up, but I wanted them to send their educators. A good number of them did, and we ended up with 100 apostolic educators in a hotel conference room in Colorado Springs. I built the program around panels with audience participation in order to make the meeting as interactive as possible. I was amazed at the spectrum of constituencies represented there. For example, one apostolic network had been assigned by God to train leaders for churches planted in academic communities, while another school had to give oral exams to some of their students because they were illiterate!

My biggest surprise came with our panel on accreditation. At the time, I was still teaching in Fuller Seminary, and I simply assumed that striving for academic accreditation would be on the priority lists of all of the schools represented. As the panel developed, I was shocked. Every single panel member, each in a different way, said in essence that for his or her school, traditional academic accreditation was a dead-end street! Those who spoke from the audience argued that accreditation would *prevent*, not help, their institution to be all that God wanted it to be!

I introduced the next panel, but to be honest, I was still in such a state of shock over accreditation that I could not pay much attention to what the new panel was talking about. The next thing I knew, I had my yellow pad out and I was receiving amazing revelation from God as to what He wanted us to do about traditional accreditation. I stepped outside, checked a couple of things with my staff, and then I asked the leader of the current panel to finish 15 minutes early because I had an announcement to make.

My announcement was that we were going to institute a creative alternative to traditional accreditation, namely, the Apostolic Council for Educational Accountability (ACEA). I outlined how we would all become members of ACEA, and how we would hold each other accountable for excellence. We would not be governed by some relatively abstract accrediting manual, but by God's distinctive purpose for each one of our institutions. Mutual accountability would replace legalistic standardized accreditation.

Since then, ACEA has flourished. Around 50 institutions have taken out membership. They pay dues, send representatives to the annual meeting in Colorado Springs, and participate in on-site visits by peers. The apostolic educators are excited. They can be everything they believe that God wants them to be and still not feel like they are operating as Lone Rangers, isolated from the rest of the Body of Christ.

Equipping Other Saints

Because, as I have said, I am an inveterate teacher, I couldn't be content with just teaching the students in Fuller or WLI or other such institutions.

At the same time, I continually need to remind myself to avoid my tendency to be overenthusiastic about new ideas. Do you remember that in chapter 8 I made a point of my agreement with Bobby Clinton's theory of convergence, which advocates that we should stick to doing what we're good at? I knew right along that I was good at teaching in-service students such as we have in WLI, and therefore, I should have been wise enough to avoid attempting to equip pre-service students, but I wasn't.

In 2002, I became overenthusiastic about a challenge to start a new school, in partnership with Ché Ahn and Harvest Rock Church of Pasadena, California, geared toward the 18 to 25 generation. It sounded good, because it would ride on the heels of the several successful youth rallies named "The Call," which Ché and Lou Engle had been doing across the nation. Consequently, we launched The Call School of Ministry, which was a nine-month residence program for those who wished to take a year out to find themselves, to explore various ministry possibilities, to study for a week at a time with outstanding teachers and to spend a good bit of time in prayer. We enrolled 50 students, many of whom would not have traded the year for anything because it permanently changed their lives for the better. But unfortunately, the school in general did not fulfill our expectations, and we discontinued it after one year. Through it I learned a good lesson: stick to in-service training!

Meanwhile, one of our long-standing vehicles for equipping in-service saints has been our conference ministry. This began in Pasadena with Fuller Institute conferences in different parts of the nation on church growth, church planting and, later, prayer and spiritual warfare. When we moved to Colorado, we added Global Harvest ministries conferences on apostolic ministry, prophecy, deliverance, signs and wonders and, more recently, topics such as reformation, dominion, wealth and social transformation. In terms of sheer numbers, our conferences have been used to equip more of the saints than anything else that I have been involved in, numbering into the thousands each year.

Sexual Bondages
The almost uniform responses to our conferences have been more than positive, let's call them enthusiastic! I say "almost" because a few have been just the opposite. One of our most provocative conferences happened in 1993, when we announced the theme "Breaking Sexual Bondages." In Doris's ministry of deliverance, sexual issues had consistently been on the top layer of demonic activities that needed ministry, so we innocently geared a whole conference around the subject. We were not prepared to receive the volume of nasty emails and phone calls that barraged us right after our conference brochure was mailed out. Some didn't think that Christians should be talking about sex in public! A good number were so furious that they asked to be removed from our mailing list. You would think we had been advertising X-rated movies!

We were disappointed that conference registrations were very low, not even enough to pay our bills. But God helped us laugh in the midst of it when we discovered that the pre-conference orders for CDs and DVDs had broken all previous records by a good bit! One pastor's wife wrote and said that their congregation would not understand if they knew that she and her husband were going to a "Breaking Sexual Bondages" conference, but they wanted the DVDs because they had to minister to so many people in the same congregation who were harboring a good many of those bondages that needed to be broken real badly!

After the conference our mail was totally different—all positive and deeply thankful. One was from a family of five—mother, father and three adult sons—all of whom were suffering from persistent sex sins like lustful behavior, homosexuality, pornography and other addictions. The father wrote and said how free they now were to talk through these issues for the first time as a family. Then he said, "Two years ago, I lost my job and purchased a $750,000 life insurance policy to replace my corporate insurance. That policy has an exclusionary clause that makes it void in case of suicide for two years. I knew that clause would expire a day or two before the conference, and when I came I had determined that my life was so messed up and impossible to redeem that the best thing for me to do was to just kill myself, spare the family any further heartache and give them financial resources to get on with rebuilding their lives. Cindy Jacobs's message reminded me of that suicidal vow, which I immediately broke before God on Friday night!"

That family is on the road to recovery and doing well! Whatever it takes, I want to continue equipping saints like these for whatever ministry God has for them in the future!

Part 5: Dominion, Wealth and Reformation

I thought that my mind-stretching paradigm shift from affirming the traditional, denominational pattern of church government to what I now consider a more biblical apostolic/prophetic foundation of the church was the last uncomfortable change in thinking and teaching that I would ever have to make. After all, I was 63 when it started, and 71 when I felt that the Second Apostolic Age had sufficiently come into place in 2001. Isn't that a career? I thought I would then have plenty of time to take my chain saws into the woods and drive my tractors into the fields.

Wrong! Little did I imagine that in that same year of 2001, I would take the first steps into what I now consider to be the most radical and potentially world-changing paradigm shift of all, namely, understanding and applying God's Dominion Mandate. The last book I published before this one has as its title *Dominion!* and it summarizes what I have learned over the last few years. One of those things I have learned, as you can imagine, is no longer to plan on this being the last paradigm shift. If more come, I am ready. If not, fine. I still have my chain saws and tractors!

A McGavran Revisionist
Back in chapter 7, I made a brief reference to Cindy Jacobs's rather shocking contention that we should pray for the healing of *nations* and expect God to answer our prayers. As I mentioned, the idea of healing whole na-

tions was different from my understanding that we should go into the nations expressly for the purpose of saving as many individuals as possible and gathering the converts into Christian churches.

I did not elaborate in chapter 7 because I wanted to save it for here. Donald McGavran's consistent interpretation of the Great Commission was that Jesus sent His followers to disciple whole nations (or people groups) according to Matthew 28:19-20. This literal interpretation of the Great Commission appeared in his seminal book *Bridges of God* as well as in his textbook that I later edited, *Understanding Church Growth*. However, when I began teaching church growth, I made an independent decision, which I (probably unwisely) do not recall discussing with anyone else, especially McGavran. I felt I needed to be a McGavran revisionist! Why? Try as I might, I could not get my mind around the idea that whole social units could be transformed by the power of God. So my take on the Great Commission was simply to go into as many people groups as possible, to save as many souls as possible and to plant as many churches as possible.

Notice that changing society did not enter the picture. For better or for worse, my teaching and writing, especially in the United States, gained me more influence in the church growth field than even McGavran had, and consequently my revision of McGavran prevailed among church leaders across the board. When Cindy Jacobs mentioned healing *nations*, I was shocked, because I immediately recognized the fact that, although she had never heard of him, she was supporting McGavran, with whom I had disagreed on that particular point. Still, I was not yet ready for a paradigm shift. I never argued against either Jacobs or McGavran, but when they mentioned nations, I stubbornly added my own twist.

Saving Souls vs. Social Change

Let's carry this one step further. My view of the Great Commission was preaching the gospel and saving souls, which is commonly referred to as evangelism. Back in chapter 5, I described a 40-year running disagreement that I had with several leaders, especially some Latin American theologians, as well as John Stott, who advocated that, along with evangelism, the Great Commission mandated, just as strongly, that we should also promote social change. In order to maintain peace in our circles, the compromise for me and my followers was that we could agree to admit both, but still adhere to the *Lausanne Covenant*, which affirmed that evangelism was *primary*. That, of course, implied that social change was *secondary*, so it could easily be neglected, which it was, by and large. I, obviously, was among those who chose to neglect social change on the grounds that it might dilute our primary task of evangelism.

With this, you can see why I would have had difficulty processing McGavran's "discipling nations" and Jacobs's "healing nations." If either one were accomplished as they were projecting, we would not just see churches scattered throughout the social unit, but the society itself would be reformed. My passion was always for multiplying churches, not reforming society.

I'm including this information at the beginning of this section because a paradigm shift is not only a move *toward* a new concept but also moving *away* from an old one. I want to make sure that everyone knows my former positions and why I held them. Now I'll try to explain how God enabled me to depart from insisting on dealing with individuals over social units and on evangelism over social change. Although it is embarrassing, you will see that I now consider myself to have been wrong on both counts. And if you are one of my older students, I can only apologize and hope that you were able to make these important shifts before I did. I wish I could refund your tuition!

The Church in the Workplace

My paradigm shift to the Dominion Mandate did not come through a visit to the Third Heaven or the voice of God coming out of a burning bush or even a timely word from a prophet. Those scenarios would probably have been much simpler than the several rather tedious steps I found that I needed to take in order to navigate through the process. The first step was getting used to a concept that I had even taught against in the past, namely, that the real church exists in the workplace as well as in the religious organizations to which we are more accustomed.

Because I try to read as extensively as I can in order to keep up with events that relate to God's current assignments for me, I had become aware that there was a significant movement called by several terms, such as "Faith at Work," and that rather widespread interest in that movement had been growing. I read a bit about it and I applauded it, but from the back row. My interest in putting it on my agenda was little more than my interest in learning how to play the violin. I was a church person, not a business or workplace person. I was happy that others, not I, would be caring for things like that.

It all changed in 2001, when a Christian business couple whom I had come to know, Dennis and Megan Doyle of Minneapolis, surprised me by inviting me to speak in the Twin Cities to a group of businesspeople they had been convening for some time. My first inclination was to send apologies, since I had no experience in relating to this kind of audience. I was used to speaking to church leaders, not workplace leaders.

However, as I was contemplating this invitation and praying about it, God got my attention by speaking to me directly. As you now know from reading this book, it has been quite a bit more common for God to speak to me through prophets than directly. But this was one of those unusual cases. God said, "Son, I want you to pay strict attention to ministry in the workplace." My response? I said yes to God and yes to the Doyles!

Now I had to come up with a plan. I had no prepared teaching material on the subject, so I began to purchase and read some books. Eventually, my personal library on workplace ministries has grown to more than 100 volumes, almost all of which I have read, but back then it was only a few. As I perused them, one of the most significant discoveries was that I had been gearing my thoughts and my actions around a Greek mindset rather than the biblical Hebrew mindset. I soon repented for that, and it was a good thing, because if I hadn't changed my thinking, I now know that I could not have progressed in finally understanding the Dominion Mandate. I came to realize that in Hebrew thought there was no huge gap between the spiritual and the natural, which required words like "sacred and secular" or "clergy and laity" or "full-time ministry" or "church and world." Rather, God is personally present in all of life and He wants His children to experience Him wherever they are and in whatever they are doing.

I wish I could report that I hit a home run in Minneapolis. I might have hit an infield single, but it wouldn't be much more than that. Nevertheless, I was now firmly on the road toward where God wanted to take me. I ended up writing a whole book on the subject, *The Church in the Workplace*, and here are the main points that I had learned:

- **There is a church in the workplace.** The biblical word for church, *ekklesia,* means the people of God. Sometimes it is used for the people of God meeting together, but at other times it is used for the people of God wherever they might be found. When they are in their churches one day a week, they are truly the church; but when they are in the workplace the other six days, they are still the church. I like to call the Sunday church the "nuclear church" and the workplace church the "extended church."

- **Christian ministry is not confined to the nuclear church.** For years I assumed that the normal place for valid Christian ministry was in the nuclear church. Now I know that the saints do the work of the ministry wherever they are; not just one day per week, but seven days per week. The biblical word for ministry, *diakonia,* is equally translated "service" in the Bible. For example, when a Christian airplane pilot *serves* passengers by taking them where they want to go, that "service" is a biblical form of "ministry" as well, just as much as singing in the choir or pastoring a church.

- **God assigns apostles to the church in the workplace.** If apostles are an essential part of the biblical foundation of the church, it is only logical to conclude that He gives them both to the nuclear church and to the extended church. We have done pretty well in identifying and activating apostles in the nuclear church, but we are only beginning in the extended church.

Why would it be so important to activate apostles in the workplace? I have become convinced that they actually hold the keys for opening two strategic gates to the future: (1) the gate to social transformation or reformation, and (2) the gate to the great transfer of wealth for advancing the Kingdom and taking dominion.

The Dominion Mandate

Here is a true personal dilemma. I am nearing the end of writing these memoirs. However, at the moment, I find myself on one of the steepest learning curves of my career. When I first contemplated writing my memoirs, my thought was to include everything I've ever learned in this book. But how can I? I'm still learning! I don't have any idea how long I'll go on. This book is due to be released on my eightieth birthday, but, after all, Moses just started getting up a good head of steam when he was 80!

All these new understandings relating to the Dominion Mandate are in process as I write. My intent, therefore, is to avoid coming to too many conclusions, because new information might eventually point in other directions. This is a good reason to be as brief as I can throughout this chapter. So let me start by showing what I consider to be the big picture of the Dominion Mandate:

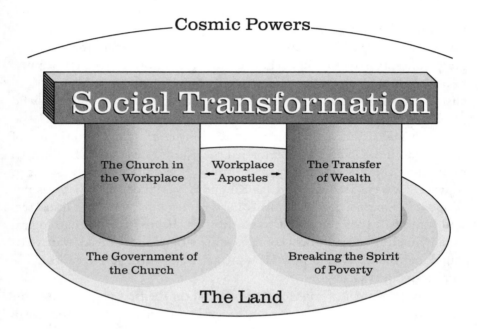

The central bar is "Social Transformation," which many are also calling "Reformation." This is our Dominion Mandate, seeing the kingdom of God actually being manifested here on earth as it is in heaven.

The whole picture is underlain with issues regarding "The Land," and is surrounded with "Cosmic Powers" actively attempting to prevent God's kingdom from coming to earth. Fortunately, we have learned a great deal about how to neutralize these forces of evil, and the details of that are found in chapter 7, chapter 8 and part 2 of this chapter.

The goal of Social Transformation rests on two indispensable pillars. One is "The Church in the Workplace," which I have just explained, and that is based on "The Government of the Church," which I dealt with in part 1 of this chapter. The other pillar is "The Great Transfer of Wealth," based on the principle of "Breaking the Spirit of Poverty," both of which I am coming to shortly.

Notice, finally, that the only component of the diagram that has arrows indicating action is "Workplace Apostles." This reflects what I said a page or two ago that it is only by activating apostles in the extended church that we will hope to see the necessary gates to reformation and wealth transfer effectively opened.

Dominion Theology

I have been trying to figure out why I was stubbornly reluctant for so long to grasp concepts like discipling whole nations and reforming society. It must have been a lingering residue of my days as a fundamentalist, a dispensationalist and a separatist. I had developed a strong repugnance for liberals who preached a "Social Gospel" and who devalued soul-saving evangelism.

I now realize that it took me much too long to grasp the significance of the kingdom of God. I had memorized the Lord's Prayer and I had prayed many times, "Your kingdom come, Your will be done on earth as it is in heaven." However, in my mind the Kingdom was something that was not supposed to happen now, but rather in some distant future after Jesus' second coming. It took me awhile to go through the necessary eschatological paradigm shift to eventually come to realize that God, indeed, wants His kingdom to come to earth now. He wants us to be reformers. He wants to use us to transform society!

A deep theological root for this is found on the first page of the Bible where we read that God first creates the world then creates Adam and Eve in order to give them dominion over the whole creation. However, Satan succeeds in persuading Adam to disobey God, which allows him to usurp the dominion. That is why he is called "the god of this age." Jesus then came to reverse this process, to begin to establish His kingdom and to send us out to preach the gospel of the kingdom. I now see that our task is not only to save souls but also to retake the dominion over creation that Adam lost. I explain all this in detail in my book *Dominion!*

The 7-M Template

Obviously, Satan is not going to give up any of the territory that he has held for millenia without a fight. That is why I am so grateful for the decade of the 1990s, which was like a spiritual warfare boot camp for the Body of Christ. Now we know fairly well what the weapons of our warfare are and how to use them; but if we are going to win, we need a strategy.

A question that kept lurking in my mind was: *What are the battlefields?* I knew that the society we are mandated to reform was not just one big conglomerate, but a unified whole that is made up of several vital pieces, each one of which must take its own path toward reformation. I knew that apostles in the workplace would be the generals, but apostles have spheres. I didn't know how to identify the spheres or the battlefields.

Then came my friend, Lance Wallnau, a pastor, an apostle and a business consultant. Drawing on insights from leaders like Bill Bright and Loren Cunningham, Wallnau has been able to popularize what he calls the seven mountains that shape societies. Here is his warfare strategy: "If the world is to be won, these are the mountains that mold the culture and the minds of men. Whoever controls these mountains controls the direction of the world and the harvest therein."[9]

Wallnau's seven mountains or seven molders of culture are (1) Religion, (2) Family, (3) Education, (4) Media, (5) Government, (6) Arts and Entertainment, and (7) Business. These are the major battlefields for taking dominion over society.

Remember in the Social Transformation diagram that workplace apostles are the only component with action arrows? This is why. We nuclear-church apostles have influence in the Religion Mountain and some (decreasing) influence in the Family Mountain here in the United States. But, by and large, the kingdom of God will only be extended in the six non-Religion mountains under the leadership of extended-church apostles—apostles of the workplace. Wallnau says, "Look at your occupational field and see it as a mountain. What companies and people are at the top of the mountain? What skills, knowledge, and personal characteristics are needed to occupy that position? What would need to exist for you to occupy the top of that mountain?"[10]

I believe this is the battle plan we must follow for sustained reformation. When I said earlier that I am still on a learning curve as I conclude this book, discovering how to implement this and how to measure the results toward our goal are still huge challenges.

Wealth

Did you ever notice or pay much attention to Solomon's wisdom when he said, "Money answers everything" (Eccles. 10:19)? Throughout most of my life, this verse of Scripture impacted me about as much as the one in Deuteronomy 14:21: "You shall not boil a young goat in its mother's milk"! A major reason for this is that I had naively succumbed to the influence of the spirit of poverty. Money or wealth, in my mind, was not particularly pleasing to God! Sufficiency was all that a spiritual believer should expect.

It is not hard to analyze why poverty would have gained such a tight grip on me. I was born when the Great Depression began, suffered the rigors and hardships and rationing of World War II and, just when the national economic system began to improve, Doris and I left for 16 years on the mission field with a subsistence income. Poverty had been our way of life. When I started teaching in Fuller Seminary at 41, we had no material assets except for the minimal down payment on a car and some furniture we had bought in Mexico. We had to borrow from a friend the down payment on our first home. Even though Fuller paid a good salary, I still bought my clothes from the Salvation Army Thrift Store and refused to allow air conditioning to be installed in our family automobile!

How was I delivered from that repugnant spirit? God used several people in the process, one of whom was Bill Bishop Hamon. We were together in a conference in 1996 when God spoke directly to him about my poverty bondage. Bishop then gathered some of his friends, took me to a side room and loudly decreed that the spirit of poverty would no longer have an influence on my life. He then pulled some money out of his pocket and told the others to do the same. He then handed me $170 in cash and said that it was a prophetic act for me personally. I was not to give it away, nor was I to tithe it; but I was to spend it on myself and my wife. So Doris and I wined and dined in an elegant restaurant and I paid the bill with the literal cash I received, with some change left over. That was a huge turning point for us!

But Hamon wasn't through. Nine years later, I was leading the closing session of the International Coalition of Apostles when he asked my permission to do a prophetic act from the platform. Much to my surprise, he announced that, since I had never taken a salary from ICA, it was time for the members who were present to bless me with financial gifts. He brought Doris up with me and challenged the apostles to come forward and lay money at the feet of their apostolic leader. The result? We left with thousands of dollars in our pockets! When our plane landed in Colorado Springs, I said, "Doris, your Camry is way over 10 years old. Let's stop in the Toyota dealer and buy a new one before we drive home!" We were able to pay over half the money necessary for Doris's new Camry! And, yes, it had air conditioning!

Why do I tell these stories? Because I don't believe God would use us in the transfer of wealth unless and until we had broken the curse of the spirit of poverty. Don't forget the pillar of Wealth that is supporting the bar of Social Transformation in the graphic. Its foundation is Breaking the Curse of the Spirit of Poverty.

The Great Wealth Transfer

I think that it is time we began agreeing strongly and openly that we cannot expect to be agents in God's hands for massive and sustained reformation unless we control huge amounts of wealth. In all of human history, three things, above all others, have changed society: violence, knowledge and wealth. And the greatest of these is wealth!

It wasn't until 2004 that I began sensing a direction from the Lord to pay more attention to the great transfer of wealth that several other leaders had been talking about. One of the first things I did was to sit down with Chuck Pierce and probe his photographic mind. I asked when God's prophets began speaking about wealth transfer, and he estimated that it was around 1992. Since 12 years had elapsed by then, I began searching for possible reasons for the delay. I concluded then, and I still believe this, that God will not release the quantities of wealth He has in mind until a critical mass of workplace apostles has been activated.

I began to picture four links in the chain of the great transfer of wealth:

The Four Links

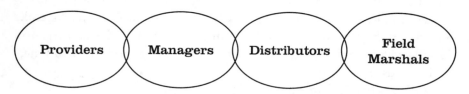

As you can see, the four necessary links in the chain of transference of wealth are: providers, managers, distributors and field marshals. I believe that three of the four links are mostly in place. The providers either have the wealth or God will give them the power to create it according to Deuteronomy 8:18. The field marshals who direct the extension of the Kingdom on the front lines around the world are numerous. Distributors are of two kinds: Narrow-band distributors are in contact with field marshals in their apostolic spheres; wide-band distributors are in contact with the most effective narrow-band distributors.

Our weakest link has been managers, and here is where workplace apostles are absolutely necessary. Before the wealth from the providers goes further down the chain, it should be multiplied several times, as did the faithful money managers in Jesus' parable in Matthew 25. In fact, I look forward to the day when our Kingdom-minded ministries will establish ministry revenue funds that will be large enough and be managed aggressively enough to cover a substantial amount of a ministry's annual budget. I would love to see ministries' finances eventually come through revenue-based funding rather than donor-based funding as most have been using up to now. Very few nuclear-church apostles would know how to manage such revenue funds. It takes extended-church apostles to do it well.

Conclusion

I hope you are beginning to see what I meant earlier when I said that this section of the book presents a dilemma for me. If God does favor me with the opportunity to undertake a new assignment from Him at age 80, it might well be in this area of wealth transfer, particularly in the distribution link of the chain. I have a great deal more that I would like to share here, but the timing is not right. It could be that a future book on the subject is in the incubator. Before that happens, however, I need to learn a lot more and I need to log much more hands-on experience than I presently have.

One thing I am as sure of as I can be: God wants His kingdom to come here on earth as it is in heaven. He is raising up an army of Kingdom-minded and Kingdom-motivated people whom He will empower to retake from Satan the dominion of the 7 mountains that mold our culture. And He will provide all the tools, the resources, the strategy and the wealth necessary for us to accomplish the task!

With all that, it's time to talk about transitions.

Notes

1. C. Peter Wagner, *Your Spiritual Gifts Can Help Your Church Grow* (Ventura, CA: Regal, 1979), p. 261.
2. C. Peter Wagner, "Church Growth" in *Dictionary of Pentecostal and Charismatic Movements*, edited by Stanley M. Burgess and Gary B. McGee (Grand Rapids, MI: Zondervan Publishing House, 1988), pp. 180-195.
3. C. Peter Wagner, *Dominion!* (Grand Rapids, MI: Chosen, 2008), p. 31.
4. Bill Hamon, *Apostles, Prophets and the Coming Moves of God* (Shippensburg, PA: Destiny Image, 1997), p. 10.
5. See Philip Jenkins, *The Next Christendom* (New York: Oxford University Press, 2002) and *The New Faces of Christianity* (New York: Oxford University Press, 1996).
6. Sandy Simpson and Mike Oppenheimer, "An Answer to Ted Haggard: Response to Ted Haggard's Email Rebuttal to our *Open Letter to the NAE*," April 23, 2003, p. 1.
7. Luis Bush, *Raising Up a New Generation from the 4/14 Window to Transform the World* (Flushing, NY: Transform World New Generation, www.4to14window.com, 2009), p. 4.
8. Personal correspondence, March 13, 2009.
9. Lance Wallnau, "A Prophetic, Biblical, and Personal Call to the Workplace," privately circulated paper, nd., np.
10. Ibid.

10

Transitions

Research from the leadership expert, Bobby Clinton, confirms the unfortunate fact that a majority of Christian leaders do not finish well. I remember how surprised I was when, years ago, he first gave me that information. In fact, "finishing well" happened to be an entirely new concept to me at that time. Even though I was relatively young, I still determined then and there that I would strive be one of those who do finish well. Have I succeeded? Obviously I can't know the answer to that because I haven't yet finished!

Getting old is a fascinating phenomenon. It's an extremely gradual process. I often say that I can't quite remember when my wild oats began turning to prunes and bran! Long ago, I resolved not to resort to denial when, if I happened to be among those so fortunate, old age finally arrived. They say that you're only as old as you feel, and there is probably something to that. Unlike others I know, passing 40 or 50 or 60 or even 70 were not notable events for me. I disallowed birthday parties. I actually never felt much different after those supposed milestones than before. However, for reasons that somehow I am unable to explain, I did actually begin feeling old when I turned 76. You're only as old as you feel? Well then, I'm 79 for sure, because I *feel* 79!

Some friends still scold me when I bring this up. One reason, I know, is that they love me and they never want me to leave them. I honor this and, frankly, it's very touching. Then we sometimes begin playing a game. They say, "Well, you don't look 79!" I respond, "Yes, I do!" After we argue about it for a moment or two, I firmly establish my point by pulling out my driver's license and saying, "This government ID says I'm 79. When you look at me you see 79!" So we proceed to change the subject.

A Vision for Transitions

Whatever we might think of this, finishing well requires some planning. Obviously, the planning needs to be done ahead of time, but the problem is that no one knows when "the time" will come. I have no plans for retirement. Many people are still playing tennis in their eighties. We have a physician in Colorado Springs who is actively seeing patients in the poor areas of town at the age of 90! I want to be like him! Meanwhile, let's be real. Because long-range plans are unrealistic at this point, my short-range plan is to take some concrete steps toward the future, envisioning and taking action steps toward practical transitions.

Of course, transition means change. I have never been a stranger to change. You may recall that circumstances took me to 13 schools for my first 12 grades. As a youngster, I got to like changes and even look forward to them. I think this may be why transitions have been a bit easier for me than they are for some. I tend to be a forerunner. I'm always curious to discover what's on the other side of the mountain. God works in seasons, and if He has a new season for my life, I want to move into it rather than maintain the status quo in an old season, good as it might have been for the time. I can identify with the apostle Paul, who said, "Forgetting those things which are behind and reaching forward to those things which are ahead, I press toward the goal for the prize of the upward call of God in Christ Jesus" (Phil. 3:13-14).

The principal transitions for me, not counting the two major ones of salvation in Christ and marrying Doris, can fall into two categories: theological transitions and ministry transitions. Let's look at them one at a time.

Theological Transitions

Theological transitions are often described as paradigm shifts. That's because they require a "renewing of your mind," as the Bible says in Romans 12:2. A paradigm is nothing but a mental grid through which certain outside information is processed before it gets into the mind. Many things enter into forming paradigms, which frequently outlive their usefulness. Fortunately, when they do, they can be changed. But the change isn't always easy. Sometimes it is so radical that we call it a "paradigm *shift*." I like to think of the theological transitions I have made throughout my ministry as paradigm shifts.

This is no place to deal with theological issues in any kind of depth. I did some of that in previous chapters. All I want to do here is to list my theological paradigm shifts and add only a sentence or two of explanation. For me, they all were important transitions, and I'll list them in chronological order.

- **Shifting from the two-channel theory to recognizing Jesus' full human nature.** My first understanding of the two natures of Christ was that He would regularly switch between using His human nature and using His divine nature. My Fuller theology professor, Edward John Carnell, convinced me that, based on Philippians 2, we can be sure that, while He was on earth, before the cross, Jesus used only His human nature. I explained in chapter 2 how this caused problems in my ordination examination.

- **Shifting from human abilities to spiritual gifts.** It was during my jungle missionary days, with the help of a missionary friend named Ken Decker, that I began to understand how the Body of Christ is meant to function with every member using his or her spiritual gifts. Teaching this in person and through two of my books, *Your Spiritual Gifts Can Help Your Church Grow* and *Discover Your Spiritual Gifts,* may turn out to be the most helpful contribution I will have made to the Church across the board. The books have continued in print for 30 years and are still doing well.

- **Shifting from theological education to equipping the saints.** Ralph Winter's model of theological education by extension (TEE) began the process of shifting from traditional methods of teaching pre-service students theological and biblical theories to equipping in-service students for practical ministry. I explain TEE toward the beginning of chapter 5. This led to the formation of Wagner Leadership Institute, which you will find in part 4 of chapter 9.

- **Shifting from passive evangelism to pragmatic evangelism.** My most life-changing educational experience was completing my degree in missiology under Donald McGavran at the Fuller School of World Mission in the late 1960s. He taught me to focus our attention, not on our evangelistic efforts per se, but on the measurable results that our efforts actually produce. You can find this detailed in a section called "Shifting Paradigms" in chapter 5. My book *Strategies for Church Growth* explains this concept more fully.

- **Shifting from monocultural theology to cross-cultural theology.** Before I became a missiologist, I took for granted that the theology developed in Europe and North America would be valid for the church all over the world. It was almost like unintentionally equating theology to Scripture. However, when I began bringing cultural anthropology into the picture, mostly under the tutelage of Chuck Kraft, my view of theology became a bit more tentative. Please allow me to deviate from my pledge of brevity in these items of theological paradigm shifts and expand a little more on this one.

Seminary students normally take a course in the history of dogma. This unfolds the story of leaders like Augustine (fifth century) and Thomas Aquinas (thirteenth century) and John Calvin (sixteenth century) and many other figures who did their best to explain biblical principles to the church at large. The only point I want to make here is that, at least until modern times, when concepts of globalization have begun to penetrate the intellectual world, the general assumption was that valid theological principles were only developed in the Western world. Missiologists, whose focus is mainly on the churches of the non-Western world, of course would take exception to that notion.

This leads to an interesting story about how I flunked my tenure exam in Fuller Seminary. As many would know, one reward for faculty in institutions of higher learning who teach for a certain amount of time and who maintain certain standards of competence is to receive academic tenure. This means that their institution trusts them to develop and teach their ideas without threat of being dismissed by the institution. In plainer language, it means that tenured professors cannot be fired.

At Fuller, a requirement for being granted tenure was passing a theological exam administered by professors of the School of Theology. Although this was a bit of an irritant to us who were professors in the School of World Mission and in the School of Psychology, we had no choice. My exam was going well until one of the theologians, Paul King Jewett, asked, "What do you think of systematic theology?" My rather naïve response? "I would prefer using the plural 'systematic theologies.'" There was a brief silence, and things started going downhill from that point on.

When they asked me to explain, I suggested that competent theologians from non-Western parts of the world might use the same Scriptures and come to some conclusions different from the standard dogma of the Western world. In such cases, their points of view should be given as much consideration as those of their Western counterparts. By way of example, I brought up Islamic theology. I stated the fact that sincere, intelligent, good-hearted Islamic scholars truly believe that Christians are polytheists, worshiping three gods. Because they obviously are wrong, I suggested that perhaps our Christian systematic theologians could restate our doctrine of the Trinity so that Muslims could better understand that we are truly monotheists, not polytheists, and that it might take a non-Western Christian theologian to accomplish such a thing. The examination was quickly concluded, and I was informed that I would not be awarded academic tenure at that time!

Parenthetically, I need to enter into the record that a while afterward, I was invited back to be reexamined. This time I was wise enough to evade all questions that might have had cross-cultural implications, and I passed with flying colors. Consequently, I enjoyed academic tenure for the rest of my career!

- **Shifting from programmed evangelism to power evangelism.** I turned one of the most significant corners of my thinking when John Wimber came on the scene and began ministering in signs and wonders. Before he came, I believed in the Holy Spirit, but I thought that effectiveness in evangelism came from applying the right principles at the right time. Wimber's success in Anaheim Vineyard and his teaching in Fuller drove me back to the Scriptures and to the conclusion that spiritual power was the principal key to effective and sustained evangelism. Incidentally, this has been verified over the past 30 years by the explosion of Christianity in the Global South. My best book on this is *How to Have a Healing Ministry in Any Church*, and you can find more details in the chapter "The Wimber Era."

- **Shifting from tolerating Satan to a declaration of war.** Throughout my early ministry, I conceived of Satan as merely a nuisance in our efforts at spreading the gospel. Then, as I related in chapter 7, my contact with Cindy Jacobs and others awakened me to the reality of literal spiritual warfare. Far from being a mere nuisance, Satan is a formidable enemy who must and will be defeated in the several theaters of spiritual warfare. My theological position on this is found in *Confronting the Powers,* and my practical position is found in *Warfare Prayer.*

- **Shifting from Reformed sanctification to Wesleyan holiness.** Once I became involved in spiritual warfare, I found that the Reformed view of sanctification that I held would not be sufficient.

So I shifted to John Wesley's view that we could and should live lives of purity and holiness, thereby shutting many doors through which Satan's demonic forces could enter and thwart our effectiveness. A small book I wrote on this is out of print, but I also explain it thoroughly in chapter 10 of *Changing Church*.

· **Shifting from denominational government to apostolic government.** As soon as I began taking seriously the biblical teaching that the foundation of the church is apostles and prophets, I began shifting my paradigm from democratic forms of government, typical of traditional churches and denominations, to apostolic leadership, which holds that the Holy Spirit delegates considerable amounts of authority in church affairs to individuals whom He calls and assigns to specific tasks. My textbook on the change is *Churchquake!,* while my latest thinking is summarized in *Apostles Today*.

· **Shifting from a church vision to a Kingdom vision.** Most of my early career focused on the church. More recently, however, I began to realize that Jesus' emphasis was not so much on the Church as on His kingdom. He never sent out His disciples to preach the gospel of the *church*, but rather the gospel of the *Kingdom*. The kingdom of God is not confined to the four walls of the local church. I will not forget that after I published what I considered one of my best books, *Church Growth and the Whole Gospel,* Ray Bakke commented that I had not mentioned the Kingdom even once in a book on the church's social responsibility. I looked back and he was right! Since then I have not made that mistake again. Check out, for example, *Changing Church*.

· **Shifting from the extension of the church to the reformation of society.** The Great Commission says that we are to make disciples of all the nations. I used to think that it meant that we are to go into nations to win as many souls as possible and to multiply churches. I now take the Great Commission literally to mean that we should reform the *nation* (or people group) entirely so that the whole society begins to reflect the values of the kingdom of God. I now believe in the Dominion Mandate, and I explained more about that in part 5 of chapter 9.

- **Shifting from classical theism to open theism.** I was taught that God has determined and therefore knows ahead of time everything that ever happens. However, once I began flowing with the prayer movement in the 1990s, I began to believe strongly that our prayers can actually influence what God will do next. They can change God's mind. I presented my theological argument supporting this open theism in chapter 4 of my latest book, *Dominion!*

- **Shifting from ministry in the church to ministry in the workplace.** Up until a few years ago, I believed that all Christian ministry was congregationally based. This was one of my worst mistakes. I even thought that spiritual gifts could only be used in church activities. I have now repented of this because I understand that the church also exists in the workplace and that what believers do in the workplace is a legitimate form of ministry. I tell all about this paradigm shift in my book *The Church in the Workplace.*

- **Shifting from escapist eschatology to victorious eschatology.** This most recent paradigm shift was a long time coming. I think I was still in Bolivia when I began questioning the premillenial, pretribulation Rapture eschatology that I had been taught. The idea was that the world would get worse and worse and at just the right time, we would be raptured out and the Antichrist would take over. I didn't think I really believed that, but I simply put the issue on the back burner for decades. However, when I started understanding the Dominion Mandate, it became clear that I needed a better view of the end times. The light came on when I read Harold Eberle and Martin Trench's *Victorious Eschatology,* and their partial preterist view is what I now believe. I have yet to write anything substantial on the subject.

Someone once told me that I have shifted so many theological paradigms that my gears must be stripped by now! They are probably right. But, as I said up front, I definitely do not want to miss God's next season for me or any new assignments He might attempt to give me. If any of this requires another "renewing of my mind," I am ready to do it!

"There Is No Success Without a Successor!"

I will not forget a statement I heard John Kelly make a few years ago: "There is no success without a successor!" As soon as he said it, I was rather startled because it made me realize that I had never given that much thought to my successors (please note the plural!) even though I was over 70 at the time. From that day on I began seriously thinking and praying about passing my batons.

In order to help orient myself to the challenge, I scheduled a panel-driven session on "Apostolic Succession" for one of the annual meetings of the International Coalition of Apostles. It was quite enlightening. I also read what I could find on the subject. For example, Jeff Myers reports that "Five hundred of the largest companies can expect to lose 50 percent of their senior management by 2010, and 40 percent of companies don't have a leadership succession plan."[1] This was both comforting and alarming. It was comforting to know that I wasn't the only one who had weaknesses in this area, but it was alarming to realize what a disservice many of us are liable to perpetrate on future generations. I now agree with Myers when he says, "The winners in the race of life are those who successfully pass the baton of godly faithfulness to the next generation."[2]

In John Maxwell's classic book *The 21 Irrefutable Laws of Leadership,* his twenty-first law is "The Law of Legacy." Unfortunately, his research, like Bobby Clinton's, also found that "Leaders who practice the Law of Legacy are rare."[3] Maxwell is very realistic. Here is his wisdom: "Every leader eventually leaves his organization—one way or another. He may change jobs, get promoted, or retire. And even if a person refuses to retire, he is going to die."[4] In one of his teaching tapes, Maxwell elaborates on this by talking about "Level 5 leaders." He says, "Level 5 leaders routinely select superb successors. In other words, they are vitally concerned with passing the leadership baton to others. . . . Level 5 leaders basically say, 'I want to make sure that I leave somebody behind who can continue to be successful in the mission and the vision that I have.' "[5]

I am now so convinced that I want to obey the Law of Legacy that my question is, "Why doesn't everybody do this?" Maxwell answers it this way: "Level 4 leaders say, 'I don't care what happens to the organization after I'm gone—I just want to get everything I can for myself.' They don't have a sense of longevity. They don't have a perspective of the big picture."[6] I definitely want to be remembered as a Level 5 leader, not a Level 4 leader. And I realize that it is my responsibility, no one else's. Jeff Myers says, "In a relay race, the responsibility for passing the baton falls to the one who is carrying it, not the one who is receiving it."[7]

Our Daughters Are Our Friends

Many leaders I know have chosen family members as their successors. Among them, passing the baton from father to son has been the most common. This is not the way it has worked out with Doris and me. Over the pages of this book you have met our three daughters, Karen, Ruth and Becky. As we move into the sunset years, one of the elements of our lives that we are most thankful to God for is that our family remains intact. We never had a case of adolescent rebellion. Karen, Ruth and Becky are not just our daughters; they are our friends. All three are serving the Lord in the assignments He has given them. They each have given us three grandchildren, and we now have three great-grandchildren as well, waiting for many more.

None of our daughters has been assigned by God to succeed us in leading the ministry. Becky was on our staff for a long time, and she handled a short-lived publishing company that we founded called Wagner Publications. Her husband, Jack Sytsema, was the first dean of Wagner Leadership Institute. Ruth is currently Information Technology Manager for Global Harvest Ministries and she lives in a section of our house.

Though they are not our ministry heirs, our daughters are clearly our family heirs. We have family conferences with them, they are in personal contact with our estate attorney and they have access to our wills and other papers. We love our daughters and do not want to surprise them when we leave them. For us the simplest procedure is to leave our estate to our daughters and allow them to determine what goes to grandchildren.

During one of our family conferences, they suggested that we prepay our funerals, which we immediately did. We even have our engraved tombstone on our plot in Evergreen Cemetery. We do not think it would be fair to burden them with an assortment of emotionally loaded decisions while they are grieving.

So much for our family transitions. Now for ministry transitions.

Ministry Transitions

When I mentioned the common phrase that there is no success without a successor, I stated that in my case, I needed to identify successors—plural—

rather than just one successor. How many? Realistically we are talking about 8 or possibly 10.

This, I think, relates directly to the assignment God has given me to serve as a "horizontal apostle." I explained in part 1 of chapter 9 how the concept of "horizontal apostle" opened the door for me to recognize openly that God had given me the gift of apostle. I had been given a supernatural ability to bring Christian leaders together for Kingdom purposes, which is what horizontal apostles do.

Andes Evangelical Mission

As I started thinking and praying seriously about transitions, my mind went back to other transitions in which I had been involved through the years. For example, I had served as a missionary to Bolivia for almost 16 years when I sensed God's leading toward joining the faculty of the Fuller Seminary School of World Mission. By then I had assumed the position of Field Director of the Andes Evangelical Mission under the authority of General Director Joseph McCullough whose office was in the United States. For years I had come to appreciate the work of my colleague, Ron Wiebe, some years my junior. I built a personal relationship with him and we admired each other greatly. McCullough agreed that Ron should be my successor, so I began to mentor him and prepare him for the future. When I left, Ron stepped into my place and the transition was seamless.

Charles E. Fuller Institute

My second significant transition was not nearly as seamless. You may recall that when I returned to the United States to begin teaching in Fuller, Dan Fuller, the son of the late founder of the seminary, Charles E. Fuller, asked me also to take leadership of his father's legacy, the Fuller Evangelistic Association. I told all about this in chapter 5. First I had the privilege of distributing much of the Fuller wealth to cutting-edge missionary projects around the world. When these funds began diminishing, I changed the thrust of the organization to the Charles E. Fuller Institute of Evangelism and Church Growth (CEFI) with the intent of doing church consultation and offering national church growth conferences. One of the first colleagues I hired to assist me was John Wimber. When he left to start the Vineyard Movement, I replaced him with Carl George, a pastor from

Gainesville, Florida, whom I considered one of the most brilliant and articulate proponents of church growth theory and practice in the country. I had in mind that Carl would be my successor in CEFI, but unfortunately, I was blindsided by a skillful and hostile takeover of CEFI on his part, forcing me to resign from the board. When I began to see it coming, I fought fiercely, but I lost! Carl took over and he ran the organization until it disbanded a short time later. Not a good transition!

McGavran Chair of Church Growth

The third transition was a bit different because it happened within the rarified atmosphere of professional academia. I was aware that I needed to mentor a colleague and potential successor in my chair of church growth. Because I was moving into areas of the spiritual aspects of church growth such as signs and wonders, my first choice was Grant McClung, a Pentecostal professor I had mentored through his doctoral program. It was considered a done deal until he appeared for his routine theology exam administered by the theologians from the School of Theology. Much to my surprise, and that of my School of World Mission colleagues, he was disapproved! The traditional Reformed theologians could not appreciate his Pentecostal mindset. I must say that this experience was among the half dozen most profound disappointments of my career. McClung is now President of Missions Resource Group and a member of the World Missions Commission of the Pentecostal Word Fellowship.

My next choice was an Anglican from the U.K., Eddie Gibbs, as I mentioned in chapter 8. Eddie and I had built a close personal relationship through his participation in the Doctor of Ministry program, and I recognized him as one of the most creative and articulate advocates of church growth that I had met. I helped him get financial backing from Billy Graham so that he could move to California and join the SWM faculty. He managed to pass the theology exam with flying colors! We worked together very productively for a good while until a new seminary provost, Larry Den Besten, took office. Den Besten, as a Fuller board member, had previously developed a strong dislike for me because of bringing John Wimber into the school. In his view, I was a troublemaker, and he did not attempt to disguise his hostility. He used his executive power to transfer Eddie Gibbs from the School of World Mission to the School of Theology, successfully removing him from under my mentorship. Another huge disappointment! Eddie soon resigned from Fuller to take a pastorate for a period of time in order to gain more ministry experience in the United States. After I left California for Colorado, Gibbs was asked to return to the School of World Mission (the hostile provost by then had passed away), and he did become the second Donald McGavran Professor of Church Growth as planned. This was a good transition, but not a smooth one.

The Church Growth Movement

During the 1970s and 1980s, I somehow became recognized as the de facto leader of the church growth movement nationally and internationally. As I detailed in chapter 5, I convened and founded the American Society of Church Growth (ASCG) in 1986. Transition was no issue here because I designed ASCG to have a new president every year. But as to the de facto leadership of the movement as a whole, my choice of a successor was Gary McIntosh of Talbot School of Theology. His approach to the theory and teaching of church growth on the graduate level was very similar to mine. I even recommended him to the Fuller School of Theology as the director of their Doctor of Ministry program, but unfortunately they never were able to reach an agreement. I worked with John Vaughn, the first national expert on megachurches and president of Church Growth Today, to establish the *American Journal of Church Growth*, and Vaughn became the initial editor in 1990. Gary McIntosh then took the editorship in 1995 and continued through 2008. This, along with his prolific writings, has solidified his position as the de facto leader of the church growth movement. He currently teaches Church Growth in six additional seminaries besides Talbot. McIntosh is also projecting the first biography of Donald McGavran, and I have recently given him all my personal files as well as my complete collection of McGavran's writings. This was a symbolic passing of the baton, and a touching moment for me.

120 Fellowship

I have mentioned my 120 Fellowship adult Sunday School class at Lake Avenue Church from time to time. The 120 Fellowship was more of a molder of my spiritual growth and subsequent career than most Sunday School classes might be. I taught every Sunday morning for 13 years, with occasional normal absences. During those years I would not accept invitations to speak in other churches because I felt I needed to be with my "congregation" in LAC. Over those years, I researched and developed the material for what I consider my best book, *The Book of Acts*. I transitioned out of 120 when it became clear that Doris and I would make the move from California to Colorado. The transition was simple. I had developed a strong leadership team over the years. We knew each other well, and the team was committed to move ahead with the vision. One of the team members was Dave Rumph, who, along with his wife, Jane, were charter members of our Global Harvest Board. It soon became evident to the leadership team that Dave should move into my place as class leader, and Dave has taken the class forward through the years. It is still an important component of Lake Avenue Church.

The Present and the Future

The transitions I have just described are in the past. As you can imagine, it is a bit more challenging to shift to transitions that are either just recently completed, in process or yet to complete as I write to meet the publisher's deadline for this book. If this were to be released on my ninetieth birthday instead of my eightieth, I could calmly look back and evaluate these transitions as I have done with the earlier ones. But knowing that this is not possible, my publisher, Bill Greig III, has proposed that I consider writing one or more supplements to these in the years to come. Let's see if this ever works out!

Global Harvest Ministries (GHM)

As you know, beginning in 1991, the legal and organizational base for Doris's and my ministries has been Global Harvest Ministries (GHM). Our current assignments have changed from season to season, but the focus has always been to advance the kingdom of God through the spiritual gifts and personal networks that God has given us through the years. Obviously, the most important transition of all for us would be delivering GHM to the next generation. A little while ago, I mentioned that our daughters are not the ones to receive the torch of this ministry. So we have gone outside our natural family to our spiritual family in which Chuck Pierce is one of our spiritual sons.

You undoubtedly have noticed that the chapter "The Pierce Era" is so long that it needed to be divided into 5 sections. This is one of the indicators of how our lives and ministries have been intertwined with Chuck for

almost 20 years. Beginning in 1997, Doris and I started mentioning to
each other the possibility of Chuck's being our successor. Among other
things, he was just beginning his writing career and working with our
daughter, Becky, as his initial coauthor. Because Becky lived in our house
at the time, we had a good bit of personal contact. A couple of years later,
we began to be a bit more explicit to Chuck as well as to others about succession. We kept testing this idea, and our feelings that it was the direction
that God wished us to take continued to increase. Finally, in 2002, I wrote
a memorandum of understanding to our GHM Board of Directors ex-
pressing our desire that Chuck be our successor, and the board supported
the plan. We were all in agreement that when the time came for the legal
corporation of Global Harvest to be dissolved, the assets (if any remained)
and the ministry legacy would go to Pierce.

Chuck is president of Glory of Zion International in Denton, Texas.
He has felt that the proposed transfer of GHM would not fit into the existing Glory of Zion framework, so he called us in to help him start a new
organization called Global Spheres, Inc. Chuck is president, I am vice president, and Doris is a board member. But Global Spheres goes far beyond
receiving GHM. Global Spheres is a new wineskin for apostolic-prophetic
alignment. By now most leaders in our charismatically inclined evangelical segment of the Body of Christ understand that biblical alignment is
necessary for the power of God to flow through them in order to fulfill
their divine assignments with excellence. But many of them, representing
the Religion Mountain as well as the other six mountains, have not yet
found the alignment that they know they need. Global Spheres is providing a new wineskin for apostolic alignment with Chuck and me for those
with whom we have developed a personal connection.

Proper timing for a major transition like this is of the essence. As I
have mentioned, this memoir is scheduled to be released to the public on
my eightieth birthday, August 15, 2010. Chuck Pierce had been prophesying that 2010 would be a year for "digging new wells," so after some discussion, it seemed right to all of us to make the transition from Global
Harvest Ministries to Global Spheres at the time of my birthday.

The Global Prayer Movement

You will recall that Global Harvest was founded in 1991 with a single purpose in mind, namely, to help steer the AD2000 United Prayer Track

through the decade of the 1990s. It was my responsibility to assume the apostolic role of leadership for this prayer movement, even though we were not using that terminology at first. Part of the Prayer Track was the Spiritual Warfare Network (SWN). I asked Cindy Jacobs to lead the U.S. division of the SWN in the early 1990s, and she expanded it to the U.S. Strategic Prayer Network (USSPN). Later, I transferred the leadership to Chuck Pierce, and the name became U.S. Global Apostolic Prayer Network. By the beginning of 2008, both Chuck and I knew that our roles with the global prayer movement had come to an end. Cindy Jacobs then stepped up and initiated the Reformation Prayer Network, which has been catalyzing the prayer movement across the United States ever since. Chuck continues to deploy high-level prophetic intercessors internationally with his green-beret Eagles of God, visiting several nations per year with them. With these and other such entities, the global prayer movement carries on with great strength.

The Apostolic Council of Prophetic Elders (ACPE)

As I mentioned in part 1 of the last chapter, Cindy Jacobs was the one who originally cast the vision for ACPE in 1999, and then she asked me to take on the apostolic leadership. I managed and convened the group from then until the annual meeting of 2008, when I laid hands on Cindy and passed the baton of leadership to her. Our GHM office transferred all the records to her office at Generals International, and the transition was complete. Her one condition was that Doris and I remain active members of ACPE, to which we readily agreed. ACPE continues moving forward with a strong prophetic voice for our nation.

The Apostolic Council for Educational Accountability (ACEA)

In part 4 of the last chapter, I told how I was able to organize the Apostolic Council for Academic Accountability (ACEA) in 1998. Rather than being an offshoot of the prayer movement, ACEA was a group of educators from different parts of the apostolic movement. My successor, then, needed to be an educator from the apostolic stream. One of the members of ACEA from the beginning was Leo Lawson who had apostolic alignment with Rice

Broocks. Rice's network at that time was called Morning Star International, based in Nashville, Tennessee, and the school was the Graduate School of Campus Ministries. Their assignment was to multiply churches on American college campuses, and Leo had developed a superb training program, affiliated with Fuller Seminary, in which I was privileged to teach on a yearly basis. I came to admire Leo greatly, and in due time, I became convinced that he was the one whom God wanted to be, first of all, my close colleague and, second, my successor in ACEA. When I approached him about this, he, like Cindy Jacobs, agreed on the condition that I remain active in ACEA. In the ACEA annual meeting in May 2009, I handed Leo, who is the age of my children, the gavel. He has organized a very competent council of educators, and together they are taking ACEA into its new season with a number of new thrusts that would never have occurred to me.

The International Coalition of Apostles (ICA)

The transition of ICA was a no-brainer. You may recall that in the first part of the last chapter I told how John Kelly met with other apostles in Singapore and then founded ICA. I have had the wonderful privilege of serving as presiding apostle since 2000, and now is the time to turn this dynamic gathering of apostles back to its founder, who is also the age of my children. Kelly and I agreed to make the announcement of this transition at the ICA Annual Meeting in December 2009, with 2010 as the year when the transfer from my office would be completed. Fortuitously, the administrative transfer was made early in the year. The act of passing the ceremonial gavel is planned for a gathering to be hosted by Chuck Pierce in Denton, Texas, commemorating both my eightieth birthday and the release of this memoir.

The International Society of Deliverance Ministers (ISDM)

Doris has been the point person for the International Society of Deliverance Ministers (ISDM), and I have supported her in every way possible. Through recent years we have established close personal relationships with Bill and Janet Sudduth whom we consider in the top tier of deliverance ministers and teachers of deliverance in the nation. Bill was over the deliverance arm of the Brownsville revival. He and Janet moved from Florida to

Colorado Springs to be near us, they have set up offices in our building and we regard them as a spiritual son and daughter. Early in 2010, Doris and I turned ISDM over from Global Harvest Ministries to their organization, Righteous Acts Ministries (RAM). As of the annual meeting of ISDM in September 2010, Sudduth will be formally installed as president of ISDM. Doris and I, of course, will continue as active members.

Wagner Leadership Institute (WLI)

Part 4 of the last chapter tells the complete story of Wagner Leadership Institute (WLI). WLI is the largest of the entities under GHM, and it is the only one that carries my name. Thus, I felt that it was extremely important to seek God's direction for my successor. It needed to be a person who had some educational credentials, who knew me well, who had a passion for promulgating my legacy, who was called to equip the saints, who believed in our new wineskin for training, and whom I admired and trusted. I prayed about this for a considerable period of time until around the middle of 2009 I believe I heard clearly from the Lord that my successor in WLI was to be Ché Ahn.

Who is Ché Ahn? While I was teaching at Fuller in the 1980s, this young pastor who had moved to Pasadena, California, from back east made an appointment. Among other things he shared that he was planning to plant a charismatic church and he was believing that it would grow to 5,000. Because I was professor of church growth, when I heard that, I wanted to be his friend. We both knew that Pasadena had historically been a graveyard of charismatic churches, and I welcomed a person of faith who had the potential of breaking that curse. Well, we bonded, I became a spiritual father and I nurtured him through his M.Div. and D.Min. degrees at Fuller.

Ché planted Harvest Rock Church, a flourishing congregation that now owns the famous performing arts center, Ambassador Auditorium, in Pasadena. It is not quite 5,000, but it is well on its way. Meanwhile, Ché founded a vertical apostolic network, Harvest International Ministries (HIM), which counts more than 5,000 churches in some 35 nations. When I established Eagles Vision Apostolic Team (EVAT) to provide primary apostolic alignment, Ché became a charter member. I am a member of his HIM board.

When WLI opened the door for regional WLIs in America, Ché was one of the first to move with us, establishing WLI Pasadena, which has become one of our strongest. Ché was a key to starting WLI Indonesia. Using his Korean-American heritage and his apostolic ministry in Korea, Ché helped launch WLI Korea with Apostle Hong Jung Shik, arguably the strongest WLI in the world today. Here in America, Ché has supervised the start-up of WLI Korean-American Los Angeles, WLI Korean-American Seattle, WLI Korean-American Chicago, and WLI Korean-Canadian Vancouver. Ché is fully committed to WLI and he wants to expand it nationally and internationally.

Before I go on, let me insert another encouraging word about prophecy, which has been a recurring theme in this book. Many times, God will use prophecy to confirm a significant decision such as the WLI successor. This actually happened, much to my delight.

Cindy Jacobs is also on Ché's HIM board. During our meeting in Pasadena, in October 2009, she lapsed into one of her characteristic prophetic modes. Keep in mind that the only people who knew that Ché would be my successor at that time were Ché, his wife, Sue, Doris and me. No one else. Here is what Cindy said: "And the Lord would say, 'Peter Wagner, you have a mantle to bestow upon Ché Ahn. There is a mantle you have from the School of World Mission. It is a new wine mantle.' And the Lord says, 'I desire to use HIM with their equipping mantle. What the School of World Mission did I am going to give to you in the new wine school.' And the Lord says, 'You are going to train and equip, train and equip, for you are moving into the training and equipping season.'" When I spoke to Cindy later, she admitted that she had WLI in mind, but (wisely) hesitated to speak it out!

Other Transitions

The Eagles Vision Apostolic Team (EVAT) is my personal group of apostles who have chosen to align with me apostolically. I provide them with what has been called "apostolic covering" by some. As I mentioned previously, the 20 to 25 EVAT members are my closest circle of co-workers. There is no reason for making a transition in EVAT, so I have no plans for doing so. When I ultimately leave the scene, EVAT will simply disband.

The Fourth Career

Come to think of it, when this book is released, Doris and I will be starting our fourth career. We will not be retiring; we will be reloading. After all, Moses just got going when he was 80! Sometimes I feel like a roll of toilet paper—the nearer it gets to the end, the faster it goes! Here is how I see the progression:

Career #1: Missionary service in Bolivia, 1956-1971
Career #2: Teaching at Fuller Theological Seminary, 1971-2001
Career #3: Leading Global Harvest Ministries, 1991-2010
Career #4: Advancing God's kingdom through Global Spheres, Inc., 2010 onward

My vision is to move as widely throughout the Body of Christ as I can, using my gifts of apostle and teacher. I feel that I can help God's people understand more clearly some of the things that the Holy Spirit is currently saying to the churches. I can see the army of God being mobilized in highly strategic ways to push back the forces of darkness and help establish the kingdom of God here on earth as it is in heaven.

In this chapter on transitions, I do not have much to report on the great transfer of wealth. I actually have established some infrastructures for large-scale wealth distribution, which I feel might be a part of my agenda for this fourth career. However, I am not mentioning the names of some of the groupings that I have already established because I do not want to be premature in any conclusions. In any case, I am ready to become proactive in what I like to call (leaning on some of Bruce Cook's terminology) "sophisticated philanthropy for apostolic distribution" as soon as the wealth is released.

Conclusion

I do not intend to conclude these memoirs with a premature obituary. Someone else will write an authentic one when the time comes. I do, however, believe that "there is no success without a successor," and I have seriously undertaken that process of transition, as you have just read. To the best of my ability, I will continue to be faithful to John Maxwell's Law of Legacy.

Perhaps I should mention the great encouragement that came at the time Doris and I first met with our corporate attorney, Stuart Lark, to initiate the legal details for these hopefully seamless transitions. Stuart, who had previously read a preliminary memo that we had drafted, started the meeting with a fairly extended speech during which he became a bit choked up. He told how unusual it was for him to help terminate a ministry that had so carefully anticipated and planned out the details. The much more usual case was for him to be called upon to pick up the pieces and try to repair the damage that typically characterized "messy" closings of similar ministries. It brought to mind Bobby Clinton's sad statistic that only one out of four Christian leaders finish well.

I now can only trust and pray that during my fourth career God will continually provide divine assignments through which I can glorify His name and help advance His kingdom.

If I may have a final word, it is to fellow Christian leaders who pass their seventieth birthday. If you have reached or if you are approaching that plateau, here is my word for you: Please think seriously about writing your memoirs. As I mentioned in the first chapter, I resisted this call for a long time on the mistaken assumption that doing so might be a transgression of true humility. To the contrary, I now believe that if we fail to leave behind us written memoirs, we are neglecting an essential part of our responsibility for intergenerational impartation. None of us knows when the end will come, but we all know for sure that it will come. So I strongly, even apostolically, urge you to begin using a significant portion of your time researching, analyzing and getting on paper how God has worked in your life to bring you to the honored position of Christian leadership that so many recognize and that you now enjoy.

My prayer is that this memoir, which by the grace of God, I humbly submit, will be an encouragement to my generation and a challenge for the next generation to diligently pursue excellence in moving toward the destiny that God has for each and every one!

Notes

1. Jeff Myers, *Handoff* (Dayton, TN: Legacy Worldwide, 2008), p. 17.
2. Ibid., p. 22.
3. John C. Maxwell, *The 21 Irrefutable Laws of Leadership* (Nashville, TN: Thomas Nelson Publishers, 1998), p. 218.
4. Ibid., p. 222.
5. John Maxwell, Maximum Impact audio tape, "Going from Good to Great" (vol. 6, no. 3, 2001).
6. Ibid.
7. Myers, *Handoff*, p. 31.

Books Published by
C. Peter Wagner

With a Running Commentary from the Author

1. *The Condor of the Jungle* (with Joseph S. McCullough). Old Tappan, NJ: Fleming H. Revell Co., 1966. Two printings. German, British English (2 editions) and Australian English. This is the biography of Australian Walter Herron, actually the first full-time missionary pilot ever recorded. He was a member of AEM and based in Concepción, located in the jungle area of Bolivia where we spent our first term.

2. *Defeat of the Bird God.* Grand Rapids, MI: Zondervan Publishing House, 1967. Two printings. Reprinted by William Carey Library, 2 printings, Condensed version reprinted by Good News Publishers. Five printings. During my 1961-1962 furlough in Princeton Seminary, I decided to cut my literary teeth on missionary biographies. This was the first book I wrote, a biography of Bill Pencille, SAIM missionary to the Ayoré Indians. Because of Joseph McCullough's influence, Herron's biography (#1) was written second, but published first. As an unknown author, it took me awhile to get a contract for this one.

3. *Latin American Theology: Radical or Evangelical?* Grand Rapids, MI: William B. Eerdmans Publishing Company, 1970. Spanish. I wrote this in order to encourage Latin American evangelicals to strive to become recognized theologians on the level of their liberal counterparts. However, I was blindsided by the negative criticisms on the part of some pioneer Latin American evangelical theologians, because I stressed evangelism and church growth to the neglect of Christian social responsibility. I have since changed my views.

4. *The Protestant Movement in Bolivia.* Pasadena, CA: William Carey Library, 1970. This was the dissertation for my MA in Missiology (Church Growth) from the Fuller School of World Mission under Donald McGavran. I had gathered and filed enough material to produce this, the only history of the early missionary work in Bolivia.

5. *An Extension Seminary Primer* (with Ralph Covell). Pasadena, CA: William Carey Library, 1971. Two printings. Ralph Winter mentored me in a new wineskin for equipping the saints through theological education by extension (TEE). I joined Ralph Covell of Denver Seminary in an extensive overseas tour to introduce the concept to several other nations. This book compiles the teaching information that Covell and I developed. TEE was the early educational philosophy that now undergirds Wagner Leadership Institute.

6. *A Turned-On Church in an Uptight World.* Grand Rapids, MI: Zondervan Publishing House, 1971. Aka, *Our Corinthian Contemporaries.* Five printings. Chinese (2 editions) and Spanish (2 editions). While I was studying at Fuller in the early fifties and teaching at Bell Friends Church, I specialized in the book of First Corinthians. After teaching this over and over for 15 years, I compiled my thoughts in this work, one of the few Bible study books I have done.

7. *Frontiers in Missionary Strategy.* Chicago, IL: Moody Press, 1972. Six printings. Korean. When I transferred from field missionary service to teaching at Fuller, the first course I began to teach was Strategy of Missions. I developed material based on 16 years on the field in Bolivia and produced this textbook, which was used in many other Bible schools and seminaries throughout the United States and Korea.

8. *Church/Mission Tensions Today* (editor). Chicago, IL: Moody Press, 1972. One of the objectives of responsible missionary work is to plant churches and other ministries in the target culture and turn the work over to the nationals as soon as possible. Around 1970, missiologists had become aware that too many missions and missionaries were staying too long on the field, controlling the churches there instead of turning over the work and leaving. This led to a top-level consultation at Green Lake, Wisconsin, to discuss the matter, including the rela-

tively new thought of Third World churches sending out their own cross-cultural missionaries. I was asked to edit the book containing the addresses from this conference.

9. *Look Out! The Pentecostals Are Coming*. Carol Stream, IL: Creation House, 1973. Aka, *What Are We Missing?* Three printings. Spanish, Portuguese and British English. One of the most important paradigm shifts that I experienced during my career was recognizing that God was indeed at work among the Pentecostals and charismatics. Previously, I had been anti-Pentecostal along with the majority of my fellow evangelical missionaries. When I discovered that the growth of Pentecostal churches far exceeded ours, I began to research the movement and develop relationships with their leaders. I wrote this book to help fellow evangelicals consider the same paradigm shift, and many did. However, to my surprise, my new Pentecostal friends purchased and used this book much more than evangelicals.

10. *Stop the World, I Want to Get On*. Ventura, CA: Regal Press, 1974. Three printings. Reprinted by William Carey Library, two printings; five printings in all. When I started teaching at Fuller, I began traveling extensively overseas and learning a great deal about how world missions were being conducted by different streams. This book was a basic introduction to what was happening in world missions in the early 1970s, and many schools used it as a textbook.

11. *Your Church Can Grow: Seven Vital Signs of a Healthy Church*. Ventura, CA: Regal Press, 1976, 1984. Twenty-four printings. Korean, Japanese, Chinese, Indonesian, Spanish and Italian. As professor of church growth, I not only researched and taught about the growth of churches on the foreign fields, but also in the United States. This is my main textbook for American church growth, and a large number of evangelical pastors still have it in their libraries.

12. *Unreached Peoples '79* (edited with Edward R. Dayton). Elgin, IL: David C. Cook Publishing Company, 1978. As a major part of my activities as the leader of the Lausanne Committee (LCWE) Strategy Working Group, I worked with Ed Dayton of MARC at World Vision to compile data and publish annual editions of information about unreached

people groups in general as well as statistical charts of the people groups. This is the first one.

13. *Your Spiritual Gifts Can Help Your Church Grow*. Ventura, CA: Regal Books, 1979, revised editions 1994, 2005. Forty-six printings. Spanish, Chinese, Japanese, Korean (2 editions), Burmese, Dutch, German, Indonesian (2 versions), Arabic, Finnish, Portuguese, Italian, British English, and Indian English. Of all my books, this needs to be recorded as the most helpful one for equipping the Body of Christ. For one thing it is the most widely circulated of all my books, with more than a quarter million copies in English alone. It helps people find their God-given purpose in life by defining each of the 28 spiritual gifts and providing a 135-question questionnaire to assist them in getting an idea of what their gifts might actually be. This is still in print.

14. *Your Church Can Be Healthy*. Nashville, TN: Abingdon, 1979. Eight printings. I always taught that there was a direct relationship between church health and church growth. Healthy churches grow! In this book, I attempted to do a pathology of church growth, identifying and analyzing eight diseases that affected church growth. Some of them were terminal, but I suggested action steps to prevent and cure the others.

15. *Our Kind of People: The Ethical Dimensions of Church Growth in America*. Atlanta, GA: John Knox Press, 1979. You may recall that toward the end of chapter 5, I expressed my disappointment that many leaders would not accept the "homogeneous unit principle of church growth" that I, following Donald McGavran, had been teaching, even though it was then and still is a valid sociological phenomenon. Most of the objections were ethical in nature, so when I launched out for my PhD in Social Ethics at the University of Southern California, I decided to do my dissertation on the subject. This book is my dissertation, slightly revised. Some of the leaders who read it have told me that they think it is the most convincing book I have written. Sadly, however, it failed to change the world!

16. *Unreached Peoples '80* (edited with Edward R. Dayton). Elgin, IL: David C. Cook Publishing Company, 1980. The second annual volume in the series on unreached peoples.

17. *The Church Growth Survey Handbook* (with Bob Waymire). Santa Clara, CA: The Global Church Growth Bulletin, 1980. Numerous printings. Spanish, Swedish, Arabic, German and Portuguese. This is a step-by-step guidebook for leaders who wish to do research on the growth of their churches as well as churches within a certain region. It gives a practical foundation for planning strategy for future growth.

18. *Unreached Peoples '81* (edited with Edward R. Dayton). Elgin, IL: David C. Cook Publishing Company, 1981. The third annual volume in the series on unreached peoples. This one highlights Asian people groups. This is the last volume I did with Ed Dayton. He found others to do one or two more before the series was discontinued. The task was then transferred to the Joshua Project under the AD2000 Movement.

19. *Church Growth and the Whole Gospel.* San Francisco, CA: Harper & Row; England, Kingsway, 1981. Two printings. Korean and British English. I had become so frustrated with criticisms about my strong promotion of the clause in the Lausanne Covenant stating the primacy of evangelism over social action that I decided to write a scholarly apologetic defending my position. In this polemical book, I named and harshly refuted a number of leaders who disagreed with me. This was my last polemical book, since, after it was published, the Lord spoke to me and told me never to write in a polemical tone again. Ironically, I have now actually changed my position and I see that evangelism and social responsibility are equal components of dominion theology. I have apologized to some I refuted.

20. *Effective Body Building: Biblical Steps to Spiritual Growth.* San Bernardino, CA: Here's Life Publishers, 1982. Portuguese and Korean. This is a re-writing of the material on First Corinthians that first appeared in *A Turned-On Church in an Uptight World* (#6 above). I consider it different enough from the previous title that it deserves to be listed as a separate book.

21. *Church Growth Bulletin: Third Consolidated Volume* (edited with Donald McGavran and James Montgomery). Covers September 1975 through November 1979. Santa Clara, CA: Global Church Growth. 1982. Donald McGavran's in-house newsletter for the Church Growth Movement

was the *Church Growth Bulletin*. In his later years he asked Jim Montgomery, one of his first disciples, and me to assist him with the editing and publishing of this valuable primary source.

22. *On the Crest of the Wave: Becoming a World Christian*. Ventura, CA: Regal Books, 1983. Nine printings. Indonesian. Over a period of almost 10 years, the material in *Stop the World, I Want to Get On* was becoming outdated. World missions in general had gone through many significant changes. The publisher and I agreed that, instead of attempting to revise *Stop the World*, a new update on what was happening in the missiological world was necessary, and this book is the result.

23. *Leading Your Church to Growth: The Secret of Pastor/People Partnership in Dynamic Church Growth*. Ventura, CA: Regal Books, 1984. Thirteen printings. Korean (2 editions), Japanese, British English (2 editions), Philippines English, German, French, Indonesian and Spanish. The subtitle of *Your Church Can Grow* is *Seven Vital Signs of a Healthy Church*. After much research I became convinced that leadership was the number one vital sign. This is my only book on leadership per se and pastors still tell me how much this book changed the course of their lives and ministry. Looking back, I now realize that I was advocating apostolic-type rather than pastoral-type leadership, although I did not know the terms then.

24. *Spiritual Power and Church Growth*. Altamonte Springs, FL: Creation House, 1986. Three printings. Spanish, Portuguese, Korean, Indonesian, Norwegian, German, British English, and Chinese. The lessons learned and applied by Pentecostals around the world needed to be spread more widely throughout the Body of Christ. *Look Out! The Pentecostals Are Coming* had long since stopped circulating and this attempt to revive the ideas, coming after John Wimber began to make his impact, was well received and it went into seven other languages.

25. *Church Growth: State of the Art* (editor). Wheaton, IL: Tyndale Press, 1986. Five printings. Korean. By the mid-1980s, the field of church growth had grown vigorously throughout U.S. seminaries and Bible schools and denominational leadership. I recruited a number of those who had been teaching and writing on church growth to join together and share their expertise in this compilation and reference work.

26. *Strategies for Church Growth: Tools for Planning Evangelism and Missions*. Ventura, CA: Regal Books, 1987. Eleven printings. Indonesian, Portuguese, Chinese, British English, German, and Thai. I had been learning about and teaching strategy of missions for almost 20 years. *Frontiers in Missionary Strategy* was long out of print. This book, which became widely used in seminaries and Bible schools, was an update to the Body of Christ on what I had been learning over those years.

27. *Signs and Wonders Today*, revised edition (editor). Altamonte Springs, FL: Creation House, 1987. Spanish, Japanese and Portuguese. One of the major factors in disseminating the paradigm shift initiated by John Wimber's teaching at Fuller was the decision of Robert Walker to dedicate an entire issue of his magazine, *Christian Life*, to the ripple effects of the course MC510: Signs, Wonders and Church Growth. This issue broke all records for sales, and he also published it out in a separate magazine-format edition. I was asked to revise and update the material and issue it in book form. The book contains chapters both pro and con.

28. *The Third Wave of the Holy Spirit*. Ann Arbor, MI: Servant Publications, 1988. Six printings. Chinese and Japanese. How I made my paradigm shift into power ministries through MC510 at Fuller and how I coined the term "Third Wave."

29. *How to Have a Healing Ministry Without Making Your Church Sick*. Aka, *How to Have a Healing Ministry in Any Church*. Ventura, CA: Regal Books, 1988. Seven printings. German, Korean, Japanese, Chinese, Philippines English (2 editions), Swedish, British English, Indian English, and Indonesian. Under the influence of John Wimber, I started to develop teaching materials and courses on physical healing, and I soon felt that my students needed a new textbook on the subject. This book stayed in circulation for quite a while, and many leaders used it to help their people move out into new areas of faith healing.

30. *Wrestling with Dark Angels* (editor with F. Douglas Pennoyer). Ventura, CA: Regal Books, 1990. Eleven printings. British English, Korean, Portuguese, Indonesian and German. This is the compilation of presentations to the Academic Symposium on Power Evangelism, which I convened at Fuller Seminary. It helped to establish academic

respectability for teaching power ministries in evangelical seminaries and it showed that Wimber's influence had penetrated more widely than many had thought.

31. *Understanding Church Growth* by Donald A. McGavran, Third Edition revised and edited by C. Peter Wagner. Grand Rapids, MI: Wm. B. Eerdmans Publishing Co., 1990. Four printings. German and Portuguese. Donald McGavran's *Understanding Church Growth* is the basic international textbook for the whole Church Growth Movement, originally released in 1970. After 20 years, the ideas were as relevant and cutting-edge as ever, but the literary format left much to be desired in the contemporary world, starting with the use of gender-exclusive language. I felt very privileged that McGavran would entrust me with a revision of the book. I conscientiously avoided introducing any of the fine-tuning I had been making of McGavran's original concepts in my own teaching and writing. I did add a chapter incorporating a printed talk that he had delivered on faith healing and church growth. It is truly a classic, and I hope it remains in print forever.

32. *Church Planting for a Greater Harvest*. Ventura, CA: Regal Books, 1990. Eleven printings. German, Korean (2 editions), Indonesian, Spanish and Portuguese. I introduced the first-ever course on church planting in Fuller Seminary, and many theology students as well as missions students elected to take it through the years. I needed a textbook for the course, so I wrote this book. I should note that it was focused on church planting in America rather than overseas. Many denominations used the book to train and motivate their own church planters.

33. *Engaging the Enemy* (editor). Ventura, CA: Regal Books, 1991. Seven printings. British English (as *Territorial Spirits*), Japanese, German, Czech, Indonesian, Chinese, Hungarian, Portuguese (2 editions) and Spanish. When I first became aware of strategic-level spiritual warfare and territorial spirits, in 1989, I began scouring the literature to find any previous references to the phenomenon. Surprisingly, I found quite a few, and I compiled them in this introductory work.

34. *Warfare Prayer*. Ventura, CA: Regal Books, 1992. Twenty-one printings. Reprinted: Shippensburg PA: Destiny Image, 2009. British English (2

editions), German, Japanese, Portuguese, Chinese, Korean (2 editions), Indonesian, Spanish, Arabic, Polish, Russian, Thai and French. This is the first of the *Prayer Warrior Series*. It is my basic introduction to strategic-level spiritual warfare and a textbook for the courses I taught in Fuller on the subject. It stayed in print with Regal for 15 years, and it has now been re-issued by Destiny Image.

35. *Prayer Shield*. Ventura, CA: Regal Books, 1992. Twenty-eight printings. British English (2 editions), Chinese, German, Indonesian, Korean (2 editions), Japanese, Spanish, Portuguese, French, Russian, Thai, Polish and Arabic. This, the second book of the *Prayer Warrior Series*, was likely the first book specifically on intercession for leaders. The idea has spread widely, and most leaders I know have by now recruited teams of personal intercessors. The term "prayer shield" has become a technical term, and most would not know that it was derived from this book's title.

36. *Breaking Strongholds in Your City* (editor). Ventura, CA: Regal Books, 1993. Sixteen printings. British English, Indonesian, Japanese, Spanish, Korean, Traditional Chinese, French, Russian, Portuguese and Polish. Spiritual mapping had become such a rapidly developing and highly useful part of the prayer movement that I decided to change my original plans for the *Prayer Warrior Series* and introduce this extra volume. George Otis, Jr., the recognized expert on spiritual mapping, has the first chapter, and I follow with the second. There are several other contributors.

37. *Churches That Pray*. Ventura, CA: Regal Books, 1993. Eleven printings. Indonesian, Japanese, Spanish, Korean (2 editions), Portuguese, Thai, French, Russian, Chinese and Polish. This fourth book of the *Prayer Warrior Series* looks into the prayer ministries of outstanding local churches in the United States and other nations. Interestingly enough, no matter how hard I tried, I could never discover a direct correlation between strong prayer ministries and the growth of churches.

38. *Spreading the Fire: A New Look at the Book of Acts*. Ventura, CA: Regal Books, 1994. Four printings. Norwegian, Japanese, Korean, Spanish and Indian English. I started teaching the book of Acts in the 120 Fellowship

Sunday School class, in 1992. Researching this and getting the material into book form was by far the most extensive writing project of my career. Regal agreed to publish this first attempt in three volumes in order to avoid one huge book. This volume covers Acts 1 to 8.

39. *Lighting the World*. Ventura, CA: Regal Books, 1995. Three printings. Norwegian, Japanese, Korean, Spanish and Indian English. Volume two of the Acts series covers Acts 9 to 15.

40. *Blazing the Way*. Ventura, CA: Regal Books, 1995. Three printings. Norwegian, Japanese, Indian English and Korean. Volume three of the Acts series covers Acts 15 to 28.

41. *Praying Through the 100 Gateway Cities of the 10/40 Window* (edited with Stephen Peters and Mark Wilson). Seattle, WA: YWAM Publishing, 1995. Afrikaans, Spanish, Chinese and Korean. This was the prayer guide for the AD2000 United Prayer Track's Praying Through the Window II initiative, October 1995, as described in chapter 8 and part 3 of chapter 9. We estimate 36 million believers prayed together through the month.

42. *Confronting the Powers*. Ventura, CA: Regal Books, 1996. Five printings. Korean, French, Russian and Spanish. The fifth book of the *Prayer Warrior Series*, this is my theological apologetic for strategic-level spiritual warfare. While it did not convince as many as I would have liked, it did seem to cool the intensive debate that had been going on for some time.

43. *The Healthy Church*. Ventura, CA: Regal Books, 1996. Two printings. Korean and Portuguese. When Abingdon discontinued *Your Church Can Be Healthy* (#14) after 8 printings over some 15 years, my Doctor of Ministry students persuaded me to rewrite it and issue it with Regal. I was disappointed that they sold only two printings, but by this time the Church Growth Movement per se had undoubtedly passed its peak.

44. *Praying with Power*. Ventura, CA: Regal Books, 1997. Seven printings; Shippensburg PA: Destiny Image, 2008, one printing. Total eight printings. Korean, Indian English, Indonesian, French, Portuguese and Spanish. The sixth and final book in the *Prayer Warrior Series* summa-

rizes the new things that we learned during the prayer movement of the 1990s. I was delighted when Destiny Image decided to put it back in print, and it deserves to stay with us for a while. There is no substitute for the basic teachings it contains.

45. *The Rising Revival* (edited with Pablo Deiros). Ventura, CA: Renew Books, 1998. Two printings. Dutch, Spanish, Chinese, Korean and Thai. Doris and I made numerous mission trips to witness and participate in the Argentine Revival, which was notable because it lasted more than 15 years, much longer than most revivals. Pablo Deiros joined me in compiling the first-hand stories of the major players in this historic book.

46. *The New Apostolic Churches* (editor). Ventura, CA: Regal Books, 1998. Four printings. Japanese, Chinese, Korean and Indonesian. After convening the National Symposium on the Postdenominational Church in 1996, I asked 18 pioneer apostles to write firsthand accounts of their personal apostolic networks. I opened with a summary of the common characteristics of this new wineskin for doing church. This was my first book on apostles and apostolic ministry.

47. *Confronting the Queen of Heaven*. Colorado Springs, CO: Wagner Publications, 1998, 2000. Three printings. Spanish (2 editions), Portuguese, Japanese, German and Czech. As the results of spiritual mapping continued to pour in from many nations of the 10/40 Window, it became clear that one of Satan's chief principalities of darkness was the Queen of Heaven in her many different deceptive adaptations. This book exposes a number of them and gives guidelines for aggressive warfare.

48. *The Everychurch Guide to Growth* (with Elmer Towns and Thom S. Rainer). Nashville, TN: Broadman and Holman, 1998. One of the most popular conferences that we did through CEFI in many parts of the country for years was "Breaking the 200 Barrier." The Southern Baptists invited me to put my thoughts into writing in this book, along with sections by Elmer Towns on the middle-sized church and Thom Rainer on the large church.

49. *Radical Holiness for Radical Living*. Colorado Springs, CO: Wagner Publications, 1998. Three printings. Spanish, Indonesian, Korean and

Bulgarian. For a long time, I have been disappointed that the Body of Christ has taken a distorted view of personal holiness due, to a large extent, to adopting the "Reformed doctrine of sanctification." This book attempts to correct that through a Wesleyan view of holiness with the premise that we can, in fact, please God by living a life of true holiness.

50. *Hard-Core Idolatry: Facing the Facts*. Colorado Springs, CO: Wagner Publications, 1999. Two printings. Spanish. I feel that we have tended to water down the biblical meaning of idolatry by defining it as just about anything at all that might stand in the way of giving God preeminence. Idolatry is, in fact, nothing less than idol worship, as the term implies. However, for reasons I can't quite understand, I was never able to convince many people of this important viewpoint. Of course, it could be that I am wrong!

51. *Churchquake! How the New Apostolic Reformation Is Shaking up the Church as We Know It*. Ventura, CA: Regal Books, 1999. Six printings. Spanish, Korean (2 editions), Indonesian, Swedish, Polish and Chinese. I wrote this as my textbook on the different aspects of the paradigm shift from denominationalism to the New Apostolic Reformation. Even though I consider it one of my best-researched and written books, it never sold as many copies as I would have hoped. I was disappointed.

52. *Revival! It Can Transform Your City*. Colorado Springs, CO: Wagner Publications, 1999. Japanese, Korean and Portuguese. This is one of my early writings on social transformation as our goal.

53. *Apostles of the City: How to Mobilize Territorial Apostles for City Transformation*. Colorado Springs, CO: Wagner Publications, 2000. Two printings. German and Spanish. The idea that some apostles have been assigned geographical territories as their sphere of authority has been new to some. In this book, I attempted to give a biblical and theological rationale for the concept. One error, since corrected, is assuming that pastors are the spiritual gatekeepers of the city. I now see that apostles are the gatekeepers, but more of that comes in later books (e.g., #68).

54. *The Queen's Domain: Advancing God's Kingdom in the 40-70 Window* (editor). Colorado Springs, CO: Wagner Publications, 2000. Romanian,

German, Czech and Hungarian. When we switched from the 10/40 Window to the 40/70 Window, it became obvious that the Queen of Heaven had been disproportionately victorious over many of those nations, largely because of the relentless pressure of Mariolatry from the Catholic Church. In this book, several of our experienced intercessors record what they have learned about this distressing phenomenon.

55. *Apostles and Prophets: The Foundation of the Church.* Ventura, CA: Regal Books, 2000. Two printings. Korean and Indonesian. Even though we were entering the Second Apostolic Age, I was surprised that probably a substantial majority of apostles had never cemented positive relationships with one or more prophets as partners in ministry. In this book, I tried to analyze some reasons why and suggest steps to correct the trend. Somehow the book did not catch on as much as I had hoped, and it soon went out of print.

56. *Pastors and Prophets: Protocol for Healthy Churches* (Editor). Colorado Springs, CO: Wagner Publications, 2000. Two printings. Korean and Indonesian. Even more than apostles, I found that pastors, for the most part, had an aversion to allowing close ministry relationships to prophets. Much of this was due to certain prophets not understanding proper protocol in local church ministry. Some of the relatively few pastors who have done well in this area contributed very helpful chapters.

57. *Seven Power Principles that I Didn't Learn in Seminary.* Colorado Springs, CO: Wagner Publications, 2000. Reissued by Regal Books as *7 Power Principles I Learned After Seminary*, 2005. Two printings. Korean, Spanish and Chinese. My arguments as to why traditional evangelicals should consider switching to more biblical views concerning the operating of the supernatural in their lives and ministries.

58. *Acts of the Holy Spirit: A Modern Commentary on the Book of Acts.* Ventura, CA: Regal Books, 2000. Two printings. Revised and updated with the new title *The Book of Acts: A Commentary,* in 2008. This is my *magnum opus.* This 500+ page commentary on Acts does not attempt to duplicate the information found in the classic exegetical-historical scholarly commentaries, but rather it attempts to show how modern revelation of the missiological and power dimensions of the text and context help

us understand the book better and allow a practical application to missions and church growth today.

59. *Destiny of a Nation: How Prophets and Intercessors Can Mold History* (Editor). Colorado Springs, CO: Wagner Publications, 2001. There is no doubt in my mind that the most convincing explanation of George W. Bush's narrow election victory in 2000 is a direct answer to the prayers and spiritual warfare of Christian intercessors. Several key players contribute chapters.

60. *What the Bible Says About Spiritual Warfare*. Ventura, CA: Regal Books, 2001. Largely in response to the negative fallout from John Paul Jackson's *Needless Casualties of War*, I decided to summarize and update the arguments in favor of the need for strategic-level spiritual warfare. After Regal took this out of print, we incorporated it in the new Destiny Image edition of *Warfare Prayer* (#34).

61. *Humility*. Ventura, CA: Regal Books, 2002. Two printings. Dutch, Portuguese, Korean, Spanish and Indonesian. Virtually everyone I knew affirmed the need for humility in their speaking and writing, but I found that no one in my generation had developed the subject in book form. With this, I hoped to fill the gap.

62. *Discover Your Spiritual Gifts*. Ventura, CA: Regal Books, 2002, revised 2005. Seven printings. After my first book on spiritual gifts had been circulating for more than 20 years (see #13), I was shocked to discover that research showed a lower level of understanding of spiritual gifts among believers in general than previously. So I decided to add a smaller book for those who would be unlikely to read such a long book as the other one.

63. *Spheres of Authority: Apostles in Today's Church*. Colorado Springs, CO: Wagner Publications, 2002. Spanish and Indonesian. This book summarized my understanding of the ministry of apostles as of 2002. It was later replaced by *Apostles Today*, in 2006.

67. *Out of Africa: How the Spiritual Explosion Among Nigerians Is Impacting the World* (edited with Joseph Thompson). Ventura, CA: Regal Books, 2004.

Two printings. Some of the strongest and most effective Christian leadership today is found among apostles in Nigeria. Here they tell their fascinating stories. I am the only non-Nigerian who has a chapter.

68. *Changing Church: How God Is Leading His Church into the Future.* Ventura, CA: Regal Books, 2004. Two printings. Indian English, Spanish, Korean and German. *Churchquake!* (# 51) tells of the paradigm shift from denominationalism to the New Apostolic Reformation. This book describes some of the more significant changes that have occurred since.

69. *Freedom from the Religious Spirit* (editor). Ventura, CA: Regal Books, 2005. Dutch, Spanish and Korean. The Holy Spirit began revealing to many leaders in my sphere the pernicious and disproportionate influence that the spirit of religion had been exercising in our midst to keep us from moving into God's new seasons. In this book, several of us share our findings on the roots and cures for this malady.

70. *The Church in the Workplace: How God's People Can Transform Society.* Ventura, CA: Regal Books, 2006. Two printings. Bulgarian, Korean, Chinese, Portuguese and Spanish. I began catching on to workplace ministry around 2001, and in this book I share the thoughts I had been developing on this crucial subject over the first five years. Many testify to changing their paradigm after reading it.

71. *Apostles Today: Biblical Government for Biblical Power.* Ventura, CA: Regal Books, 2006. Two printings. Korean. This is my sixth and final book on apostles and apostolic ministry. It incorporates material from the other five and essentially renders them obsolete.

72. *Let's Laugh: Discovering How Laughter Will Make You Healthy.* Shippensburg, PA: Destiny Image Publishers, 2007. Hey! Let's take a break! For about 30 years I established the pattern of telling jokes (by reading them!) to introduce my classes and my public addresses. This is the most fun book I ever wrote. After four light-hearted chapters on the theory of humor, I go on to include the best 64 jokes in the world. I'm sure they're the best because I discarded at least 6,400 other jokes throughout my selection process.

73. *Dominion! How Kingdom Action Can Change the World.* Grand Rapids, MI: Chosen Books, 2008. Korean. Since around 2004, I became convinced that the Dominion Mandate was the most accurate biblical framework for a true understanding of the Great Commission. Our goal goes beyond saving souls and multiplying churches to transforming the society in which we live. This is a biblical and theological framework for understanding why.

INDEX

Contact C. Peter Wagner at

Global Harvest Ministries
P.O. Box 63060
Colorado Springs, CO 80962

Phone: (719) 262-9922
Fax: (719) 262-9920
Email: info@globalharvest.org

Find out more about C Peter Wagner and
Global Harvest Ministries at

globalharvest.org
wagnerleadership.org